Corporate Governance, Enforcement and Financial Development

To Jingran and my parents

Corporate Governance, Enforcement and Financial Development

The Chinese Experience

Ding Chen

University of Newcastle, UK

Edward Elgar

Cheltenham, UK • Northampton, MA, USA

Published by
Edward Elgar Publishing Limited
The Lypiatts
15 Lansdown Road
Cheltenham
Glos GL50 2JA
UK

Edward Elgar Publishing, Inc.
William Pratt House
9 Dewey Court
Northampton
Massachusetts 01060
USA

A catalogue record for this book
is available from the British Library

Library of Congress Control Number: 2012951763

This book is available electronically in the ElgarOnline.com Law Subject Collection, E-ISBN 978 1 78100 481 4

ISBN 978 1 78100 480 7

Typeset by Columns Design XML Ltd, Reading
Printed by MPG PRINTGROUP, UK

Contents

Tables

Figures

Abbreviations

ABC	Agriculture Bank of China
ADR	American Depositary Receipt
AMC	Asset Management Corporation
BOC	Bank of China
BP	British Petroleum
CAO	China Aviation Oil
CAOHC	China Aviation Oil Holding Corp
CBRC	China Banking Regulatory Commission
CCB	China Construction Bank
CCP	Chinese Communist Party
CCTV	China Central Television
CICC	China International Capital Corporation
CNPC	China National Petroleum Corporation
CPA	Certificated Public Accountants
CPD	Propaganda Department of the Central Committee of the Communist Party
CSDCC	China Securities Depository and Clearing Corporation
CSRC	China Securities Regulatory Commission
Deloitte	Deloitte Touche Tohmatsu
EU	European Union
GDP	gross domestic product
GMD	Guo Min Dang
Guo Jin	Guo Jin Securities Company

HKICAC	Hong Kong Independent Commission against Corruption
HKSE	Hong Kong Stock Exchange
Huijin	Central Huijin Investment
ICBC	Industrial and Commercial Bank of China
IMF	International Monetary Fund
IPO	initial public offering
Jianyin	China Jianyin Investment
JSC	joint stock company
KPMG	Klynveld Peat Marwick Goerdeler
LLC	limited liability company
LSE	London Stock Exchange
M&A	merger and acquisition
MBO	management buy-out
MOF	Ministry of Finance
NASDAQ	National Association of Securities Dealers' Automated Quotations
NETS	National Electronic Trading System
NIE	New Institutional Economics
NPC	National People's Congress
NPL	non-performing loan
NYSE	New York Stock Exchange
OECD	Organisation for Economic Co-operation and Development
OTC	over-the-counter
Pacific	Pacific Securities Company
PBOC	People's Bank of China
P/E	price–earnings ratio
PEI	private equity investment

PetroChina	Petrol China Company Limited
PICC	People's Insurance Company of China
Ping An	Shenzhen Ping An Insurance Company
PLA	People's Liberation Army
PLC	Party's Political-Legal Committee
PLCs	public listed companies
PORC	Public Offering Review Commission
PRC	People's Republic of China
PSE	Prague Stock Exchange
PSL	private securities litigation
PwC	PricewaterhouseCoopers
QFII	qualified foreign institutional investors
RMB	Ren Min Bi
ROA	return on assets
ROCE	return on capital employed
ROE	return on equity
SARFT	State Administration of Radio, Film and Television
SARS	Severe Acute Respiratory Syndrome
SASAC	State-owned Assets Supervision and Administration Commission
SCB	State-owned Commercial Bank
SCRES	State Committee for the Restructuring of the Economic System
SDB	Shenzhen Development Bank
SEEC	Stock Exchange Executive Council
SETC	State Economic and Trade Commission
SGX	Singapore Stock Exchange
SHSE	Shang Hai Stock Exchange
SIAS	Singapore Securities Investor Association

Sinopec	China Petroleum & Chemical Corporation
SOE	state-owned enterprise
SPC	Supreme People's Court
SPPA	State Press and Publication Administration
SRO	self-regulatory organization
ST	Special Treatment
STAQ	Securities Trading Automated Quotations
SZSE	Shen Zhen Stock Exchange
TBF	treasury bond future
TBs	treasury bonds
TSOE	traditional state-owned enterprise
TVE	township and village enterprise
UBS	Union Bank of Switzerland
UK	United Kingdom
US	United States
WSOLLC	wholly state-owned limited liability company
WTO	World Trade Organization
Zhong Jing Kai	China Economic Development Trust Investment Company

Acknowledgements

China's remarkable performance over the past three decades has won its gradualist approach a great deal of proponents. For instance, Rawski (1999, 153) claimed that 'we are all gradualists now'. A leading textbook on economic transition cites the Chinese experience as the most robust example of the gradualist model and claims that such a model is more complete and adequate than the big-bang approach, otherwise known as the 'Washington Consensus' (Roland, 2000).

However, such a claim sounds over-optimistic to some insiders. Before moving into academia, as the section chief of the Prevention Bribery and Embezzlement Section at Jiangmen People's Procuratorate, I spent three years studying the corruption issue, which has become systemic and penetrated almost every cell of Chinese society over the past decade. I therefore have deep concerns about the future of China, and I am not alone.

Probably there is nowhere better than China's stock market to see the limits of the gradualist approach. As will be shown in this book, the potential efficiency gains that could be brought about by a healthy, well-functioning stock market have been completely outweighed by the consideration of maintaining survival of the ruling party. The study on corporate governance and the stock market provides us a lens through which to scrutinize China's transition.

My deepest gratitude goes to my supervisors, Professor Frank Stephen and Dr Rilka Dragneva-Lewers for their patience and inspiration. I would also like to express my thanks to Professor Roman Tomasic, Mr David Williamson, Professor Emilios Avgouleas, Dr Andrew Johnston, Mr Bill Hebenton, Dr Jackson Maogoto and my mentors at Renmin University, Professor Zhu Daqi and Professor Wang Zongyu, for their comments and encouragement.

I am deeply grateful to my dear friends Li Yang, Lin Feng, Si Ningning, Li Xia, Su Bing, Lee Jiecui, Zhu Huixiao, Zhang Huili, Li Zhaohui and Jiao Yanhong for their unflagging support. My warm thanks also go to my Ph.D colleagues at Manchester Law School, Long Long, Lin Wangwei, Han Tianzhu, Sun Fang, Xie Bo, Gao Xuan, Qin Xiaojing, Huang Haiming, Stephie Fehr, Ann Richter and Sarah A. Che Rohim, with whom I shared joys and sorrows, ups and downs. Finally, I thank my editors, Mathew Pitman and Laura Seward for their hard work, and Carolyn Cox for language correction.

Table of statutes and regulations

Table of cases

United Kingdom

United States

Introduction

I. THE CHINA PUZZLE

China set up its two stock exchanges, the Shang Hai Stock Exchange (SHSE) and Shen Zhen Stock Exchange (SZSE) in 1990 and 1991 respectively. After about 20 years' growth, by the end of 2008, there were a total of 1625 companies listing on these two stock exchanges and the combined market capitalization reached 12.13 trillion yuan. Investors' accounts totalled 152 million, 107 securities companies had been set up with total assets of 1.1912 trillion yuan (The China Securities Regulatory Commission,[1] 2008 Annual Report). In terms of market capitalization, it ranked as the second largest market in Asia, next only to Japan, and fourth in the world.[2]

The rapid expansion of the Chinese stock market represented a sharp contrast to the failure of its former socialist counterparts such as the Czech Republic. In 1995, the Prague Stock Exchange (PSE) had 1716 listings (*Int'l Herald Tribune*, 17 March 1999). By early 1999, the number of listings on the PSE had fallen by more than 80 per cent to 301 and fewer than a dozen of them enjoyed any liquidity (Coffee, 1999a, p. 9). So the question arises, how did the Chinese stock market develop in this form? What makes the difference between it and other transition countries?

Law and finance scholars, such as La Porta, Lopez, Shleifer and Vishny, based on considerable empirical evidence across countries, claimed that strong legal protection of investors is the determinant of capital market development (1997, 1998, 2000a, b). However, Allen et al., (2005), and Pistor and Xu (2005) found that legal protection of

---

[1]   Referred as the CSRC hereinafter.

[2]   The calculation does not include Hong Kong Stock Exchange (HKSE). In July 2009, the market capitalization of the Chinese stock market once overtook Japan and became the second largest in the world. See *Financial Times Chinese*, 17 July 2009. However, it must be noted that the prevalent figure does not reflect the real size of the Chinese stock market. In the Chinese stock market, two-thirds of shares are non-tradable whose value should be heavily discounted. This issue will be discussed in detail in Chapter 4.

shareholders in China's stock market is very weak. In fact, the level of investor protection in China is not only significantly below developed countries, it is also not ahead of any of the other major emerging economies[3] (Allen et al., 2005). Apparently, the growth of the Chinese stock market cannot be explained by the 'law and finance' school. Instead, it raises a serious challenge for the law and finance literature.

Pistor and Xu (2005) made an attempt to explain the growth of China's stock market. They argued that the quota system that was adopted during 1993–2000 (de facto until 2004) by the CSRC, created an incentive for the regional bureaucrats to select more over less viable companies to list and thereby operated as an alternative to legal protection of investors in information disclosure. Nevertheless, as will be discussed in this book, Pistor and Xu's argument is based on unsound assumptions and ignores some important factors which render it problematic. As a result, the development of China's stock market thus far still remains a puzzle. The purpose of this book is to try to solve this puzzle.

II. THE SIGNIFICANCE OF THE QUESTION

Explaining the development of China's stock market has important implications, most directly, for corporate governance study. Corporate governance study has become a mainstream concern in the past two decades, as a result of the worldwide wave of privatization; the takeover wave of the 1980s; the 1998 East Asia, Russia and Brazil crises; pension fund reform and the growth of private savings; deregulation and the integration of capital markets; a series of US and European scandals that triggered some of the largest insolvencies in history (Becht, Bolton and Roell, 2005). Empirical evidence confirmed that good corporate governance is critical to economic growth through increasing access to external financing by firms (Demirguc-Kunt and Maksimovic, 1998); lowering the cost of capital and enhancing the valuation of firms (La Porta, et al., 2002; Claessens, et al., 2002; Caprio et al., 2003); resulting in better allocation of resources and better management (Beck et al., 2000; Beck and Levine, 2002; Wurgler, 2000); reducing risk of financial crises (Claessens, 2006).

Although the importance of corporate governance has been widely recognized, the question of how to achieve good corporate governance

---

[3]   Allen et al. (2005) showed that China's corruption index is the worst among the seven developing countries, while its measures of anti-director rights (creditor rights) is only higher than that of India and Mexico.

still remains in debate. But in the past two decades, the Anglo-America shareholder model seems to gain some advantage over its competitors. As a result, a good number of corporate governance codes, principles that were based on the Anglo-American model have been produced by various organizations and spread across countries. The Anglo-American model has different versions: apart from the 'law and finance' school which emphasizes legal protection of shareholders, the 'law and economics' version suggests that corporate governance can be effectively addressed through private contracting and contractual arrangements, regulation is unnecessary or even harmful (Easterbrook and Fischel, 1991) and the role of law is marginal (Easterbrook and Fischel, 1991) or even trivial (Black, 1990). Both schools attracted many followers and had a significant influence on policy making internationally.

A study of the Chinese stock market development provides us with an opportunity to test the effectiveness of the prevailing theories. As already noted, if the growth of China's stock market cannot be explained by the 'law and finance' literature, then, can it be explained by the 'law and economics' literature? If not, what can? Does China represent an alternative approach to stock market development? What experience can other economies learn from it? I believe this research has both theoretical and practical significance to corporate governance study.

More broadly, explaining stock market development has significant implications for the 'rule of law' debate. Recent economics literature, echoed in the pronouncements of the World Bank and similar multilateral organizations, emphasized that the rule of law is crucial in fostering economic development (Hall and Jones, 1999; Acemoglu et al., 2001; Rodrik et al., 2004).[4] In spite of its poor 'rule of law' profile, China has been the fastest growing country over the past three decades and its economy has already become one of the most important in the world. For the 'rule of law' advocates, China is a question that they cannot avoid. The study of the development of China's stock market can shed light on the 'rule of law' issue.

III. METHODOLOGY

In order to explain the development of China's stock market, we need a conceptual framework which allows us to examine various governance mechanisms on a unified base. However, such a framework does not exist

---

[4] Such emphasis dates back to Max Weber and is carried forth by Douglass North (1990).

in current research. Previous studies have normally focused on some governance mechanisms while ignoring others, in particular, little attention has been paid to the relationship between different governance mechanisms. Relying on the insights of New Institutional Economics (NIE), an analytical framework under which the role of various governance mechanisms could be better evaluated is established.

The framework runs as follows: looking through agency theory, corporations can be treated as a nexus of contracts (Jensen and Meckling, 1976), among which I focus on the financial contract between external financiers and corporate controllers. The corporate governance problem thereby could be regarded as an enforcement issue, i.e. how to enforce the financial contract between external investors and corporate controllers. Based on the knowledge on contract enforcement that has been accumulated by NIE scholars in the past few decades, we can first establish a conceptual framework for contract enforcement in general. Under this framework, contract enforcement can be divided into self-enforcement and enforcement by third party. Self-enforcement includes enforcement in one-shot games and in repeat games; third-party enforcement contains non-state third-party enforcement and state enforcement. Corporate governance is then brought into this framework: various corporate governance mechanisms are now turned into enforcement mechanisms and reconsidered in an enforcement context.

The next step is to apply this framework to the Chinese stock market and examine the effectiveness of each enforcement mechanism. Based on this comprehensive study, I will try to identify the driving forces in the development of the Chinese stock market.

This methodology has some distinct advantages. First, I believe it catches the essential issue in developing/transition countries. As previous studies have shown, there is often a big gap between 'law in practice' and 'law in books' in these countries. Thus, more attention should be paid to enforcement than to substantive laws. Second, it allows various governance mechanisms to be evaluated in one unified framework. By doing so, it helps to clarify an important question: What is the relationship between these governance mechanisms?

IV. STRUCTURE OF THE BOOK

The book is divided into five chapters. The first chapter lays down the theoretical framework of the book. This chapter finds that since effective enforcement requires various enforcement mechanisms to work together, for the sustainable development of the stock market, formal enforcement, i.e. the enforcement by the state, and informal enforcement such as large shareholders and stock exchanges must work together. However, formal enforcement might not be necessary in the early stage. Informal enforcement could support the market's growth to a certain extent. This finding is different both from the 'law and economics' school which downplays the role of formal enforcement, and the 'law and finance' school which seems to misplace the formal enforcement.

The second chapter provides the background settings of China's stock market and listed companies. It finds that, in order to realize the party-state's goal of using the stock market to finance state-owned enterprises (SOEs) without losing control, the Chinese stock market is dominated by state-owned listed companies, two-thirds of the shares are not tradable, the market is artificially segmented and most market players are owned by the state.

The third chapter presents a comprehensive study on enforcement in China's stock market. Various enforcement mechanisms are examined here. It finds that state ownership has fundamentally undermined the foundation of self-enforcement mechanisms. The tradition of centralization has weakened the function of non-state third-party enforcers such as stock exchanges. Formal enforcement is inherently weak in a state where the elites are only constrained by the power of others, not by the rule of law. As a result, neither formal nor informal enforcement is effective in the Chinese stock market.

The fourth chapter provides a critique of Pistor and Xu's (2005) argument and suggests an alternative explanation to the development of China's stock market. It argues that the Chinese stock market growth is a result of state guarantee, financial repression, institutional rent seeking and speculation by investors. In the absence of effectual enforcement, although the Chinese stock market expanded quickly in size, it is highly inefficient and unsustainable.

The final chapter outlines the broad conclusions of the book. It summarizes the central arguments and major contributions of this book, highlights relevant policy implications and briefly discusses the future of the Chinese stock market.

1. Theoretical framework

INTRODUCTION

This chapter establishes the theoretical framework of this book. Section 1 provides a brief review of the concept and significance of corporate governance. Section 2 outlines the agency theory – the approach taken in this book to look at the corporate governance problem. Section 3 examines the various ways proposed in previous studies to dealing with the agency problem. Section 4 is the main body of this chapter. First, based on empirical evidence, it establishes the centrality of enforcement in corporate governance, at least in transition or developing countries. Second, relying on the insights of New Institutional Economics (NIE), it sets up an analytical framework for contract enforcement in general. It divides enforcement mechanisms into self-enforcement and third-party enforcement. The former could be further divided into self-enforcement mechanisms in a one-shot game and in a repeated game; the latter could be further divided into enforcement by a non-state third party and by a state. Specific mechanisms in each sub-category will be examined and a discussion regarding the relationship between private ordering and public ordering will also be included. Third, it applies this general analytical framework to the corporate context. Various corporate governance mechanisms like large shareholders, gatekeepers will be examined in this enforcement framework. The discussion between private ordering and public ordering will also be extended to the corporate context.

I. CORPORATE GOVERNANCE: CONCEPTION AND SIGNIFICANCE

Although corporate governance has become an extremely popular topic in the past two decades, there is no uniform definition of it. The many definitions could be generally grouped under two heads. One group of definitions is concerned largely with issues of control and corporate behaviour. For example, the report of the Committee on the Financial

Aspects of Corporate Governance (The Cadbury Report) defines corporate governance as 'the system by which companies are directed and controlled'. Margaret Blair (1996, p. 3) calls it 'the whole set of legal, cultural, and institutional arrangements that determine what publicly traded corporations can do, who controls them, how the control is exercised, and how the risks and returns from the activities they undertake are allocated'. Berglof and Von Thadden (1999, p. 11) define it as 'the set of mechanisms that translate signals from product markets and input markets into firms' behaviour'.

Under the broad definition, the objective of corporate governance would be to maximize the contribution of firms to the overall economy, including all stakeholders. Corporate governance then would include the relationship between shareholders, creditors and corporations; between employees and corporations; and between financial markets, institutions and corporations. It could also encompass corporate social responsibility.

This book adopts a narrow type of definition in focusing on the relationship between corporate financiers and corporate controllers. Corporate governance is 'the set of mechanisms – both institutional and market-based – that induce the self-interested controllers of a company (those that make decisions regarding how the company will be operated) to make decisions that maximize the value of the company to its owners (the suppliers of capital)' (Denis and McConnell, 2003, pp. 1–2). Or, stated more simply, it is about the key question: How can financiers make sure that, once they sink their funds, they will 'get anything but a worthless piece of paper back from the manager' (Shleifer and Vishny, 1997, p. 741).

The reason for adopting this definition is that the main interest of the book is to explore this question: how to promote the development of a stock market which has now been proved to exert a first-order impact on long-run economic growth. In order to encourage people to invest their money in the stock market rather than leave it in banks, the first thing one needs to do is to ease their fear of being cheated by people who control the way corporate funds are used. It by no means indicates that the interests of other stakeholders are not important, they are. But it is beyond the scope of this book.

II. THE AGENCY THEORY OF CORPORATE GOVERNANCE

This book takes an agency perspective on corporate governance. The agency problem is an essential element of the contractual view of firms, developed by Coase (1937), Jensen and Meckling (1976), Fama and Jensen (1983a, b). The agency relationship is a pervasive fact of economic life. As long as one party (the principal) engages the other (the agent) to perform some service on his behalf and to delegate some decision-making authority to the latter, there is an agency relationship. The agency problem arises from the fact that the agent commonly has better information than does the principal about the relevant facts; the principal cannot easily assure himself that the agent's performance is precisely what was promised. As a result, the agent has an incentive to behave opportunistically[1] which will reduce the value of the agent's performance to the principal, either directly or indirectly because the principal must engage in costly monitoring of the agent (Ross, 1973; Milgrom and Roberts, 1992).

In the corporate context, the essence of the agency problem is the separation of management and finance, or, in more standard terminology, the separation of ownership and control. An entrepreneur or manager might find the need for raising funds from external investors, either to put them to productive use or to cash out their holdings in the firm. The financers, on the other hand, need the managers' specialized human capital to generate returns on their funds. A critical question arises, therefore, as to how investors can be assured that their funds are not being wasted or stolen and ultimately that they are repaid by the entrepreneurs or managers. The agency problem in this context 'refers to the difficulties financiers have in assuring that their funds are not expropriated or wasted on unattractive projects' (Shleifer and Vishny, 1997, p. 741).

In an ideal world, the financiers and managers could sign a contract that specifies exactly what managers do in all states of the world, and how the profits are allocated. Nevertheless, most future contingencies are hard to describe and foresee. As a result, complete contracts are technologically difficult and prohibitively expensive (Grossman and Hart, 1986). Because of these problems in designing their contracts, the manager and the financier have to allocate residual control rights – i.e. the rights to make decisions when unforeseen circumstances arise that were unanticipated in the contract (Grossman and Hart, 1986; Hart and Moore, 1990).

---

[1]   The term 'opportunism' following the usage of Williamson (1985), to refer to self-interested behaviour that involves some element of guile, deception, misrepresentation or bad faith.

Financiers could give funds to the managers only on the condition that they retain all residual control rights. Thus, any time some unexpected thing occurs, they get to decide what to do. But this might not work since the financiers are not informed or qualified enough to decide what to do – the very reason they hired the manager in the first place. As a consequence, the manager ends up with significant control rights and discretion over how to allocate investors' funds (Shleifer and Vishny, 1997, p. 741). Once they are entrusted with the funds, they can expropriate shareholders.

Expropriation can take a variety of forms. In some instances, the insiders simply steal the profits. In other instances, expropriation take more elaborate forms such as transfer pricing, asset stripping, investor dilution, diversion of corporate opportunities, excessive compensation, shirking, consumption of perquisites, empire-building, entrenchment etc.

III. DEALING WITH THE AGENCY PROBLEM

Previous studies proposed various methods of dealing with the agency problem. Gomes (1996) and Kreps (1990) argue that managers repay investors even if this is not obligatory, because they want to come to the capital market and raise funds in the future, and hence need to establish a good reputation in order to convince future investors to give them money. Delong et al. (1989, 1990) found that external finance could occur without effective governance if investors are sufficiently optimistic about short-term capital gains and prepared to part with their money without regard for how the firm will ultimately pay them back.

A more far-reaching approach is provided by the traditional 'law and economics' scholars. Admitting that contract is inherently incomplete and the agency problem does exist, they argue that financial contracts take place between sophisticated issuers and sophisticated investors. Thus, on average, investors recognize a risk of expropriation, penalizing firms that fail to contractually disclose information about themselves and to contractually bind themselves to treat investors well. Because entrepreneurs bear these costs when they issue securities, they have an incentive to bind themselves through contracts with investors so as to limit expropriation (Jensen and Meckling, 1976).

The legal system does have a role to play in this contractual model, but it is at best of secondary importance (Easterbrook and Fischel, 1991), or even trivial (Black, 1989). It holds that the legal system should simply enforce private contracts. As long as these contracts are enforced by the courts, regulation is unnecessary or even detrimental to financial markets since regulators are often captured by the incumbent firms and use their power to deter entry (Stigler, 1964, 1971; Easterbrook and Fischel, 1991). For these theorists, corporate law should be confined only to providing 'standard terms' for contracting parties so as to reduce transaction costs (Easterbrook and Fischel, 1991).

As opposed to the 'law and economics' school, the 'law and finance' scholars have claimed that in many countries, courts cannot be expected to effectively enforce contracts because they are often underfinanced, unmotivated, inexperienced, politicized or corrupt. Even in the United States where the role of courts is more extensive than anywhere else in the world, the so-called Business Judgement Rule often keeps the courts out of the affairs of companies. They suggest that rather than complete reliance on court-enforced contracting, it may be socially efficient to provide a detailed legal framework which standardizes contracts and tells judges what facts to look for and how to interpret them in light of the law (Glaeser et al., 2001; La Porta et al., 2000b; Glaeser and Shleifer, 2003).

Even with such a framework, however, the vagueness of laws and a lack of precedents may still make it too costly for a court to learn enough about a situation to figure out how the law actually applies. Statutes typically rely on broad language, such as honest trading or material information, and leave it to the courts to decide whether specific conduct constitutes a violation. Yet assessing the honesty of trading or the materiality of information is often difficult and expensive – even clean courts are unable to make timely decisions (Glaeser and Shleifer, 2003). Therefore, it may be socially efficient to create a regulatory framework which not only prescribes certain rules, but also empowers a regulator rather than a judge to interpret and clarify them, as well as to decide, within limits, what conduct constitutes a violation (Glaeser et al., 2001).

The idea that laws are critical to corporate governance has received strong support from comparative research over the last decade. An influential set of articles by La Porta et al. (1997, 1998, 1999, 2000a, 2000b, 2002) and a large amount of follow-up research have now well established the link between the legal system and financial development and economic growth. It could be summarized as follows: the historically determined differences in legal origins continue to shape private property rights and investor protection laws. These laws and the quality of their enforcement is a critical determinant of a country's financial development, which, in turn, exerts a first-order impact on long-run economic growth.

La Porta et al. (1998) discuss a set of key legal rules protecting shareholders and creditors and document the prevalence of these rules in 49 sample countries around the world. They also aggregate these rules into shareholder rights (anti-director)[2] and creditor rights indices[3] for each country, and consider several measures of the effectiveness of enforcement.[4] La Porta et al. used these variables as proxies for the content of the law towards investor protection to examine the variation of legal rules and enforcement quality across countries and across legal origins. They found that common law countries provided strongest protection to shareholders, French civil law countries are the weakest and German civil law countries in between. As a result, common law countries were found to have outperformed other countries in terms of financial development (La Porta et al., 1997, 1998).

---

[2] La Porta et al. created the 'anti-director index' as a summary measure of shareholder protection. This index ranges from zero to six and is formed by adding one when: the country allows shareholders to mail their proxy vote to the firm; shareholders are not required to deposit their shares prior to the general shareholders' meeting; cumulative voting or proportional representation of minorities on the board of directors is allowed; an oppressed minorities mechanism is in place; the minimum percentage of share capital that entitles a shareholder to call for an extraordinary shareholders' meeting is less than or equal to 10 per cent; shareholders have pre-emptive rights that can only be waived by a shareholders' vote.

[3] The creditor right index is a summary measure of creditor protection. This index ranges from zero to four and is formed by adding one when: the country imposes restrictions, such as creditors' consent or minimum dividends to file for reorganization; secured creditors are able to gain possession of their security once the reorganization petition has been approved (no automatic stay); secured creditors are ranked first in the distribution of the proceeds that result from the disposition of the assets of a bankrupt firm; the debtor does not retain the administration of its property pending the resolution of the reorganization.

[4] It evaluates the quality of enforcement by efficiency of the judicial system index, corruption index and accounting standards. 'Efficiency of the judicial system' is an index ranging from 0 to 10 then representing the average of investors' assessments of conditions of the judicial system in each country between 1980 and 1983. Corruption is an index representing the average of investors' assessments of corruption in government in each country between 1982 and 1995. Accounting standards is an index created by examining and rating companies' 1990 annual reports on their inclusion or omission of 90 items falling in the categories of general information, income statements, balance sheets, funds flow statement, accounting standards, stock data, and special items.

IV. CORPORATE GOVERNANCE AS AN ENFORCEMENT ISSUE

In this book, the corporate governance problem is looked at from a different angle. As noted above, under agency theory, the corporation is regarded as a nexus of contracts, thus, the corporate governance problem could be understood as an enforcement issue: how to enforce the financial contract between external financiers and corporate controllers? Good corporate governance therefore means effective enforcement of financial contracts. I choose to focus on enforcement as I believe it better catches the key issue of corporate governance, at least in transition and developing countries.

1. The Centrality of Enforcement in Transition/Developing Countries

One of the critiques of the 'law and finance' literature is that it places too much emphasis on the substantive laws (law on the books), and gives little attention to their effectiveness (law in practice) (Jackson, 2006, 2007; Jackson and Roe, 2009; Coffee, 2007; Dam, 2006a).

By contrast, Pistor et al. (2000) studied the impact of legal changes (also focusing on shareholder rights and creditors rights) on external finance in 24 transition economies in Eastern Europe and the former Soviet Union from 1992 to 1998.[5] They found, primarily as a result of legal technical assistance,[6] many of these countries have experienced impressive legal changes both in shareholder rights and creditor rights. By 1988, the transition economies scored higher on the La Porta et al. shareholder rights index than the three civil law families in the La Porta et al. sample and are surpassed only by the common law countries.[7] In terms of the creditor rights index, transition countries are well above the

---

[5]   They use various indicators. As to shareholder rights indices, they use La Porta et al.'s anti-director index along with five additional indices, called VOCIE, EXIST, ANTIMANAGE, ANTIBLOCK and SMINTEGR (stock market integrity index). Regarding creditor rights, they also added CREDCON, REMEDY and COLLAT to La Porta et al.'s creditor rights indices.

[6]   The American aid agency (USAID) has been particularly active in many countries of the former Soviet Union. Countries wishing to join the European Union (EU) are required to harmonize extensive parts of their laws with European standards.

[7]   By 1998, transition economies score 3.13, compared to the French civil law family (2.33), German civil law family (2.33), Scandinavian civil law family (3.0) and common law family (4.0).

world average and the average score for any of the four legal families.[8] Thus, in terms of law on the books, transition economies can boast higher levels of investor rights protection on the books than some of the most developed market economies, such as France and Germany.

However, when turning to effectiveness of these legal rules, it is found that high levels of formal legal protection achieved in many transition countries by 1998 are not mirrored in similar improvements in the effectiveness of legal institutions. Rapid improvements in formal legal protection are not necessarily associated with improvements in law enforcement. When they examined the impact of legal institutions on external finance, they found no evidence that formal legal indicators are correlated with financial market development. In contrast, they found legal effectiveness had overall a much higher explanatory power for the level of equity and credit market development. Therefore, it suggests that a major determinant for equity market development in the region is not primarily the law on the books, but the effectiveness of legal institutions (Pistor et al., 2000).

Of course, the most vivid example as to the disparity between law on the books and its effectiveness is Russia. Russian corporate law has largely borrowed (in a simplified fashion) the principal features and protections of US and UK corporate law (Black and Kraakman, 1996).[9] However, the Russian legal environment seems even closer to the Hobbesian state of nature with the looting of corporations and financial institutions being a fairly common event. Apparently, massive expropriation can occur even when the law on the books is nearly optimal[10] (Coffee, 1999a, p. 6).

Johnson et al. (2000) in the study of the Asian financial crisis concluded that weak enforcement of shareholder and creditor rights had first-order importance in determining the extent of exchange rate depreciation in 1997–1998. The three indices of legal institutions – which it termed 'efficiency of the judiciary, corruption, and the rule of law' – were found to better predict the change in exchange rates in emerging markets than did the standard macro measures. Other measures reflecting the

---

[8] Common law family scores 3.11; French civil law family 1.58; German civil law family 2.33; Scandinavian civil law family 2.0; transition countries 3.23.

[9] Russian company law has borrowed heavily from US and UK sources and, in its current version, was heavily influenced by a model developed by two American law professors. See Black and Kraakman (1996).

[10] Judging by the rules proposed by La Porta et al.

strength of shareholder rights were also found to be significantly correlated with the severity of the financial crisis, but only as long as these
measures reflect how rights are actually enforced.

Bhattacharya and Daouk (2002) found that the actual prosecutions for
insider trading did reduce the cost of capital in a jurisdiction, but that the
passage of an insider trading law did not. A large international study
found that the level of enforcement is much more important than the
quality of law on the books in explaining the turnover of CEOs (Defond
and Hung, 2003).

More recently, Dam (2006a) reports additional empirical evidence
from financial markets on the positive correlation between a strong and
effective judiciary, acting as an important formal contract enforcement
institution, and economic development. In particular, he cites the World
Bank's World Development Report of 2005, which argues that within
individual countries in Latin America, firms doing business in the
provinces of Argentina and Brazil that have competent courts enjoyed
greater access to credit. Similarly, the larger and more efficient firms in
Mexico can be found in Mexican states that have superior court systems.
The World Bank report attributes these favourable economic outcomes to
the fact that better courts reduce the risks firms face, and increase the
firms' willingness to invest more.

In their latest study, Jackson and Roe (2009) developed a series of
enforcement variables that had superior explanatory power to common
law origins in explaining stock market capitalization. They found that
common law origins no longer had any significant relationship with stock
market capitalization once they controlled for their various enforcement
variables. Thus, it suggests that legal origin influences contract enforcement and the quality of the judiciary, and it is through this channel
instead of legal rules that it affects financial development.

In reality, it is hard to entirely separate legal rules from enforcement.
The available evidence suggests that both good rules and their enforcement matter, and that the combination of the two is generally most
effective (Djankov, Hart et al., 2008; Djankov, La Porta et al., 2008; La
Porta et al., 2006). The quality of laws also has some impact on their
enforcement. But the degree of the divergence between 'law on the
books' and 'law in practice' is considerably different in developed
countries from that in developing/transition countries. In the former, once
laws are enacted, their enforcement is of less concern. By contrast, in the
latter, laws are often a 'facade without a foundation' (Murrel, 1996,
p. 34). For example, the *New York Times* (1 June 2000) reported that there
were 25 million cases pending before the courts in India, and even if no
new ones are filed, it will take 324 years to clear the backlog.

It is relatively easier to enhance the quality of substantive laws, after all, good laws can be found by simply searching the internet. It is much more difficult, if not impossible, to transplant the institutions that enforce laws, such as courts and regulators. As Nobel Laureate Douglass North (1990, p. 54) pointed out: 'the inability of societies to develop effective, low cost enforcement of contracts is the most important source of both historical stagnation and contemporary under-development in the Third World'. Therefore, at least for transition/developing economies, it is quite plausible to put enforcement rather than substantive laws in the centre when studying corporate governance.

2. A Broad Approach to Enforcement

The above discussion has highlighted the significance of enforcement. However, it focuses only on implementation of legal rules. I believe the study of enforcement should not be restricted to legal enforcement. In this book, I take a much broader approach to enforcement. Following Barzel (2002, p. 35), who defines enforcement as 'the credible threat to induce compliance', enforcement, in my understanding, consists of a set of institutions that could impose a threat on corporate controllers so as to make the incomplete contracts credible. As will be seen below, legal enforcement is only one of such mechanisms and by no means always the most important one. Over the past few decades, NIE has accumulated considerable knowledge on contract enforcement. relying on this knowledge, a general conceptual framework for contract enforcement will first be established and then applied to the corporate context.

V. A GENERAL FRAMEWORK FOR CONTRACT ENFORCEMENT

Even though enforcement is generally agreed to be critically important to economic performance, and there is a vast literature on the subject, no simple framework for thinking about enforcement exists. We can consider several ways of classifying the issues related to enforcement. Enforcement could first be divided into self-enforcement and third-party enforcement, which could be further divided into state enforcement and non-state third-party enforcement. Self-enforcement along with non-state third-party enforcement could be classified as informal enforcement as opposed to state enforcement that could be termed as formal enforcement. Moreover, self-enforcement and non-state third-party enforcement are sometimes called private ordering, state enforcement as public ordering which includes private enforcement of law and public enforcement.

All these enforcement mechanisms, more or less, can be found in almost every country. But the role of each mechanism varies significantly across countries. Even for the same country, it varies from time to time, from transaction to transaction. Also, each means has a comparative advantage under different circumstances, and no single means is likely to be preferable to all the others all the times (Barzel, 2002, p. 25). Therefore, there is no simple answer to the question of what is optimal.

1. Self-enforcement

Realizing the gains to be had from specialization requires exchange, and exchange agreements must be enforced. However, enforcement cannot be taken for granted. Whenever the full performance of an exchange requires time (on one or both sides), the party who finishes first will find himself having to rely on the promise of the trading partner to get what he has bargained for. The trading partner, after receiving his agreed gains, finds it is in his interest to renege on the agreement. If there is no other means to mitigate this risk arising from opportunism, only simultaneous exchanges could take place.[11]

Simultaneous exchange, as we observed, only constitutes a small subset of overall economic exchanges. People do find various ways to get agreements enforced. Sometimes, the parties themselves may enforce the agreements. Self-enforcement, however, works well only for some agreements. Under what conditions will contracts tend to be self-enforcing? In a wealth-maximizing world, the answer is that 'contracts will be self-enforcing when it pays the parties to live up to them – that is, in terms of the costliness of measuring and enforcing agreements, the benefits of living up to contracts will exceed the costs' (North, 1990, p. 55).

1.1 Self-enforcement in one-shot games

Even in a one-shot transaction, self-enforcing is made possible by changing the balance of benefits and costs facing the second mover. The party who finishes first can make the breach more costly by demanding hostages or collateral. The party who receives the gains first could make his promise more credible by tying his hands (Williamson, 1983).

---

[11]   The exchanges must be strictly simultaneous, which means that the goods or services in question must have immediately verifiable attributes and qualities. If the measurement requires time, the exchanges will still be forgone.

1.1.1 Hostages The party who finishes first could require a hostage *ex ante* from the trading partner. The essential characteristic of a hostage is that it is valued by the hostage-giver but not necessarily by the recipient or anyone else. Taking a hostage gives the recipient some power to coerce the trading partner to perform by threatening to destroy it. The trading partner has to take the value of the hostage into account when he decides whether to default or not. As long as the value of a hostage to him exceeds the costs of performance, he will choose to perform.

However, the characteristic of a hostage limits its role in securing transactions. An ideal hostage would be something that had no independent value to the recipient or anyone else. Otherwise, it will simply transfer the risk from one party to another since the recipient might want to keep the hostage either as substitute for performance, or in addition to it.[12] On the other hand, the hostage holder still finds himself to be vulnerable to opportunism. Since the hostage is worth nothing to anyone but the giver, if the giver lied about its value, the recipient would be no better off than he was at all. Even if the giver did not lie, the only power that a recipient can use to coerce the hostage-giver is to threaten to destroy it. But the actual destruction of the hostage will do no good to him as he will lose the only thing that makes performance possible. Being aware of this, the hostage-giver could force the recipient into a bargain that is potentially disadvantageous to the latter (Kronman, 1985, pp. 12–15).

1.1.2 Collateral Instead of asking for a hostage, the party could demand collateral. What distinguishes a hostage from collateral is that the latter not only has value to the giver, but also to the recipient. In the case of a breach, the recipient can directly realize its value through use or trade without dealing with the giver. Therefore, collateral could free the recipient from the *ex post* breach negotiations and thus eliminate the opportunism arising from the using of a hostage.

However, the use of collateral might create opportunism of another form. If it is to provide complete protection for the recipient, the asset must be worth as much to him as the performance he has been promised. But this creates risk of opportunism on the recipient's part. Since the collateral has equal value to the recipient as the promised performance, while valued more to the giver (otherwise it would already be sold or traded in the first place), now the recipient is in a position to force the

---

[12] If the return of hostage and performance does not occur simultaneously, the recipient might refuse to return the hostage after he received the agreed gains.

giver into a bargain in his favour. If the recipient is under-collateralized, he will be put back to the situation associated with hostage giving (Kronman, 1985, pp. 15–18).

1.1.3 Hands-tying   Hands-tying is similar to hostage giving in the way that in each case, the promisor does something at the outset that will make a subsequent breach on his part more costly. As a result, his incentive to perform is strengthened and the confidence of the other party increased. However, there is an important difference between the two. In the case of hostage giving, it requires the promisee himself to take action to punish the breach – namely, to destroy the hostage he holds. By contrast, hands-tying makes punishment self-executing. If the breach occurs, the promisor will automatically incur the added cost of doing so without requiring the promisee to do anything (Williamson, 1983; Kronman, 1985, pp. 18–20).

The party could make some investments whose value will be lost or largely reduced in the case of breach. Investing in transaction-specific assets and advertising are most often observed examples of this kind. A transaction-specific asset becomes useless or can only be used for other purposes by incurring additional costs if the party breaks the agreement with the current partner. The whole advertising expenditures would be largely wasted if the reputation of the party was tarnished in one single transaction. The prospective loss in either case would deter the promisor from being opportunistic in the current exchange.

Its automaticity makes hands-tying a superior means to hostage and collateral. It frees the promisee from taking any action to punish the promisor, on the other hand, it protects the promisor from blackmail that might happen in using collateral. But hands-tying still has the same fundamental limitation as hostage and collateral. Ultimately, they all depend on the promisor's own calculation of costs and benefits to decide whether or not to adhere to the agreement. None of them could prevent the party from breaking his promise if he determines to do so.

1.2 Self-enforcement in repeated games

As shown above, even a one-shot transaction could be self-enforced under certain conditions. However, the most likely and indeed empirically observable state in which contracts are self-enforcing is that in which the parties to exchange have a great deal of knowledge about each other and are involved in repeated dealings. Repeated transactions can be self-enforced because the immediate gains from behaving opportunistically can be offset by future losses caused by a collapse of the long-term relationship and therefore to lower future payoffs. This has been well understood both in the theory of repeated games and in practice (Axelrod, 1984; Abreau, 1986; Abreau et al., 1990).

1.2.1 Bilateral relationship Consider the case in which one party wants to exchange for something whose true quality cannot be easily observed at the time of exchange. In a one-shot game, the exchange will more likely be forgone because the party has no way to rescue if the quality turned out to be poor later. But in a repeated game, the party will be more confident with the exchange, not only because he knows the seller better (after dealing with the same person many times), but more importantly, he knows that he has the ability to punish him if being cheated. He can punish the cheater by cutting off the relationship between them. The future loss caused by the break-up of a long-term relationship could deter opportunistic behaviour. For the same reason, the party who finishes first has less concern about the performance of the other party in non-simultaneous exchanges which would otherwise be difficult in a one-shot game.[13]

1.2.2 Reputation An agreement in which the two parties have a direct long-term relationship can be self-enforced. In some cases, an agreement can also be self-enforced where both parties belong to the same group, even if there is little long-term relationship between them. Parties benefit from being a member of a certain group. In each transaction, the party has an opportunity to cheat the partner who is also a group member. Although the partner himself is unable to punish the cheater because there is no long-term relationship between them, the cheater's misconduct becomes known through the group and no other group member will transact with him in the future. The actions by the group have the effect of punishing the cheater on behalf of his current partner. Thus, a party's good reputation ensures the opportunity to benefit from future transactions, and inversely, the prospect of future beneficial transactions induces cooperative behaviour. In game-theoretic terms, 'the assurance of *ex post* sanctions against cheaters allows transactors to commit credibly to follow merchants that they will fulfil their contractual duties' (Richman, 2004, p. 2335).

---

[13] A literature on relational contracts, where both the terms and the enforcement of an agreement are embedded within a bilaterally dependent relationship, emerged in the 1970s and involved both legal and economic scholars. For instance, see Macneil (1974); Goetz and Scott (1981); Klein (1980); Williamson (1983).

For the reputation mechanism to work, the group needs a good information network and credible multilateral punishment strategies. Both conditions can be fulfilled in stable and cohesive groups or networks, which might be defined by business ties (Greif, 1993; Bernstein, 1992, 2001); ethnicity (Casella and Rauch, 2002; Rauch, 2001) and so on.

Reputation is widely used in enforcement.[14] Examples range from Maghribi merchants (Greif, 1989, 1993) and merchant guilds (Milgrom et al., 1990) in the early days, to the contemporary New York diamond industry, which is dominated by the Orthodox Jewish network (Bernstein, 1992); from the National Grain and Feed Association in the United States (Bernstein, 1996) to Mexico's footwear industry (Woodruff, 1998); from domestic organizations such as the New York Stock Exchange (NYSE) to Chinese merchants in Southeast Asian trading communities (Landa, 1981). Reputation has proved to be an effective enforcement mechanism both in the past and present, in domestic and international trade, in developed and developing countries.

However, reputation also has its own limitations. It works well in small, close-knit groups, but with the increase of the size of the group, its effectiveness decreases. As noted above, the success of reputation crucially depends on the transmission of information[15] and effective punishment.[16] However, as the size of such a group increases, both the quality of information and the credibility of punishment degrade. This has been vividly illustrated by the case studies of Ostrom (1990) and the contrasting case studies of two merchant groups by Greif (1994, 1997). The numerical calculations on the theoretical models of Kandori (1992) and Ellison (1994) also show similar tendencies. Therefore, when trading opportunities expand beyond the close group, reputation becomes less effective and alternative means are required.

---

[14]   In his famous examination of the practices of American businessmen, Macaulay (1963, p. 63) even claimed that social pressure and reputation are more widely used than formal contracts and judicial enforcement in executing mutually beneficial agreements.

[15]   Both the speed and accuracy of information transmission are important. The speed is important, otherwise the punishment would become more distant in time and get discounted more heavily in potential miscreants' calculation. The accuracy is also important: if punishment may be unleashed in error even if one has not deviated, then the deterrent effect is lessened (Dixit, 2004, p. 60).

[16]   Participation in the collective action of punishing a miscreant is sometimes individually costly; this turns the punishment process into another prisoner's dilemma game which requires its own solution (Dixit, 2004, p. 60).

1.3 Self-enforcement: its edge and limitation

Self-enforcement has an informational edge over third-party enforcement. Information is crucial to enforcement. Among other things, an enforcer must be able to observe at least some measures of the agreement he enforces in order to know what to enforce. Information could be divided into three types, private, observable and verifiable information. Information is private when it is available to one of the parties but not the other (Dixit, 2004, p. 26).[17] Information is called observable when it is available symmetrically to both parties, and verifiable when it can be proved to third parties such as a court (Dixit, 2004, p. 27).[18] Private and observable information are subjective in the sense that they are limited to parties; verifiable information is objective as it can be proved to others. Self-enforcement can be based on private, subjective information that might make collecting and proving information unnecessary. In contrast, the fact that third-party enforcement can only rely on verifiable information indicates that some subjective information must be forgone. The process of collecting and proving information therefore makes the enforcement more costly.

The fundamental limitation of all sorts of self-enforcement mechanisms is that, ultimately, they have to rely on the individual himself to decide whether to perform or not. Neither hostage-giving nor reputation could stop the party from being opportunistic if he determines to do so. As shown above, self-enforcement works by creating a future cost to the individual of taking an action that brings him an immediate personal benefit. The nature and the size of the cost can vary widely across different situations. The common requirement is that 'the future cost should outweigh the immediate benefit in the individual's own calculation based on his own preferences, whether for material things, social standing, internal guilt, or whatever' (Dixit, 2004, p. 60). But the future cost does not always exceed the immediate gains. In the strict logic of game theory, repetition must be infinite or at least indefinite, because in any fixed and finite sequence of repetitions, cooperation will unravel from the end. However, in reality, an infinite repeated game is rare; when the relationship is about to terminate, self-enforcement becomes difficult, if not impossible – an alternative mechanism is needed.[19]

---

[17] The theory of asymmetric information has been well developed and is now a standard part of economic theory.

[18] The distinction is, in practice, a matter of cost. The costs of verifying private, observable information are prohibitively high.

[19] However, as Barzel (2002, p. 36) pointed out, 'the primacy of self-enforced relationships must be made clear. In an early society at the onset of

2.   Third-party Enforcement

Self-enforcement is insufficient when immediate gains exceed the future costs, and a third party therefore becomes necessary to enforce the agreement. In the presence of a third-party enforcer, the individual will perform even when his direct gain becomes negative. The reason for this is simply that he is unwilling to incur the even greater penalty that the third party would impose if he did not perform. A variety of institutions, legitimate and illegitimate, can be used to enforce agreements and resolve disputes.

2.1   Non-state third-party enforcement

Non-state institutions can act as the third-party enforcer, either by using violence, or by employing non-violent methods to enforce agreements.

2.1.1   Criminal organizations   Among their other activities, 'criminal organizations engage in the enforcement of agreements using physical power for enforcement, in this they resemble the state' (Barzel, 2002, p. 75). The enforcement by criminal organizations has been seen throughout history. It usually operates at times or in niches where the state is absent. For instance, the origins of the Mafia's enforcement role could be traced back to the 19th century in Sicily. After the abolition of feudalism, publicly provided security was inefficient and banditry was widespread. Landowners began to hire guards of former feudal lords and some of the tougher bandits to protect their property (Bandiera, 2003). In Japan, when the government had collapsed after being defeated in World War II but the occupying US forces had not yet restored order in August– September 1945, the Yakuza played a major role in getting markets restarted (Whiting, 1999, pp. 10–11; Dower, 1999, pp. 140–148). Similar activities are found in Russia and other transition economies (Varese, 2001).

---

interactions, all agreements must be self-enforced, because no external organization yet exists to offer third party enforcement. Indeed, ultimately, all agreements in any setting must be self-enforced. Third party enforcement, including that by the state, can be embedded within self-enforced agreements. Being a bootstrap operation, third party enforcement requires agreements between clients and the would-be third party enforcers. These agreements must also be self-enforced. In their relationships with one another, then, the third parties and their clients must perceive, individually or collectively, that the gain from maintaining their relationships in future will exceed whatever gains they could reap from reneging on their agreements in the present.'

The use of criminal organizations to enforce agreements is obviously problematic. Among other things, there is no external mechanism to ensure the honesty of the enforcer. That has to be self-enforcing, based on reputation considerations in a long-term relationship (Dixit, 2004, p. 13). Long-term relationship is less effective to bind the enforcer who is specialized in using violence. If not constrained, the enforcer is likely to benefit from confiscating the gains that his enforcement will generate.

2.1.2 Private arbitration Trade organizations usually centralize some of the operations of merchants or other specialists operating within a well-defined trade. The specialists voluntarily join the organization and agree to abide by its rulings. Normal services provided by trade associations include the setting of standards and lobbying for the industry. A few trade organizations also act as private arbitrators which provide the service of enforcing agreements among members (Barzel, 2002, p. 74).

Private arbitrators have no coercive power to ensure that their decisions are obeyed. Their enforcement power primarily comes from their role in disseminating information about individual reputation. Milgrom et al. (1990) studied the private judges in Champaign Fairs and showed that arbitration rulings in private ordering systems serve more as mechanisms to signal the quality of a merchant's reputation than as genuine instruments to enforce contractual obligations. A merchant who is found by a private court to have breached a contract but fails to pay receives publicity as a bad actor, leading other merchants to respond to the public ruling by refusing to deal with the transgressor. If the arbitrators also have power of expulsion, it can be a more effective sanction than the fines the courts will impose.[20] Bernstein (1992, 1996, 2001) gave examples of modern trade associations that provide similar functions to their members with her studies of the cotton industry, the National Grain and Feed Association and the New York Diamond Industry. It is shown

---

[20] Private arbitration panels (such as the Memphis Cotton Exchange and the New York Diamond Dealers Club) generally invite state courts to enforce their rulings (Bernstein, 1992, p. 125; 2001, p. 1737). In fact, however, 'very few private disputes spill into state court and are instead enforced exclusively of private enforcement to the likelihood that an individual who contests an arbitration decision and forces a fellow merchant to seek a ruling in state court will suffer doubly – by prompting his own expulsion from the trade association while additionally earning a reputation as litigious, uncooperative member of the merchant community. So, despite the alleged enforceability of the arbitration rulings in state court, the real enforcement power comes from the reach of the arbitrators only to those beholden to the prospect of future transactions' (Richman, 2004, footnote 32).

that effective enforcement within these industries is achieved by publicizing non-compliance and by expulsion.[21]

Arbitration works on the basis of the reputation mechanism, but unlike the pure reputation mechanism, or to use Williamson's (1991, p. 159) term, 'spontaneous private ordering',[22] arbitration represents an organized private ordering in which there is an organizing central body that collects and disseminates players' reputational information.[23] As noted above, the effectiveness of pure reputation may be weakened when relied upon beyond small communities; with a body of arbitrators determining where wrongdoing occurs and publicizing the identity of the wrongdoers, arbitration makes it possible for the reputation mechanism to work well even in a larger community.

Although the presence of arbitration could extend transactional security to a broader scope, its effectiveness is limited to individuals committed to repeat interactions with the industry or merchant community. It has no reach to individuals outside the community. Therefore, the exchanges that it can facilitate are constrained by the size of the group. Moreover, since it ultimately relies on the reputation mechanism, it has the same limitation as the latter, that is, it works only for those whose gains from dealings within the merchant community outweigh their immediate loss in arbitration. In order to extend the scope of exchange beyond the community and force individuals to perform even if it is not in their

---

[21]   Bernstein (1992, pp. 128–130) and Richman (2006, pp. 406–408) describe how sanctions in the diamond industry resemble the Old West's 'Wanted' posters, where the pictures of merchants who are found to owe debts are posted on the walls of each of the world's 24 diamond bourses. Once a dealer is known to have a bad debt, he will lose future business, face expulsion from the diamond bourses, and potentially suffer a denial of religious honours in the Ultra-Orthodox community.

[22]   Ellickson's (1991) cattle ranchers represent an example of spontaneous ordering, since the neighbours' social networks naturally facilitate gossip and information-sharing that are sufficient to induce coordinated behaviour.

[23]   Arbitrations are also used in other contexts for other reasons. 'In international trade, each party may suspect that the other country's courts will be biased in favour of its nationals; this can deter them from entering into contracts that may end up in national courts. Therefore both may agree *ex ante* to settle any disputes in an agreed international forum of arbitration. These forums usually lack the expertise that industry-specific forums can provide. Therefore they are not likely to lower costs or improve verifiability and permit more complete contracts; instead, removing the suspicion of bias may be their most important function' (Dixit, 2004, p. 29). Dezalay and Garth (1996), Casella (1996) and Mattli (2001) describe and discuss several of these institutions of arbitration in international trade.

interest to do so, a third-party enforcer who can impose costs directly on the individual without requiring a long-term relationship becomes necessary.

2.1.3 Information intermediaries Collecting information about an individual's reputation is costly. As a result, some organizations emerge to exploit economies in scale of information collection. As noted above, trade associations often play an important role in collecting and providing information. However, the trade association is mainly concerned with traders among pairs of its own members, and provides information about a member's reputation with other members. There are other organizations that are concerned with interactions between a member on one side and a non-member (general public) on the other. Some collect information about cheating by a member of the general public and provide it to their members, such as credit-approval services maintained by Mastercard and Visa. Some others keep track of their members' behaviour and make this information available to the public. This enables their members credibly to create and maintain reputation (Dixit, 2004, p. 98).

In some situations, third parties charge a fee to provide information to one side of a transaction about the history of the other side. Well-known examples include agencies that rate creditworthiness of people or firms, or services that monitor the quality of goods and services provided by firms (Dixit, 2004, p. 98).

2.2 Enforcement by the state

As the scope and complexity of exchange have increased, the once-for-all exchanges (or, in North's term, impersonal exchange) become more pervasive and the foundation of the reputation mechanism has been undermined. Hostage, collateral and hands-tying, as discussed above, can enforce one-shot transactions, but are usually limited to those in which attributes of goods in exchange are easy to measure. In the absence of effective state enforcement, large-scope, complex, impersonal exchanges are likely to be foreclosed and the gains from specialization cannot be fully realized.

Even the most libertarian economists, who deny the government any useful role in most aspects of the economy, allow that making and enforcing laws that give clear definition of property rights and ensuring adherence to voluntary private contracts are legitimate and essential functions of government (Friedman, 1962, p. 2). The state, as third-party enforcer, relies on violence to enforce contracts. The cost imposed by the state is direct. Imposing it does not require long-term relationships, neither between the principals and the enforcers nor among the principals themselves. It consists in the threat of physical punishment, which can include incarceration and seizure of property (Barzel, 2002, p. 42).

As the state can impose costs on the party regardless of their cost-benefit calculus, it provides transactional security to all exchanges within its jurisdiction. With the presence of a state enforcer, transacting parties do not have to acquire information about their trading partners in each exchange, or concern themselves about the other party's reneging on contracts after performance made on their own part, or to gain member-ship of certain groups. Once a breach occurs, they can resort to courts for compensation. Complex exchanges are made possible even among com-plete strangers who never expected to meet again. As a result, this facilitates specialization and division of labour that are believed to be critical underpinnings of economic growth.

However, the state acting as an effective contract enforcer is something that cannot be taken for granted.[24] If the state has coercive force, there is always the possibility that those who run the state will use that force in their own interests at the expense of the rest of the society. Barzel (2002) criticizes the orthodox economic view of the state as a benevolent and costless monopolist in coercion. In fact, only advanced countries in recent times come anywhere near the economist's ideal picture, in which the government supplies legal institutions that are guided solely by concern for social welfare and operate at low cost. In all countries, through much of their history, the apparatus of state law was very costly, slow, unreliable, biased, corrupt, weak or simply absent. In most coun-tries this situation still prevails (Dixit, 2004, p. 3). 'To develop the state into a coercive force that is able to protect property rights and enforce contracts effectively without risking abuse of its coercive power to the detriment of society is the fundamental dilemma facing most countries' (North, 1990, pp. 59–60).

In the case of a non-state third-party enforcer, enforcement is backed by long-term relationships, and the enforcers' ability to prevent competi-tors from offering their service seems to be limited. Therefore, when people realize that the enforcer engages in extortion, they can reduce their extortion losses by 'voting with their feet', namely turning to a competing third party. This will reduce their legitimate earning ability as well as the power to extort of the enforcer and the prospects of such

---

[24]   The idea that the state was the only third-party enforcer was dominant until economics recognized the ubiquity and importance of information asym-metries and transaction costs; the usual implicit assumption was the law operated costlessly (Dixit, 2004, p. 3).

losses will constrain the enforcer (Barzel, 2002, p. 44). In contrast, the state has a monopoly of legitimate violence-using within its jurisdiction. Thus, people are less likely to constrain the state from abusing its coercive power by turning to its competitor. The state's confiscation power does not depend on clients' perceptions. However, on the other hand, the parties to agreements are not compelled to use any particular third party to enforce them, and they will not secure the services of any third party they perceive as likely to confiscate their gains (Barzel, 2002, p. 44). Before the state can credibly constrain itself from abusing power, people will not access the courts to enforce contracts. Instead, they will keep relying on alternative enforcement methods even if they are not economically optimal.[25] In more extreme cases, they just completely avoid the formal legal system by going underground: 'unofficial economies' of post-communist former Soviet states (Johnson, et al., 1997) and the informal sector in Peru (De Soto, 1990) are typical examples of this kind. Therefore, an immense difference can be observed in the degree to which people can rely upon formal contract enforcement between developed countries and Third World countries (North, 1990).

3. Mixed Enforcement

It must be pointed out that these various enforcement mechanisms are not mutually exclusive. Instead, effective enforcement often requires them to work together. Commodities, even simple ones, have many valued attributes. The agreement governing a transaction is likely to stipulate the standards for some of its attributes, but it is often too expensive or technically difficult to stipulate them all (Grossman and Hart, 1986). However, the transactors will nevertheless exploit those not covered by the agreement. Therefore, multiple enforcers are employed to enforce different attributes of a transaction.

Take the exchange between a theatre company and its patrons for instance. Attributes such as the ticket price, the identity of the leading actors, and the place and time of the performance are stipulated contractually by public notices, as well as implicitly by the ticket and therefore can be enforced by the state. On the other hand, it is normally difficult for the quality of the performance to be covered by the contract and this has to be enforced by the performers' reputation. Reputation and state

---

[25] As Greif (2006, p. 8) has observed, informal contract enforcement will most likely prevail when there is no state enforcement, 'when economic agents expect the state to expropriate rather than protect their property, or when the state is unwilling or unable to secure property rights and enforce contracts'.

enforcement are simultaneously used within a single transaction; each enforce a different subset of attributes (Barzel, 2002, p. 85). Similarly, commitments regarding consumer product quality are legally enforceable under warranty provision. However, the warranty provisions cover only basic features of the goods, and for many products it is too costly for consumers to sue to enforce even these basic commitments. Other mechanisms, in particular the manufacturer's reputation, are the major determinant of the manufacturer's adherence to commitments to maintain product quality above minimal standards (Charny, 1990, p. 394).

4.   Private Ordering and Public Order

All the enforcement mechanisms discussed above can be found in contemporary economies in both developed and developing countries. Then a question arises, why do some systems of private ordering persist in modern societies? Or conversely, if a private system enjoys certain efficiencies over public courts, then why does economic research overwhelmingly indicate that reliable public courts are central to facilitating economic growth? (North, 1990; Greif and Kandel, 1995). To answer this question, it is first important to distinguish between private ordering that reflects 'voluntary opting out' of the formal legal system, and private ordering that is 'forced out' of the formal legal system.

4.1   Private ordering in the shadow of the law

Even in modern advanced economies where a well-functioning institution of state law exists, it is found that most business transactions are conducted using various informal arrangements, such as handshakes, oral agreement, ongoing relationships, custom and practice. If disputes arise, the parties first attempt to resolve them by direct negotiation. Recourse to the law is often the last, rather than the first, resort (Macaulay, 1963; Williamson, 1996). Ellickson (1991) did a field study of the way in which rural residents of Shasta County, California resolved disputes arising over trespass damage done by stray livestock. He found that the residents almost never resorted to legal redress, but instead relied on an elaborate structure of informal constraints to resolve disputes. This leads to the concept of 'private ordering in the shadow of the law'.[26]

Such private ordering in the shadow of the law arises for different reasons. The most often-mentioned reason is the cost of using the formal

---

[26]   Martin Shapiro (1975) deserves credit for first using the shadow imagery. The phrase was popularized by Mnookin and Kornhauser (1979) in their study of negotiations surrounding divorce settlements.

legal system. Bernstein (1992) discusses this in detail and illustrates the cost in the case of the diamond industry. The cost arises in many ways. First, even in countries with well-functioning state laws, obtaining and enforcing a judgment in the court system takes a long time – three years is not uncommon. Second, parties may find themselves under-compensated in the formal legal system. In its calculation of damage, the court may underestimate or even leave out items like lost profit that are speculative and can be overstated by the plaintiffs. Third, judges in state courts have to cover all conceivable matters that could arise under civil law, and therefore lack the expertise that insiders would be able to acquire about a specific industry. As a result, their verdicts in commercial disputes can be less predictable than those available in alternative specialized forums. Finally, courts may require public disclosure of information about business opportunities, costs and profits that the parties would prefer to keep secret. Sometimes the parties wish to avoid public knowledge of the mere fact that they were involved in litigation, which may cause their potential trading partners to think of them as inflexible and unwilling to renegotiate deals in response to changed circumstances (Bernstein, 1992, pp. 134, 149; Dixit, 2004, pp. 25–26). Bernstein (1992) uses the customs of the New York diamond trade to suggest that reputation and trust can be used at a low enough cost to allow private transactions to take place outside the domain of the formal legal system.

Another important reason for using private ordering is information. Alternative institutions may enjoy informational advantage over the public courts. As noted above, contracts enforced by courts must con-dition on verifiable information. As a result, private and observable information that might affect the accuracy of judgement has to be left out. Even compared to a non-state third party that also relies on verifiable information, the courts are still disadvantageous. Arbitration forums specialize by industry, geographic region, and so on, in the range of disputes they take up. They acquire expertise in their special areas. They can adopt procedures and rules of evidence that suit their specific concerns. State courts must stand ready to consider all matters that could arise under the law, and although some attempts can be made to assign cases to judges on the basis of their expertise, the rules and procedures must remain the same for all cases. For these reasons, arbitrators are better able to obtain, interpret and use information pertinent to the dispute than are the state courts (Bernstein, 2001, pp. 1729, 1741; Dixit, 2004, p. 11).

Therefore, in a well-functioning legal system, people often voluntarily opt out of the formal system for reasons of cost and information. Optional private ordering usually does not imply dysfunctional public order, and indeed is often rendered workable by an effective, background formal legal system that enforces contracts when necessary. There is a complementary relationship between the formal legal system and informal system (North, 1990; McMillan and Woodruff, 2000; Lazzarini et al., 2004). Indeed, in most developed countries, the vast majority of litigated civil cases, including contract disputes, result in settlement before adjudication in the shadow of the formal law. Lazzarini et al. (2004) found that courts facilitate the self-enforcement of non-contractible dimensions by enforcing contractible exchange dimensions. This complementary effect is particularly important when repetition is unlikely and thus self-enforcement is difficult (2004, p. 264). Accordingly, they argue that at least in non-repeat relationships, formal contract law and enforcement may have a 'crowding in' effect on informal enforcement mechanisms, such as norms of reciprocity.

In addition, courts recognize the informational advantage of the alternative institutions. Therefore when a relational or implicit contract serves such an informational purpose, courts refuse to intervene to modify its terms, or to insert missing provisions, or to overrule the availability of discretion to one party (Schwartz, 1992). They also enforce the awards of industry arbitration tribunals, using the government's power of coercion to obtain compliance if the loser in the arbitration attempts to defy the ruling. This has been so since 1920 in the United States (Bernstein, 2001). In the international context, over 100 countries have now acceded to the 1958 New York Convention on the Recognition and Enforcement of Arbitral Awards (Mattli, 2001).

4.2   Private ordering under dysfunctional public order

Private ordering also prevails when reliable state-sponsored contract enforcement is unavailable, namely under dysfunctional public order. Examples of this kind include those in early commercial societies, which pre-dated modern state institutions and contract law (Gray, 1997; Greif, 1989, 1993; Milgrom et al., 1990), modern communities in Third World societies where contract law and independent judiciaries are not yet well developed (Fafchamps, 1996; McMillan and Woodruff, 1999; Woodruff, 1998), and members of mafia or other criminal networks whose trans-actions involve illegal activity (Milhaupt and West, 2000). These com-mercial networks resort to self-enforcement because state contractual enforcement is not a reliable option.

Relying on empirical evidence that emphasizes the major role played by social norms and networks in rendering private transactions self-enforcing, some scholars argued that many economic activities that foster economic development do not need a means of formal third-party enforcement (Bernstein, 1992, 1996, 2001; Greif, 1996; Landa, 1981; Upham, 1994; Jones, 1994). Greif (1996, p. 241) stated 'many exchange relations in historical and contemporary markets and developing economies are not governed – directly or indirectly – by the legal system'. By making this argument, however, the fact has been largely ignored that as a result of the unavailability of an effective formal legal system, forced private ordering can be highly inefficient and carries detrimental effects for long-term institution building.

The most critical challenge to the formal legal system (or more generally to the rule of law) orthodoxy is presented by the well-known 'East Asian Miracle'. The successful development achieved by countries in the region such as Japan, Korea, Taiwan, and more recently China, led Jones (1994, pp. 212–213) to make the claim that 'informal alternatives to legal regulation may be more efficient than the competitive markets based on law', because the four dragons have been dominated by a 'rule of relationship' rather than rule of law and yet have enjoyed remarkable economic growth. She therefore concluded that 'formal rational law may not be quite as crucial to capitalism as Weber imagined' (Jones, 1994, p. 215).

A similar argument was made by Upham (1994, p. 237) who suggests that 'the experience of Asian economies demonstrates that the strict judicial enforcement of property and contract rights is not necessary to economic growth'. He offered evidence that formal contract enforcement is not a prerequisite to a nation's economic development in his analysis of Japanese economic development. He pointed out that while Japan underwent dramatic economic development through the second half of the 20th century, it simultaneously experienced a shrinking of its legal system, measured in part by a decrease in the number of professionals that work in the system and a corresponding decrease in litigation rates (Upham, 2002, pp. 23–24).

In China, the absence of a consistently enforced legal framework largely prevents the state from being a credible third-party enforcer of contracts, which North suggests to be necessary for economic development. However, it has experienced an almost consistent 9–10 per cent economic growth rate over approximately two decades. Allen et al. (2005) argued that the weakness of the Chinese formal legal system does not inhibit the development of its private sector, which has been the driving force in China's economic growth in the past 30 years. Actors in the private sector have made their way by using informal mechanisms

In conclusion, formal enforcement is fundamental to sustained economic growth. It matters not only because it has comparative advantages over enforcing a certain category of contracts, namely anonymous exchanges, but also because it enhances the effectiveness of informal mechanisms. Under a well-functioning public order, people can employ the benefits of private ordering without suffering from its dark side. Under a dysfunctional public order, exchanges can still expand to a certain degree, but it has to incur considerable costs that prevent it from fully realizing its potential.

VI. ENFORCEMENT IN CORPORATE CONTEXT

Above, we have established an analytical framework regarding contract enforcement. Now we apply it to the corporate context. The primary concern of this book is the contractual relationship between external financiers and corporate controllers (either managers or large shareholders) who have control over using the raised funds. Put another way, it concerns how investors enforce the contract between corporate controllers and themselves so as to assure being repaid.

In the contract between external investors and corporate insiders, as the investors sunk their funds at the outset, there left no chance for them to behave opportunistically. Only corporate controllers have the opportunity to make an extra private gain by not living up to their promise. That is therefore a one-sided prisoner dilemma (Dixit, 2004).

1.   Self-enforcement Mechanisms

Of course, the controllers could promise that they will be honest, but in the absence of some form of governance, the promise is not credible. As a result, investors may choose not to invest. In order to reduce investors' concerns, controllers can employ a variety of commitment mechanisms to make contracts self-enforced. As discussed above, these measures include the use of hostage, collateral and hands-tying.

1.1   Self-enforcement in a one-shot game

1.1.1 Hostage   As noted before, a hostage should be an asset that is valuable to the provider but not to the holding party. Given assets of this specific nature are often in short supply and the strictness of timing requirements, hostage exchanges are difficult to arrange. Thus, it is very rare to find specific examples of using hostages that improve corporate governance of firms towards outside investors.[28]

1.1.2 Collateral Collateral is probably the most important mechanism between firms and creditors. Creditors usually require the firm to provide some assets, such as property or equipment as collateral. If the firm defaults, the creditor can realize its debts by selling the collateral in the market or making use of it.

However, as noted before, the use of collateral cannot eliminate opportunism. Rather, it could create opportunism of other forms. In the corporate context, it may incur an additional social cost because it is particularly disadvantageous to newly established firms which often lack assets that could be used as collateral. Moreover, collateral might reduce the creditors' incentive to monitor since they now have less concern about the company's performance. Minority shareholders might find it disappointing because they could otherwise free ride on the monitoring effort of creditors.

1.1.3 Hands-tying As a second mover, a firm can do something at the outset that will make the subsequent breach on its part more costly so as to make its promise more credible. It can take action to create valuable assets which would be lost in case of violation of earlier agreements or standards.

In the corporate context, the most common method is to establish reputation through costly advertising such as employing a world-class accountant or investment banker, or cross-listing on overseas securities exchanges. By doing so, the company reinforces investors' confidence because these expenditures will be wasted if they are proved to be untrustworthy. For example, Vimpelcom, a Russian telephone company went public in the United States and listed on the NYSE. This effort helped its shares to trade at a higher multiple of earnings than a comparable Russian company that follows domestic rules (Black, 2000, p. 1596).

Another hands-tying method is to include certain investment strategies, which can only pay off if the firm continues to have access to external

---

[28] Berglof and Claessens (2004, p. 19) have suggested that some private shareholder agreements include covenants that are of a hostage nature by, for example, requiring some assets to be held offshore. Compensating cash balances and prepayments are sometimes mentioned as examples, but they are both highly symmetric in value and typically require some third party, such as a bank or a court, determining whether the party can draw on the cash balance.

financing (which means, it leaves investors the opportunity to punish it in the future). For instance, a natural resources extraction firm may undertake a large investment with long gestation time and much sunk costs to signal its commitment to honouring current financial contracts (Berglof and Claessens, 2004, p. 17).

However, the effectiveness of hands-tying is inevitably limited. In order to convince investors, hands-tying methods need to be sufficiently costly that they can only be afforded by the largest companies. In addition, in financial markets, the gains from fraud are often sufficiently huge to offset hands-tying costs. Investors thereby will still have good reasons to be concerned about cheating. For instance, by cross-listing, Vimpelcom's shares are traded at a higher price than domestic counterparts, but they are still heavily discounted by investors compared to an American company with the same apparent prospects (Black, 2000, p. 1596).

1.2 Self-enforcement in a repeated game

1.2.1 Bilateral relationship Where there is an ongoing long-term relationship between the firm and investors, investors could enforce the financial contracts by threatening to cut off the relationship and stop financing the firm in the future, or as in many cases, rather than staying passive, they become actively involved in management.

A long-term relationship is often to be found between the firm and its creditors. Typical examples include Japanese and German main banks. Relationship banking can be beneficial to both lenders and borrowers, because the degree of information asymmetry between the two parties is smaller relative to that under arm's-length lending (Diamond, 1984). Relying on the long-term relationship, these banks can effectively protect themselves from opportunistic behaviour of the firm.

However, there is a dark side of relational banking. For one thing, it might cause opportunism on the bank's side so as to fail to relieve borrowers' credit constraints. Weinstein and Yafeh (1994) find that Japanese firms with main banks pay higher average interest rates on their liabilities than do unaffiliated firms after controlling other factors. Hoshi, Kashyap and Scharfstein (1993) find that when regulatory change enabled Japanese firms to borrow in public capital markets and not just from the banks, high-net-worth firms jumped at the opportunity. It suggests that, for these firms, the costs of bank financing outweighed its benefits. Franks and Mayer (1994) present a few cases of German banks resisting takeovers of their customer companies, either because they were captured by the management or because they feared losing profits from the banking relationship.

More importantly, it can lead to misallocation of capital. This is the costly lesson we learned from the Asian financial crisis and the long-term recession of Japan. The lack of transparency arising from relational banking covered the perverse connections between banks and borrowers and the spaghetti-like structure of cross-shareholdings in firms (The Economist, 7 March 1998b). It became more harmful when the government played a part in the relational banking. The cosy relationship between governments, banks and firms insulated business from market forces, encouraging excessive borrowing and a wasteful use of resources (The Economist, 7 March 1998a). It also encouraged cronyism and corruption. In Indonesia, much of the banking system proved to be insolvent, in large part due to connected and directed lending (Strinivas and Sitorus, 2004). In the case of Japan, it is suggested that its inability to resume consistent growth has been partly tied up with its weak banking sector, which in turn was related to the persistence of the government, and especially the ruling Liberal Democratic Party. Lending by banks quickly turned into several decades of non-performing loans (NPL) that continue to some extent today (Dam, 2006b).

A long-term relationship also exists between the firm and its large shareholders. But large shareholders' enforcing power usually does not come from the indirect threat of cutting off future financing. It comes from the direct threat of removing the management. Moreover, in many cases, large shareholders are identified with the management and there is little separation between the two. Hence, large shareholders have direct access to inside information which enables them to step in in a timely way.

Recent research has revealed that in most countries of the world, companies, even public companies, tend to have one or more large shareholders (Edwards and Fisher, 1994; Franks and Mayer, 1994 (Germany); Prowse, 1992; Berglof and Perotti, 1994 (Japan); Barca, 1995; La Porta et al., 1999 (Italy)). This indicates that the bilateral relationship is probably the most prevalent enforcement mechanism around the world. In developing/transition countries, it might be the only effective one (Berglof and Von Thadden, 1999). For large shareholders, there is little concern about enforcing the financial contracts between them and management, however, the enforcement problem between large shareholders and minority shareholders arises. Minority shareholders usually buy and sell shares at times and there is no such long-term relationship between them and the controllers (in this case large shareholders). Also, the shareholdings are often too small to grant them any meaningful influence on controllers. Therefore, they have to rely on other mechanisms.

1.2.2 Reputation It is more difficult to find a long-term relationship between the firm and any individual small investor who is usually buying and selling shares at times. However, it could be argued that there is a long-term relationship between shareholders as a whole (including both current and prospective shareholders) and the firm. Therefore, as a group, shareholders could turn a one-shot game into a repeated game and rely on the reputation mechanism to enforce the contract. If the information that the firm treats its current shareholders badly could quickly spread among the whole shareholders' group, the prospective shareholders could punish the firm on behalf of the current shareholders by not purchasing (or only do this by charging a high price) the shares of the firm in the future. The concern about facing a higher cost of capital in the future could induce the firm to give up the gains from expropriating current shareholders.

As noted before, for the pure reputation mechanism to work, the game must be played repeatedly; information must spread quickly and accurately; and punishment must be credible. All these conditions must be satisfied. In the stock market, the firm may never come back to raise capital again and thus has little concern about future costs; the related information is often too technical and complex for small investors to understand (or, it does not pay any small investor to spend enormous resources to understand, they rationally choose to be uninformed); memory in the stock market is often short — with losses to investors from previous violations already incurred and new investors coming into the market, considerations of new investment may not be affected by previous actions (Bergolf and Claessens, 2004, p. 17), therefore weakening the credibility of punishment. All these factors would undermine the function of the reputation mechanism in the stock market.

2. Third-party Enforcement Mechanisms

2.1 Non-state third-party enforcer

For corporate governance, the most important mechanism in private ordering is non-state third-party enforcement. There are various organizations in financial markets acting as third parties to enforce the contract between the firm and investors by collecting and disseminating firms' reputational information.

2.1.1 Stock exchange In stock markets, the stock exchange could play a role of third party that enforces rules protecting interests of public investors. Like many other trade associations, stock exchanges are also member-run private organizations[29] which develop norms for interactions among members, with a mechanism for punishments. The success of the NYSE illustrates that when a stock exchange plays an active role in corporate governance, it could protect investors rather well and therefore facilitate the development of the financial market.

The NYSE's unusual activism in investor protection is directly attributed to its organizational structure and its competitive position. As of the late 19th century, the NYSE still ranked well behind other exchanges in equity securities trading and therefore faced great competitive pressure. Membership could only be gained by buying a seat of an existing member. This closed structure gave its members a strong incentive to favour self-regulation that protected the value of its seats. In addition, its small size and fixed brokerage commissions led to a policy that narrowly focused on high-volume, high-quality business. Competitive pressure and its closed structure gave the NYSE a strong incentive to protect its reputation as the guardian of public investors (Coffee, 2001a, pp. 35–37).

In order to establish and preserve its reputation, the NYSE imposed high listing standards, and regularly rejected issuers' applications based on assets that were inadequate or highly risky. Under its lead, the standard of disclosure for public companies was significantly enhanced. In the 1920s it also adopted the policy of not listing non-voting common stock or companies that issued such a class of securities that prevented the separation of cash flow rights from voting rights.

In the absence of a legal framework, the NYSE imposed a mandatory disclosure obligation on its listed firms and protected shareholder voting rights that facilitated the development of the stock market. For instance, by 1907, one Wall Street firm already had 22 000 customers (Michie, 1987, p. 228), indicating that it was providing services on a mass scale.

However, the effectiveness of stock exchanges as third-party enforcers cannot be taken for granted. In history, the NYSE's activism was not the norm elsewhere. The passivity of the London Stock Exchange (LSE) and that of the European bourses stood in sharp contrast with it (Coffee, 2001a, p. 34). After all, the stock exchange is a private body that has weak incentives to enforce rules protecting third parties against its own members and clients. It also has little ability to enforce its rules against

---

[29] The case is different in China as will be discussed in Chapter 3.

non-members and some enforcement may be too costly for a private body to undertake on a thoroughgoing basis.

2.1.2 Gatekeepers   Aside from the stock exchange, in the stock market, some financial intermediaries also play the role of third-party enforcer – they are now often referred to as 'gatekeepers' (Gilson and Kraakman, 1984).

There are two kinds of definition of gatekeeper. By its original definition, the term gatekeeper refers to professionals who are positioned so as to be able to prevent wrongdoing by withholding necessary cooperation or consent (Gilson and Kraakman, 1984; Kraakman, 1986). Investment bankers, auditors and attorneys[30] fall within this definition. By a second definition, gatekeeper means 'an agent who acts as a reputational intermediary to assure investors as to the quality of the "signal" sent by the corporate issuer' (Coffee, 2006a, p. 2). Securities analysts and credit rating agencies should also be included within gatekeepers under the second definition. In this book, we take the second definition.

Recruiting gatekeepers as third-party enforcers is based on this idea: gatekeepers are repeat players in the stock market who primarily rely on their reputation to live.[31] Compared to entrepreneurs who will receive substantial gains from misrepresentation of information, gatekeepers have little to gain but much to lose (the reputational capital that they have built up over many years), thus, they have less incentive (or in Judge Easterbrook's term, it would be 'irrational'[32]) to lie about the information. By imposing liability on the gatekeepers to detect and veto misrepresentation of information, problems could be prevented before they become crises, for instance, investment bankers can refuse to underwrite the issuer's securities if they find that the issuer's disclosures are materially deficient.

---

[30]   The more typical role of attorneys is that of transaction engineer, rather than the reputational intermediary. But they can be gatekeepers when they lend their professional reputations to a transaction (Coffee, 2002, p. 1405).

[31]   Some scholars have written on the notion that intermediaries may signal product value through their individual reputations, acting as reputational intermediaries. For instance, it is stated that 'in essence, the investment banker rents the issuers its reputation. The investment banker represents to the market that it has evaluated the issuer's product and good faith and that it is prepared to stake its reputation on the value of the innovation'. See Gilson and Kraakman (1984, p. 620).

[32]   In *Dileo v. Ernst & Young*, 901 F2d 624 (7th Cir. 1990), at 629.

However, there is a gap between theory and reality. First, gatekeepers face an inherent conflict in that they are paid by the party that is to be watched. The extent to which gatekeepers can maintain their independence largely decides their effectiveness as third-party enforcers. In countries like the United States the accounting industry is dominated by four accounting firms, which have several thousands of clients and each provides essentially similar, almost standardized services to them, with no one client being material to the large accounting firms' revenues (Coffee, 2001b, p. 10). Therefore, the major accounting firms seem to be structurally independent of their clients. But this cannot be said for law or investment banking firms which often have dominating clients and provide more specialized, less fungible services, and their independence is thus more in doubt (Coffee, 2001b, p. 11). In many other countries, even accounting firms are small and lack independence, let alone law firms and investment banks. When the gatekeepers rely too much on a large client, their effectiveness will be compromised.

Second, the whole gatekeeper theory is based on the assumption that gatekeepers should always protect their reputational capital. But this is not necessarily true. As was discussed before, reputation works only when it pays. When the costs of losing reputation decline or the benefits of acquiescence in fraud increase, staying honest may not be the gatekeeper's best strategy. Especially in a market bubble where caution and scepticism are largely abandoned by investors and gatekeepers are not needed by issuing firms, 'it is simply dangerous to be sane in an insane world' (Coffee, 2002, p. 1412). Reputation will also be undermined where there is a lack of competition. In a highly concentrated market,[33] rather than competing to enhance reputation, instead gatekeepers could implicitly collude and permit their reputation to become noisy and indistinct (Coffee, 2002, p. 1414). The gatekeeper's failure in the Enron scandal is a big warning of the limits of reputational intermediaries and should not be easily forgotten.[34]

---

[33] The concentration is particularly outstanding in the credit rating industry, which is dominated by Standard & Poor's and Moody's.

[34] Coffee (2002) gave a detailed explanation of the failure of gatekeepers in the Enron scandal. First, the courts' decision together with legislation (the Private Securities Litigation Reform Act of 1995) and the SEC shifting its enforcement focus away from actions against the big five accounting firms towards other priorities appreciably reduced the risk of liability; second, in the 1990s auditor services became loss leaders, which were increasingly used to attract the much more profitable consulting services and thus exacerbate the conflicts of interest between auditors and the client; analysts' compensation came increasingly from

Third, gatekeepers themselves also face the agency problem. The firm as a whole might be big enough to be independent of any client. Individual partners, however, are often dominated by a large client. The partner might defer excessively to the client in a manner that could inflict liability on the firm (Coffee, 2002, p. 1415). In the absence of effective internal control, the agency problem could weaken the function of gatekeepers.

Last but not least, sophisticated gatekeepers with the skill and experience to catch the false or misleading information disclosure by the firms may be in short supply: this is often the case in emerging economies.

2.1.3 Media   The media collect information about a firm's reputation and charge a fee to provide information to the general public. As recent studies have shown, the media could also play an important role as third-party enforcer by imposing large reputational costs on managers and directors of firms who behave badly (Dyck and Zingales, 2002a, 2003).

Enforcement by the media could be very effective. Compared to gatekeepers, media reporters have better incentives because they serve the public rather than particular clients whom they are obligated to watch. Thus, they do not have to confront the conflicting interests. As information specialists, they can enhance the speed and accuracy of information and therefore credibly deter the opportunism of firms, insiders and intermediaries. The effect of media coverage on corporate governance is particularly clear in Russia, where corporate governance violations are plenty and there is no alternative mechanism to address this. It has been found that Hermitage's strategy of increasing the coverage of corporate governance violations in the Anglo-American press worked (Dyck and Zingales, 2008).

Nevertheless, the role of the media has some limits. Information collection is costly and difficult, thus, it may give reporters a strong incentive to enter into a quid pro quo relationship with their sources, where they receive private information in exchange for a positive spin on companies' news (Dyck and Zingales, 2002b, p. 4). Reporters may be too

---

the investment banking side of their firms which led them to make suggestions more in favour of investment bankers; the 1990s market bubble drove the gatekeepers, particularly analysts, to abandon professional standards; the highly concentrated nature of the auditor industry makes it easier for the big five to collude.

lazy or incompetent to discover the truth;[35] they are biased because they assume readers are more inclined to believe articles that confirm their prior suspicions leading them to tilt their coverage to putting a positive gloss on news (Dyck and Zingales, 2003).

Apart from these general factors that affect the effectiveness of media, in many developing countries, the government places a strict constraint on press freedom, including the financial media, which largely undermines the financial media's enforcement capacity.

2.2 Enforcement by the state

The law and finance literature has firmly established the link between formal legal institutions and development of capital markets. Formal enforcement is particularly important in this context, because in capital markets, the pay-off from cheating is often so high that it is sufficient to induce actors to forgo future gains and undermine the basis of private ordering. In order to deter opportunistic behaviour in one-shot interaction, formal enforcement must be relied on.

In a corporate context, the enforcement by the state could be further divided into two kinds: one is private enforcement of law and the other is public enforcement. Under private enforcement of law, private agents avail themselves of the framework defined by law or regulations to punish violations of contracts, using the courts to adjudicate and the state to enforce the final judgement. With public enforcement, the government not only provides the final enforcement system, but also acts as the prosecutor.

2.2.1 Private enforcement of law In most societies, it is largely private initiatives that help enforce existing laws and regulations. The government creates the rules governing private conduct but leaves the initiation of enforcement to private parties. When an individual feels cheated, he could initiate a private suit and bring it to the court or other agency (Berglof and Pajuste, 2005).

It has increasingly been accepted that private enforcement of law has certain advantages. Private claimants have better incentive to bring actions; they also have better information because they are close to the transactions at hand and the decentralized enforcement reduces problems of capture (Zingales, 2004). Thus, when it works well, it can play a

---

[35] As the CEO of the *Financial Times* once stated in an interview, 'sometimes I do think that the business press – and I include the FT in this – has not worked hard enough to ferret out these stories'. See *Daily Telegraph*, 11 October 2002.

significant role in corporate governance and financial development (La Porta et al., 2006). Moreover, when the rules are carefully designed, it has the potency of being a particularly efficient mechanism in situations with weak or ill-experienced courts (Black and Kraakman, 1996; Hay et al., 1996).

Nevertheless, a number of problems associated with private enforcement can hobble its effectiveness. First is the information difficulty. Among other things, the fact that violation occurs and causes damage must be verified before the courts. This is not easy even in some simple transactions. In the stock market, it could be extremely difficult, especially in proving the intent or negligence of managers and establishing the causality between violation and damage. Second is the cost of litigation. As noted before, the cost of litigation is one of the reasons that make private ordering prevail even in a well-functioning legal system. In securities litigation, the cost is often prohibitively expensive and hardly affordable for any private claimant. Given each of the dispersed shareholders only holds a tiny fraction of shares, the rewarded damages are unlikely to compensate the costs of litigation, therefore they are unlikely to sue. There exists also the collective action problem: each shareholder would prefer to free-ride someone else's effort of bringing lawsuits; as a result, no one does.

The state could take some actions to facilitate private litigation. It can mandate the disclosure of particular information such as profitability and ownership structure, in the prospectus. These mandates create a *prima facie* liability of issuers or intermediaries when violation occurs. It can specify the liability standards facing issuers and intermediaries when investors seek to recover damages from companies that follow affirmative disclosure rules but fail to reveal potentially material information. It can tackle the costs of litigation by allowing a contingency fee;[36] it can award punitive damages;[37] it can also help to overcome the free-riding problem by allowing class actions[38] (Black and Kraakman, 1996; Hay et al., 1996; Hay and Shleifer, 1998; Glaeser et al., 2001; Glaeser and Shleifer, 2003).

---

[36]   This means lawyers can be paid conditional on the outcome of a lawsuit.

[37]   This refers to a penalty many times the actual damage inflicted on the plaintiff. By multiplying the size of the award, it makes it more attractive to sue companies (Zingales, 2004, p. 23).

[38]   This means lawsuits in the name of an entire group of individuals, in this case, investors. By pooling the individual cases, it makes bigger the size of the potential award, making it more attractive for lawyers to pursue them (Zingales, 2004, p. 23).

In the United States, all the three legal institutions are created to encourage private enforcement. The combined effect is that it motivates lawyers to seek plaintiffs rather than the other way around (Zingales, 2004, p. 23). It even leads to a kind of legal firm that is specialized in bringing cases against companies. However, such institutions are not available in many countries. For instance, in Europe (including the UK), class actions are basically unknown, contingent fees are not permitted and a loser-pays fee-shifting rule further discourages aggregate litigation in any form (Romano, 1993; Coffee, 2007).

In addition, the effectiveness of private securities litigation (PSL) ultimately depends on the function of the courts.[39] However, the efficacy of courts is often in question. In all countries through much of their history, the courts were very costly, slow, unreliable, biased and corrupt. Even the United States' judicial system in the late 19th century was filled with corruption and scandals. It remains true today in most developing countries. Expert judges who understand highly complex, technical securities litigation and can make fast and reliable decisions may be in short supply or not available at all.[40]

Another significant problem associated with the courts is that their role can often be restrained by legislation. This is particularly problematic in civil law countries where the judges are denied law-making power. When substantive legal remedies that judges have are ill-defined, inadequate or not available at all, there is not too much that the courts can do, even they are willing.

For all these reasons, although its theoretical role has been widely admitted, until recently, active private enforcement is still a unique phenomenon limited to the United States (Coffee, 2007, p. 35).[41]

---

[39] As failings of Russian corporate law have suggested, even the carefully designed bright line rules, which rely least on courts' capacity, do not work when the judicial system is too weak. See Black et al. (2000).

[40] As admitted by a senior member of the Supreme Russian Arbitrage Court 'this share business is too complicated for us. We don't understand it. We have no laws to deal with it.' Reuters, 14 May 1995. As will be shown in Chapter 3, Chinese courts found the same difficulty.

[41] It is argued that securities litigation in the US is seriously compromised as a result of often meagre returns to wronged plaintiffs; usually their costs are not visited on the wrongdoing actors insider public firms, because the wrongdoers can usually transfer the costs to others, and often just transfer losses from one innocent group of shareholders to another innocent group, with large fees obtained by the lawyers for both sides (Coffee, 2006b; Cox, et al., 2003; Bebchuk and Neeman, 2007).

2.2.2 Public enforcement   The regulation of markets was first and foremost a response to the failure of the courts (Landis, 1938; Glaeser et al., 2001; Glaeser and Shleifer, 2003). When small shareholders are unlikely to sue and courts are unreliable, a public enforcer is needed. In the context of security markets, a public enforcer can be a securities commission, a central bank or some other supervisory body.

A public enforcer might be able to intervene *ex ante*, by clarifying legal obligations or *ex post*, by imposing its own penalties or bringing lawsuits. Public enforcement might work because the enforcer is independent and focused and thus can regulate markets free from political interference; because the enforcer has power to introduce regulation of market participants rather than remain with the legislature or the Ministry of Finance; because it can secure information from issuers and market participants more effectively than the private plaintiffs, for instance it might be empowered to command documents from issuers, distributors or accountants, and to subpoena testimony of witnesses; or because it can impose more severe sanctions, especially criminal sanctions, which is particularly important when the damages or the potential fraud are very big with respect to the size of the business, as in such cases private enforcement is insufficient to restrain opportunistic behaviour (Landis, 1938; Becker, 1968; Polinsky and Shavell, 2000; Glaeser, et al., 2001; Glaeser and Shleifer, 2003; Pistor and Xu, 2003).

However, the efficiency of public enforcement also cannot be taken for granted. The literature on regulation failure is large. Compared to a private claimant who has suffered personal loss, the salary-earning public enforcers have only mixed and often weak incentive to do their job well and they often suffer from poor information on both the general market and specific firm conditions. Regulation is costly. The costs include both direct costs of compliance and indirect costs that it imposes on private contracting.[42] Some have argued that it often imposes costs without corresponding benefits (Cheffins, 1997; Zingales, 2004). Regulators can be captured by the regulated industry (Stigler, 1971)[43] and they may lack capacity because the low-paid public job is unlikely to attract the most

---

[42]   Resources will be wasted to gain influence that facilitates or simply makes transactions possible.

[43]   Mahoney (2001) suggested that even the highly ideologically motivated Securities Act of 1933 favoured the established investment banks because it relied on them to gain the information needed for quickly drafting new legislation.

talented people.[44] Even if the regulators are dedicated and capable, they may lack resources such as manpower or budgets. All these factors cast doubts on public enforcement.

In addition, in developing/transition countries, the lack of credible constraint on state power is the primary reason that the function of courts has been undermined and there is little reason to assume the same reason will not affect the regulator.

2.2.3 The relative importance of the two Recently, there has been an ongoing debate over the relative importance of private enforcement of law and public enforcement. La Porta et al. (2006) and Djankov et al. (2008) conclude that private enforcement is central to financial development, while public enforcement is of limited value. Researchers with the International Monetary Fund (IMF) and European Central Bank conclude similarly (Bruno and Claessens, 2008; Hartmann, et al., 2007). On the other side, some scholars argue that there is no obvious winner between the two and the role of public enforcement should not be underestimated (Jackson, 2006; Jackson and Roe, 2009). Since there is by no means any conclusive evidence, equal credit is given to both in this book.

As mentioned before, for most developing countries such as China, it is very possible that both courts and regulators have failed. In the absence of credible constraints on state power, it is almost certain that the costs of state intervention will exceed the benefits it could bring about. In such cases, as suggested by Glaeser and Shleifer, the optimal policy for government is to leave the market alone and do nothing (2003, p. 411).[45]

3. An Effective Enforcement: Mixed Enforcement

In order to enforce financial contracts effectively, various mechanisms to work together are required. As discussed above, when information is private or observable, it can only be self-enforced. State and other third-party enforcement must be based on verifiable information.

Apart from the incompleteness of contracts, information asymmetry is another reason that causes an agency problem. Information asymmetry, by definition, means that some information is held by the agent privately and cannot (or only at great cost) be observed by the principal. The

---

[44] It is particularly problematic in the financial industry where complex, innovative financial derivatives tools are widely used, and because of the huge income gap between regulator and financial industries.

[45] At least it can save the costs of tackling state opportunism since the crippled state will fail to enforce contracts effectively anyway.

shareholders are less likely to observe in detail whether the management is making appropriate decisions (Jensen and Meckling, 1976). Those aspects of financial contracts, such as 'manager should work diligently', can only be self-enforced.

Even if some opportunistic behaviour of the management could be observed by shareholders, for instance, the consumption of perquisites, to bring the wrongdoers to the court, they have to prove that there exists causality between the opportunism of management and the subsequent damage that they suffered. However, it is extremely difficult to establish this causality because the observed outcome is often determined not only by the agent's action but also by some outside shocks. Under these conditions, a manager can always argue that a poor result was attributable to forces beyond his control and thus is not his fault.

Therefore, the information requirement largely restricts the role the court can play in enforcing financial contracts. It can only enforce the part of contracts that could be easily observed and verified without requiring too much interpretation. For instance, in the case of the duty of loyalty, the courts would interfere in cases of management theft and asset diversion, and they would surely interfere if managers diluted existing shareholders through an issue of equity to themselves. Courts are less likely to interfere in cases of excessive pay, especially if it takes the complex form of option contracts, and are very unlikely to second guess managers' business decisions, including the decisions that hurt share-holders (Shleifer and Vishny, 1997, p. 752).

The laws can extend the role of courts in financial contracts enforce-ment by standardizing the private contracting framework. Mandatory disclosure rules and liability rules are two major aspects of such standardization. With such rules, the originally private information is made public, and the burden of establishing causality is lessened, therefore more aspects of contracts are rendered enforceable by the external courts. For instance, investors can bring suit to the court when the firm does not comply with the disclosure rules such as including profitability and ownership structures information in its prospectus. This violation is easily observed by the public and verified in the court.

In sum, effective enforcement of the financial contracts between investors and firms requires a combination of various enforcement mechanisms. No one of them could do the whole job alone.

In addition, it is worth noting here that effective enforcement requires a combination of various enforcement mechanisms, but it does not indicate that there can be only one particular combination. The Anglo-American governance model, which is often advocated as the 'best practice' and imitated by many countries, is one that combines reputation, non-state third-party enforcement and formal enforcement. There should be other alternatives that reach equal efficiency. For instance, in Hong Kong, companies are often controlled by founders' families.[46] However, as a member of the common law family, Hong Kong offered strong legal protection to minority shareholders. As a consequence, in Hong Kong, minority shareholders could free-ride on large shareholders' efforts to monitor managers without too much concern of being expropriated by them; the stock market is also well developed.

4. Private Ordering and Public Order in a Corporate Context

Although the formal legal system can only play a limited role in enforcing financial contracts, its significance goes far beyond this. Aside from direct involvement in contracts enforcement, it also has a fundamental impact on the function of private ordering. As noted before, where an effective formal legal system exists, the formal and informal enforcement are mutually complementary and work together to make enforcement more efficient. Under a dysfunctional public order, informal enforcement is only a partial substitute for formal enforcement that inhibits full economic potential from being realized, and might be detrimental to long-term institution building.

In the corporate context, the law and finance literature has made great efforts to prove the importance of a legal system in capital market development. A great deal of empirical evidence has been generated that confirmed the previous presumption.

4.1 Private ordering in the shadow of the law
The impact of the legal system on private ordering is mainly reflected in three aspects. First and foremost, all kinds of private ordering mechanisms ultimately have to depend on the effectiveness of the legal system, to various degrees. Among others, even large investors, which are usually viewed as the mechanism that requires least legal intervention, still need some legal protection of their basic rights such as the voting rights or the power to pull collateral, in order to exercise their power over the management. Large shareholders can control the management by exercising voting rights, while the latter depends on the degree of legal protection of their votes. Management can use a variety of techniques against large investors, including requiring super majorities to bring

---

[46] In 1988, companies controlled by just four families accounted for over 36 per cent of the total market capitalization in Hong Kong (Gaylord and Armitage, 1993, p. 28).

issues on the agenda of shareholder meetings, declaring some of their shares illegal, losing voting records, and so on. In extreme case, they could just erase the name of large shareholders from registration.

Second, a formal legal system can overcome the limitation of private ordering mechanisms. Although the private ordering mechanisms play a significant role in enforcing the financial contracts, they are unable to deter opportunistic behaviour in one-shot interaction or in the last round interaction. In financial markets, huge amount of funds are usually involved that make it particularly tempting for the controllers to play a one-shot or last round game. The legal system therefore helps to overcome the limitation of private ordering by deterring the actors from behaving opportunistically when it pays them to do so. By so doing, it encourages more players to participate in repeated interactions that in turn provide the base on which the reputation mechanism works.

The role of the legal system in this aspect is particularly clear in time of crisis because crisis often triggers the last round game. Johnson et al's (2000) study of the Asian crisis of 1997–1998 provided an illustration of this. Before the crisis, when future prospects were bright, even in the absence of legal protection, insiders treated investors well because they expected more gains from continued external financing. But when future prospects deteriorated, the insiders stepped up expropriation. Aware of this, investors responded by withdrawing investment, which in turn accelerated the decline of the market. By contrast, in countries/places such as Hong Kong, there is a reliable legal system providing better protection to investors, investors had less concern about expropriation by insiders, and therefore less degree of market decline.

Last but not least, an effective legal system also facilitates the function of the private ordering mechanism by lowering the cost of information. As emphasized before, for the reputation mechanism to work well, the speed and accuracy of spreading information is the key. However, collecting information is costly and the efforts are easily subject to free-riding by other individuals, therefore it may not pay any individual investor to do it. The legal system can make information more easily and cheaply accessible to the public by mandating the disclosure of material information; as a result, it facilitates the function of the reputation mechanism. Without such rules, the reputation mechanism would be less effective.

4.2   Private ordering under dysfunctional public order

In the absence of an effective legal system, various private ordering mechanisms would arise to respond to the enforcement problem. Examples are many, such as concentrated ownership, self-regulation and relation of trust. However, they are just partial substitutes for the formal legal system and incur substantial costs in the long run.

4.2.1 Concentrated ownership As discussed before, concentrated ownership arises as a direct response to dysfunctional public order. Compared to other private ordering mechanisms, concentrated ownership seems to have some advantages. For instance, large shareholders often closely monitor the managers or are even integrated with the management, thus, the problem of information asymmetry is minor. By contrast, the reputation mechanism relies on the speed and accuracy of information which is usually very costly to obtain. Indeed, the prevalence of concentrated ownership around the world is the most convincing evidence of its effectiveness.

However, the effectiveness of concentrated ownership does not come without costs. Even block-holders themselves have to bear the cost of less diversification. Also, firms with a concentrated ownership structure are more prone to over-monitoring, which might not be a good thing (Pagano and Roell, 1998). More importantly, it impedes the development of the stock market. In the absence of legal protection, shareholders are forced to retain control because they recognize the risk of being expropriated by new controllers. As a large block is hard to sell in the secondary market, the liquidity of the market has been reduced. On the other hand, since investors will not purchase shares or only purchase at a heavily discounted price, companies are discouraged from raising capital through equity. As a result, the development of the stock market will be stifled.

In addition, the dominance of concentrated ownership might have a long-term negative impact on institution building. As long as the private benefits of control exceed its costs, they have the incentive to resist any reform that will improve the overall corporate governance quality but reduce their control benefits. Since large block-holders are usually small in number, it is much easier for them to collaborate than the diffused shareholders. As a consequence, they often win the battle. This could be widely observed around the world especially in developing countries, where the politics is often corrupt and subject to the interests of the rich (very often, the politicians represent the interests of the wealthy).

4.2.2 Self-regulation In the late 19th century in the United States, the judicial system was corrupt and incapable and provided little protection to minority shareholders. The private benefits of control appeared to be very high and resembled what has occurred in Russia and other transitional economies over the last decade (Coffee, 2001a, p. 10). Self-regulation by the NYSE therefore arose and acted as a partial functional substitute for a legal institution. As noted above, it indeed played a sizeable role in the development of the equity market in the United States.

Nevertheless, exclusive reliance on self-regulation would fall well short of optimal efficiency. First, the relatively aggressive attitude of the NYSE towards investor protection is rather unusual and mainly resulted from the competitive environment and closed internal structure. The incentive in such an activist does not necessarily persist. In the absence of competition, a self-regulation body may have less reason to enforce rules against its own members in order to preserve its reputational capital. For instance, the LSE, which faced less competition, did not make serious efforts until after World War II. In addition, members could entrench themselves and seek rents by making use of the closed internal structure (Coffee, 2001a, p. 65).

Second, severe constraints appear to exist on the ability of a private body to enforce rules against its member firms and its listed companies. Even the NYSE faced resistance from its listed companies when it sought to upgrade disclosure standards. For example, Merritt Fox has found that although the NYSE continually upgraded its listing requirement applicable to newly listed firms, it was unable to apply these new rules to earlier listed firms, which collectively constituted the great majority of the firms traded on the exchange. This is one example of the enforcement shortfall that is inherent in any self-regulatory system (Coffee, 2001a, p. 67).

Third, the self-regulation organization has no ability to sanction other than the denial of trading privileges in the case of rule violation by non-members. Yet, non-members may often be the parties most likely to engage in insider trading or other manipulative practices (Coffee, 2001a, p. 68).

The limitation of self-regulation was revealed as early as the 1920s. The US Congress found in its hearing that fraud and manipulation had been rampant in the securities markets and thus determined to strengthen the existing system of enforcement. As a result, the SEC was created and a liberalized system of anti-fraud liability borrowed in part from the United Kingdom.

4.2.3 Trust in local business community   In the United Kingdom, the common law provided little protection to minority shareholders until the first half of the 20th century. The court made two important rulings in the 1843 landmark case of *Foss v. Harbottle*.[47] The court found that while the plaintiff in the case was an aggrieved shareholder, the proper plaintiff in an action of an alleged wrong to a company was the company itself, i.e. a majority of the shareholders and not a minority. Second, it established that where a transaction could be made binding by a majority of the shareholders, no individual shareholder could sustain an action against the company. The dominance of the strict majority rule was enshrined in English law and remained so for a hundred years until 1948.[48]

Despite the lack of formal legal protection, the United Kingdom operated a large and vibrant stock market for the first half of the 20th century. Rajan and Zingales (2003) reported that between 1913 and 1999, the United Kingdom had a stock market that ranked in first or second place in six of the nine decades and in the top five for the remaining three decades. Michie (1999) recorded an increase in the number of listed companies from 200 in 1853 to 'many thousands' in 1914. How did the stock market expand in the absence of formal protection?

It is argued that the UK equity market functioned on the basis of informal relationships of trust in local business circles (Franks et al., 2005b; Mayer, 2008). Today, there are just two exchanges in the United Kingdom, but in the first half of the century there were 18 provincial stock exchanges, which collectively were as large as the LSE. Companies were very dependent on local shareholders to raise finance. Thus, their reputation among local investors was critically important to allow access to external sources of finance. Directors were keen to uphold the interests of shareholders so as to allow them to access finance for future expansion.

Moreover, the information problem was largely reduced as securities were traded in the city in which most investors resided. The securities were rarely sold by means of a prospectus and were not underwritten. They were mainly placed by private negotiation among local people who understood the trade. Therefore, the local knowledge on the part of the investor, both of the business reputation of the vendor and the prospects of his undertaking, would do a good deal to eliminate dishonest promotion and ensure that securities were sold at fair prices fairly near their investment value (Lavington, 1921).

---

[47] *Foss v. Harbottle* (1843) 67, ER 189; (1843) 2 Hare 461.

[48] The 1948 Companies Act required substantially increased disclosure from listed companies, and empowered 10 per cent or more of shareholders to call extraordinary meetings if dissatisfied with directors' activities.

Franks et al. (2005a) report that out of 33 acquisitions that occurred between 1919 and 1939, there was not a single case of price discrimination and in virtually every case almost all of the shares in the acquired company were purchased. It suggested that the rule that all shareholders in the target firm should be offered the same price for each of their shares prevailed long before it was formally enacted in law.[49] Therefore, the informal relations of trust between investors and firms acted as a substitute for a formal system that allowed equity markets to flourish and ownership to become dispersed in the United Kingdom in the first half of the 20th century.

The local stock market could support companies to grow at an early stage; however, as firms expanded, their activities would eventually develop beyond their home towns. Their shareholder base also expanded and was no longer geographically concentrated. The shareholders outside their home towns did not have the knowledge about the entrepreneur's reputation or the prospects for his undertaking. Therefore, they had to rely on more formal systems of information disclosure through company accounts and listing rules (Mayer, 2008). As a result, the 1948 Companies Act and the LSE Listing Rules were enacted to strengthen information disclosure.

However, the historical fact that the United Kingdom was successful in the transition from an informal, local, relation-based enforcement system to a formal, universal, rules-based enforcement system is something that cannot be taken for granted. Historically and contemporarily, such transition is extremely difficult. That the United Kingdom was able to make this transition should be seen as largely due to its previously existing independent and reliable legal system. Without such a legal system, the market would most likely remain compartmentalized and the local stock markets turned into obstacles to establishing a unified, nationwide market.

In sum, under dysfunctional public order, various private ordering mechanisms would arise to respond to the enforcement problem depending on specific context. The most common response is concentrated ownership and it could also be self-regulation or relations of trust in local business circles, and so on. However, they are only imperfect substitutes which may incur substantial costs and the full potential cannot be realized. More importantly, they could turn into obstacles to long-term institution building.

---

[49]   It was introduced at the end of the 1960s.

4.3 Further discussion on private ordering and public order

The previous discussion highlighted the significance of formal enforcement to private ordering, but this by no means implies that formal enforcement could replace private ordering. As pointed out before, factors such as information and costs determine that formal enforcement can only play a limited role in contract enforcement. This is particularly true in enforcing financial contracts in the stock market. The highly technical nature of financial contracts and asymmetric information in the stock market mean that the role of formal enforcement is rather limited. Private ordering, in particular non-state third-party enforcement, has obvious advantages over formal enforcement, both in capability and incentive. Private ordering, in spite of its limitations, plays a primary role in the stock market. The proper role of formal enforcement is not to suppress or replace the private ordering, but to facilitate the function of the latter. Purely relying on private ordering cannot sustain long-term growth of stock markets, nor would overwhelmingly relying on formal enforcement achieve that goal.

CONCLUDING REMARKS

Despite the enthusiasm of many countries to develop stock markets, successful examples are rare. The willingness of investors to put money in is the very precondition for developing a capital market. Enforcement, by imposing constraints on corporate controllers' opportunistic behaviour, provides an assurance to the investors that they will not be cheated, and thus makes the development of the capital market possible.

In this chapter, relying on the insights of the NIE, a conceptual framework for enforcement in a corporate context has been established. Under this framework, corporate governance is regarded as an enforcement issue, i.e. how to enforce the financial contracts between investors and corporate controllers. We find that good corporate governance requires effective enforcement, which combines some form of informal enforcement (including self-enforcement and non-state third-party enforcement) and formal enforcement, although the latter might not be necessary in the early stages. In the absence of any form of effective enforcement, a stock market is unlikely to emerge. I call this the 'enforcement matters' thesis.

This 'enforcement matters' thesis, however, is based on an implicit assumption that the company is privately owned and that the state only plays the role of third-party enforcer. However, this assumption may not hold in some cases. As will be shown in Chapter 2, in the Chinese stock market, a majority of listed companies are state owned and the state plays multiple roles other than just that of third-party enforcer. In that case, does the 'enforcement matters' thesis still hold? This will be tested in Chapters 3 and 4.

2. Historical background and characteristics of the Chinese stock market

INTRODUCTION

This chapter provides some historical background on China's stock market and introduces its characteristics. It contains three sections. Section 1 starts with a brief discussion of the general weakness associated with state-owned enterprises (SOEs); it then reviews the process of China's SOEs reform. Section 2 contains a review of the short history of the Chinese capital market and shows the entangled link between the capital market and SOE reform. It also gives a succinct description of the four characteristics of the Chinese stock market. Section 3 introduces the ownership structure of listed companies and further examines the issue of concentration ownership.

I. STATE-OWNED ENTERPRISES REFORM

To understand the Chinese capital market, one must first understand its SOE reform, as they are two sides of the same coin. Just like many other former socialist countries, before the state economic reform in 1978, SOEs dominated China's economy, particularly its industrial sector. Also like its socialist counterparts, at the beginning of the economic reform, numerous SOEs were plagued by sloth, inefficiency and waste.

1. The SOE Problem

The inefficiency of SOEs has been repeatedly illustrated by decades of practice, both in socialist countries and capitalist countries.[1] Then what is

---

[1] The collapse of former socialist countries is no doubt the best evidence of this. For capitalist countries, see The Economist, 22 January 1994, 5 February 1994; Donahue (1989); Royko (1971).

the root cause of SOEs' inefficiency? The answer lies in the state ownership per se. State ownership resulting in costly agency problems and the soft budget constraints problem – both are responsible for the inefficiency of SOEs.

1.1   The agency problem in SOEs

Looked at from an agency perspective, SOEs can be described as an example of 'concentrated control with no cash flow rights and socially harmful objectives' (Shleifer and Vishny, 1997, p. 768). The state exercises the cash flow and control rights of the SOEs on behalf of the nominal owners – the general public. However, the state is merely an abstract entity which can only act through its agents – the bureaucrats. Thus, it is the bureaucrats who gain the de facto control rights. With concentrated control rights and no cash flow rights, just like managers in the private sector, bureaucrats have the same incentive to pursue private benefits of control. In addition, bureaucrats have objectives that are very different from social welfare and dictated by their political interests. As a result, they often make use of the control rights to pursue political interests, for example, employment (Shapiro and Willig, 1990; Boycko et al., 1996; Shleifer and Vishny, 1994).

1.2   The soft budget constraint problem

Another important reason for the failure of SOEs is the soft budget constraint problem. The soft budget constraint is a concept developed most prominently by Hungarian economist Kornai. Its essence is the notion that the difference between proceeds of production and costs of production is not a matter of life and death for the firm. Therefore, it does not act as an effective constraint on firm behaviour. The major harmful consequence is that firms do not economize because nobody in the firm suffers the consequences of waste. Those consequences are externalized and are borne by society as a whole (Kornai, 1980, 1986). In the case of SOEs, unless the government decides to relinquish its control, the budget constraint will always be soft and there is no real risk of going bankrupt. As a result, managers of SOEs do not have the same incentive to enhance performance as their private counterparts who face hard budget constraints.

1.3   Public governance quality

Since SOEs are controlled by bureaucrats, the performance of SOEs is therefore closely related to the quality of public governance. In countries where public governance quality is good and bureaucrats are held strictly accountable for their performance, the inefficiency of SOEs might be restricted to a tolerable level. In very rare cases, it might operate reasonably well. In countries where checks and balances on political power do not exist, there is no accountability of bureaucrats and corruption is rampant, the costs of operating SOEs will be prohibitively high.

2. SOEs in Capitalist and Socialist Countries

It must be pointed out here that there are two fundamental differences between SOEs of socialist countries and those of capitalist countries. First, SOEs in capitalist countries are normal enterprises that happen to be owned by the state. Except for the ownership, there is no substantial difference from private enterprises, while traditional SOEs (TSOEs) in socialist countries were essentially a grassroots production unit for cost accounting, but did not have various attributes that an enterprise should have. Attached to the party and government organs, a TSOE had the basic task of carrying out all the instructions and directives from its superiors. The role of management was simply to carry out the instructions. What and how much to produce, how to produce it, and to whom the product would be sold were all determined by the government department. Apart from a productive function, a TSOE also assumed many other social functions and provided its employees with services from cradle to grave. This is the starting point of Chinese SOEs reform and this socialist legacy still affects many SOEs today.

Second, in capitalist countries, the main justification for public enterprises is that they can cure market failures that arise either from monopoly power or externalities (Atkinson and Stiglitz, 1980).[2] Even at their peak, public enterprises existed as a complement to, rather than replacement of, the private sector. The ideology underlying socialist SOEs is completely different. The very belief of socialism is to destroy private ownership and build up a new social system based on state ownership. As the foundation of the socialist system, SOEs are both economically and politically critical, or we could say, a matter of life or death for the socialist regime. Only bearing this in mind, can we understand the logic of the SOEs reform (also, the capital market) in China. Although after 30 years' reform, the ideological colour has largely faded, the significance of SOEs for the survival of the Chinese Communist Party (CCP) regime remains.

---

[2] This justification has been increasingly questioned in the past decades. For instance, Vernon and Aharoni (1981); Donahue (1989).

3. SOEs Reform Without Ownership Change

The government has attempted a series of reforms designed to improve SOE performance since 1978. At the early stage, it adopted various strategies that did not involve ownership restructuring. These strategies included granting operational rights and authority to SOEs' managers and building managerial incentives by allowing them to retain the profits of over-fulfilment after meeting the fixed target.[3] Although these measures did increase managers' and workers' incentives to maximize value at first, the positive impact was only short lived since managers and workers only took the upside of profit increases and the downside was still borne by the state (Lardy, 1998; Shirley and Xu, 2001).

Another attempt was corporatization. It is based on the belief that state assets can be better managed by transforming TSOEs into shareholding companies and installing organizational structures similar to those in Western public corporations, such as general shareholder meetings, supervisory boards and boards of directors. As a result, some selected SOEs[4] were required to convert into one of the three forms of company governed by the Company Law: joint stock company (JSC) (*Gufen Youxian Gongsi*);[5] limited liability company (LLC) (*Youxian Zeren Gongsi*)[6] or wholly state-owned limited liability company (WSOLLC) (*Guoyou Duzi Youxian Gongsi*).[7] Since the corporatization policy did not touch ownership itself, not surprisingly, it only created some companies similar to modern corporations in form.

---

[3] This is known as the 'responsibility contract system'. It is similar to managerial performance contracts used in other former socialist countries.

[4] In November 1994, the State Council decided to convene the 'National Working Conference for Experiments in Establishing a Modern Enterprise System' and to select 100 SOEs as pilot studies for corporatization. Due to the lack of emphasis on using diversification of share ownership to restructure existing SOEs into real enterprises, most enterprises involved in the experiment simply converted themselves to wholly state-owned companies. See Wu (2005, p. 155).

[5] JSCs must, unless established through the transformation of an SOE, have at least 5 initial promoters and shareholders. Until 2005 revisions to the Company Law, it was required to have registered capital of at least 10 million yuan (5 million yuan following the revisions).

[6] LLCs are relatively small companies that have no more than 50 shareholders; have a minimum registered capital of 30 000 yuan (under the 1993 Company Law, it ranged from 100 000 yuan to 500 000 yuan). The 1993 Company Law also provided for a minimum of two founding shareholders, but the 2005 revision removes this provision.

[7] A special type of LLC that may be wholly owned by a state agency.

With the frustrated effects of reform and increased competition from the non-state sector, such as Township-Village Enterprises (TVEs) and foreign-invested enterprises, by the end of 1994, more than 50 per cent of approximately 110 000 SOEs in China ran at a loss (Lincoln, 1995; Financial Times, 10 September 1997).[8] In 1996 the state industry's losses reached a record high of almost 80 billion yuan (Lardy, 1998, p. 35).

4. SOEs Reform With Ownership Change

The persistent losses of SOEs imposed a heavy fiscal burden on governments at various levels. It had become clear that the government could not control every sector and all SOEs. In 1997 the 15th CCP Congress decided to adopt a strategy of 'grasp the large and let-go the small (*Zhua da Fang xiao*)'.

4.1 Let-go the small

Under the 'let-go the small' policy, small and medium-sized[9] SOEs were allowed to determine their own path.[10] It resulted in a massive privatization of small and medium SOEs nationwide. Between the end of 1997 and the end of 2003, the number of SOEs decreased by almost half, from 262 000 to 146 000 – a reduction of 116 000.[11]

Approved methods for 'letting go' included the use of employees buyouts, sale to outsiders, reorganization, combination, leasing, contracting out and joint venture. Despite lack of nationwide statistics or surveys, it is believed that insider-dominated ownership transformation took place before 2003 (Mako and Zhang, 2007).[12] Insider privatization has typically

---

[8] Financial Times (10 September 1997) indicated that over 118 000 enterprises comprise the state sector, of which about 70 per cent lost money in 1996.

[9] In 1999, the CCP Central Committee extended the let-go policy to medium-sized SOEs.

[10] A striking fact is that there has been no specific rule to govern the privatization, which involves thousands of SOEs and employees.

[11] Data source, Finance Yearbook of China, quoted from Mako and Zhang (2007, p. 176).

[12] There are a couple of reasons for the dominance of insider privatization. First, it is less politically risky for officials who implemented the reform compared with private ownership by outsiders; second, it more readily gains support of the insiders who had gained de facto control in many SOEs; third, given the risk of large employee layoffs in outsider-led transformations, insider privatization may be easier to settle explicit and implicit obligations of the state towards employees; fourth, in the late 1990s, the poor financial condition made it difficult to attract outside investors. See Mako and Zhang (2007, p. 177).

resulted in a limited liability company with managers and employees as shareholders. In the first round transformation (1995–1998), shares were often distributed more evenly among managers and employees, but it was soon found undesirable. Thus, SOEs that underwent transformation after 1998 went directly towards concentrated management ownership (Mako and Zhang, 2007, p. 178).

Although privatization has done a lot to turn around an enterprise sector that was highly distressed, widespread irregularities accompanied privatization, in particular, insider privatization triggered a public outcry which reached its peak in the summer of 2004. Lang Xianping (Larry Lang), a Hong Kong-based economist, launched a fierce attack on several well-known Chinese entrepreneurs, accusing them of stealing state assets through disguised management buyouts (MBOs)[13] during the process of ownership transformation (Sohu Caijing, 17 June 2004, 2 August 2004; Phoenix TV, 26 August 2004). These accusations met with overwhelming popular support and sparked a heated debate over privatization that has lasted to date.[14]

In response to this debate, the State-owned Assets Supervision and Administration Commission (SASAC)[15] reviewed the implementation of SOE reform at local levels and found that in most MBO transactions, asset stripping and stealing by managers through non-transparent or unfair procedures of valuation, pricing and transfer were common. The

---

[13] MBO has a different meaning in the Chinese context. In the first place, the target firms of many MBO deals were not public companies, but state-owned, non-listed firms. Managers of these firms usually became their new owners by acquiring controlling stakes or full ownership via off-market negotiations with local governments.

[14] The debate attracted almost every well-known Chinese economist either concurring with Lang or challenging his position. Hundreds of commentaries and newspaper reports have been pouring into the public domain. For instance, See Sohu Caijing, 19 October 2004; China News Week, 1 October 2004; Securities Market Weekly, 25 September 2004; Economic Observer, 30 August 2004, 11 September 2004. In addition, Gu Chujun, the CEO of Greencool and one of the entrepreneurs criticized by Lang, brought a libel lawsuit against him which was much publicized by the media. However, the Lang–Gu debate was dramatically ended with Gu's trial in November 2006 in Guangdong Province. Gu was charged with economic crime centred on financial fraud, allegedly taking place in the process of his acquisitions of former ailing SOEs. See Caijing, 13 November 2006.

[15] The SASAC was established in April 2003. It is in charge of overseeing state assets and is entrusted with the exercise of ownership rights in SOEs on behalf of the state.

managers usually conspired with local officials who oversaw the privatized firms and accepted bribes to give the deals permission. Moreover, in some cases, it was found that managers tried to transfer risks to the buyout targets and state banks by using state shares and assets as loan guarantees to finance their MBO deals. The SASAC also pointed out that some MBO transactions harmed the rights of investors and employees as well (China Newsweek, 18 October 2004). In December 2004 the SASAC, and later, in April 2005, a regulation by the SASAC and the Ministry of Finance (MOF), banned MBOs of large SOEs and set stringent conditions for MBOs of small/medium SOEs (Financial Times, 1 February 2005). Since then, it appears that small-medium MBOs have dropped off significantly (Mako and Zhang, 2007, p. 194).

The SOEs that have not made ownership transformation face many more difficulties now. Although the government has not shifted from the general direction of ownership reform, nor dismissed privatization as a favourable policy option, the SASAC has clearly tightened its position. In addition, the 2004 debate has largely weakened the legitimacy of insider privatization, in particular through MBOs, which are now in many ways equated with the much-criticized Russian style of privatization. Ownership transformation without cooperation of insiders, however, is often very difficult to carry out. A recent tragedy during the process of Tonghua Steel's ownership reform is an illustration of this.[16]

4.2 Grasp the big

The massive privatization of small and medium SOEs documented above seems to create an impression that the *party-state*[17] has given up its

---

[16] On 24 July 2009, during the process of restructuring of Tonghua Steel (an SOE in Jilin Province), Chen Guojun, a manager who was appointed by Jian Long Steel (a private enterprise), was beaten to death by the angry employees of Tonghua Steel who rejected the acquisition. See Financial Times Chinese, 28 July 2007.

[17] The term *party-state* is used instead of *state* because it better captures China's political reality. The CCP is still the absolute power centre in Chinese politics, even if such absolute control was once weakened under Zhao Ziyang and later tightened up again by Jiang Zemin. Deng Xiaoping made the so-called Four Cardinal Principles sacrosanct in Chinese politics: the party's leadership trumps the adherence to Marxism, socialist system, and the people's democracy and dictatorship. Jiang imposed his overall guideline for China's governance: the Party stands aloof, assumes overall responsibility and coordinates all sides of the government, congress, political consultative conference, and the mass organizations. The Party commands, controls and integrates all other political organizations and institutions in China.

control of the economy. This is nothing more than an illusion. What is taking place at the same time as privatizing small-medium SOEs is the strengthening of the big ones. It is not that the party-state has changed its determination to control, it has only changed the strategy. By grasping the big SOEs, together with control of factor markets (capital, labour and land), the party-state could still assure its control of the economy, but at less cost.

The 'big' that the state determines to grasp includes SOEs in several sectors: national security-related industries, natural monopolies, sectors providing important goods and services to the public, and important enterprises in pillar industries and the high-technology sector (Economic Daily, 13 June 2003). Even a quick glance at this list would remind us of the fundamentally different role that SOEs play in China from that in developed capitalist countries. They are by no means limited to curing market failure.

By the mid-1990s, the debt-to-asset ratio of all SOEs combined as high as 85 per cent or so, and 37 per cent of non-financial SOEs were already in insolvency, even as calculated by book value (Wu et al., 1998). In order to get large and medium SOEs 'out of the difficult position in three years',[18] a series of debt-reducing and recapitalization measures were adopted. At the end of 1998, the State Council decided to establish four asset management corporations (AMCs)[19] to take over NPLs from four big state-owned commercial banks (SCBs)[20] respectively. In 1999, the four AMCs were established and took over NPLs of about RMB 1400 billion at book value from the four SCBs and the China Development Bank immediately started debt-equity conversion for about 600 SOEs chosen by the State Economic and Trade Commission (SETC). The total amount of NPLs converted to equities was about RMB 460 billion (Wu, 2005, p. 164). The main purpose of the debt-equity conversion was to convert interest payments of the debtor enterprises into profits on the books and therefore put the loss-making enterprises in the black – in essence, the government subsidized these selected SOEs (Wu, 2005, p. 164).

Other measures include increasing bankruptcy and mergers, subsidized interest rates, tax refunds, increasing investment in technical upgrading

---

[18]   On 18–24 July, 1997, the then Premier Zhu Rongji pledged to get large and medium SOEs that were in the red out of trouble in about 3 years during his inspection of 19 large SOEs.

[19]   The four AMCs are Cinda, Huarong, Great Wall and Orient.

[20]   The big four are the Bank of China, the Industrial and Commercial Bank of China, Agricultural Bank of China and China Construction Bank.

and massive layoffs. During 1998–2000, a total of 1781 bankruptcy and merger cases were approved, involving the write-off of 126.1 billion yuan of bank loans. During 1999–2000, a total of 240 billion yuan was invested in technical upgrading, financed by a combination of treasury bonds and bank loans. Between 1997 and 2003, average asset size for both centrally administered and locally administered SOEs nearly tripled. This was believed to reflect a combination of both intensive investment in fixed assets and policy-driven mergers and acquisitions (M&A) (Mako and Zhang, 2007).

Meanwhile, large SOEs were required to undertake corporatization and partial privatization.[21] In 1999, the Fourth Plenary Session of the 15th CCP Congress adopted 'The Decision on Several Important Issues Regarding Reform and Development of State-owned Enterprises' (the 1999 decision) (*Zhonggong Zhongyang Guanyu Guoyou Qiye Gaige he Fazhan Ruogan Zhongda Wenti de Jueding*). The decision is the most important document regarding SOE reform thus far. It mandated that large and medium-sized SOEs, especially well-performing ones suitable for shareholding system, should be converted to shareholding enterprises. In addition, it required that, except for a minority of enterprises that could be monopolized by the state, the rest should actively develop corporations with multiple equity-holding entities and should introduce non-state equity investment.

Complying with this requirement, most large SOEs were restructured into shareholding companies. The new three committees (shareholder's general meetings, board of directors and supervisory board) were established and co-exist with the old three committees (i.e. employee representatives meeting, labour union and party committee). Ownership has been diversified through initial public offerings (IPOs), establishment of Chinese–foreign joint ventures, issuing shares to employees and use of cross-shareholding among enterprises.

However, neither corporatization nor partial privatization indicates that the party-state has loosened its hands on large SOEs. Both corporatization and partial privatization are tools, not aims. The aim is not to reduce the state's control over key sector of the economy, but to make that control more effective (The Economist, 20 March 2004). On the other side of the corporatization and partial privatization of SOEs, was the

---

[21] The term 'privatization' has been intentionally avoided by the Party and government. They prefer to use the terms 'ownership transformation', or 'ownership diversification'.

story of China's stock market. In the past, present and future, its fate was, is and will be closely related to SOE reform.

II. THE RISE OF CHINA'S STOCK MARKET

1. The Spontaneous Experiment

Stock enterprises emerged as early as 1978. In order to raise funds, first in rural areas, later in cities, enterprises started to issue 'shares', overwhelmingly, to employees. Although, in a strict sense, these shares more closely resembled fixed income securities, investors tended to hold rather than trade such securities, having invested to obtain the steady dividend cash flow just like a fixed bank deposit or a bond.[22] By late 1986 the number of enterprises issuing shares had reached 6000 to 7000 nationwide, raising altogether around RMB 6 billion (Li, 2000) and over-the-counter (OTC) markets had sprung up in major cities.

The early 1980s' period of experimentation with corporate forms and securities was spontaneous and entirely unregulated, promoted by local governments and largely unnoticed by Beijing (Walter and Howie, 2003). SOEs and other enterprises[23] reorganized and issued shares to investors to raise funds with little government restriction. There was nothing dogmatic about which companies could or could not restructure and sell shares, nor investor restrictions, and shares could be freely transferred (Walter and Howie, 2003, pp. 6–8). All these were in sharp contrast with the later regulated market.

2. The Central Government Stepped In

The experimentation of the early 1980s increasingly raised the concern of outright privatization. As a result, beginning in 1989, the central government started to intervene and brought the experimentation period to an end. Without doubt, enterprises' restructuring activities and stock trading needed clear guidelines, however, the central government's ambition is far greater. The intention of the central government is not just to *regulate*

---

[22]   Shanghai Feile Acoustics was often given the honour of being the first to issue shares because of its relatively standardized offering procedures.

[23]   At this stage, enterprises that issued shares were mostly collective enterprises created by marginalized people. Thus, they were entirely excluded from the formal finance system. The shareholders of the first generation also belonged to this group.

the market, but to *replace* the market. As will be seen below, it started by imposing restrictions on the transferability of shares, with the central government gradually gaining control of almost every single aspect of the market. The stock market has been used to serve its various policy objectives, from financing large SOEs to financing social pension plans, and more recently, to prompt the Gross Domestic Product (GDP) growth rate. The involvement of the central government largely eliminated the liberal colour of the early stock market and replaced it with one of a planning and administrative nature.

3. Establishment of National Exchanges

One of the most important interventional steps by the central government was to establish national exchanges. Having witnessed the springing up of trading centres around the country, in particular the 'share fever'[24] in southern China, the central government came to the idea that it 'would be better to manage the situation and limit its scale inside the walls of formal exchanges' (Walter and Howie, 2003, p. 29). As a result, after years of intensive lobbying, the Shanghai and Shenzhen municipal governments finally gained the approval of the State Council to open stock exchanges. The SHSE and SZSE were opened in December 1990 and July 1991 respectively. Meanwhile, following the formal establishment of the two national exchanges, the regional trading centres were required to close down.[25]

4. Using the Stock Market to Finance SOEs

Historically, SOEs raised capital primarily through interest-free budgetary grants. Nevertheless, the fall in the central government's revenues in the early 1980s necessitated finding new sources of capital to fund SOEs. In July 1983, the government started to fund most of the SOEs' capital expenditures with bank loans rather than via free budgetary allocations.

---

[24] The 'share fever' throughout southern China was ignited by the dividend payment of Shenzhen Development Bank (SDB) for its 1988 financial year in March 1989. SDB, as China's first financial institution limited by shares, made a dud IPO in 1987 with the issue only 50 per cent subscribed. Its exceedingly generous dividend to its investors created a market for its shares almost instantaneously and investors quickly learned that there was more to shares than a simple dividend. Prices for publicly traded Shenzhen companies snowballed with funds pouring in from all across China. See Walter and Howie (2003, p. 25).

[25] Regardless of the requirement, they continued to play a role until 30 June 1999.

However, since the main banks are also state owned, many of the loans were more like grants. Debt forgiveness and payment deferrals were routinely granted (Huang, 2002).

As noted above, the persistent loss-making SOEs not only led to high debts-to-assets ratios for themselves but also accumulated a huge sum of NPLs in the SCBs.[26] Thus, the government decided to make use of the stock market as an alternative fundraising vehicle for SOEs (Wu, 2005, p. 242).[27] Before 1997 the exchanges were mainly controlled by the Shenzhen and Shanghai municipal governments and used to finance local SOEs. After 1997, with the central government taking over full control of exchanges and adopting the 'grasp large' strategy, using stock market to finance SOEs became a national policy, followed by the dramatic change of the central government's attitude towards the stock market.[28]

The policy of using the stock market to finance SOEs has a fundamental impact on the market. First, it deprives the stock market of its basic function – allocating capital. It is the government rather than the market that decides which company should get the resources. Second, the fundraising objective shifts the regulatory focus from institutional building to index (price) managing. For the same reason, the regulatory authority has to acquiesce in illegal activities such as price manipulation and false restructuring when they are the only ways to attract retail investors. Third, the series of institutional arrangements designed to raise funds for SOEs result in large-scale rent seeking, price distortion, etc.

---

[26]   The problems with banks will be further discussed in Chapter 3.

[27]   Wu, then serving as an advisor to the State Council, claimed that 'the administrative authorities ... adopted the policy that the stock market should serve the SOEs' (Wu, 2005, p. 242).

[28]   Before 1997 the central government took a very cautious, reserved attitude towards the stock market. On 16 December 1996, a People's Daily (*Renming Ribao*) front-page special editorial entitled 'Correct Understanding of the Current Stock Market (*Zhenque Renshi Dangqian Gupiao Shichang*)', warned of the market's highly speculative nature and the market commenced to collapse. Rumours named Zhu Rongji, the then vice Premier, as the editor of the piece which identified 'very abnormal and irrational trading' conditions in the market and which made explicit comparison with the American stock market just before its 1929 crash. See Green (2004). By contrast, facing a similar share frenzy starting from 19 May 1999, on 15 June 1999, in another *People's Daily* special correspondence entitled 'Strengthen Confidence, Normal Development (*Jiaqiang Xinxin, Guifan Fazhan*)', claimed that 'the recent stock market performance is reflecting the true macro-economy and market requirements, so it is normal for the market to rise', and concluded with the statement 'a good situation in the securities markets is not easy to come by, all sides should double its value'.

They also cultivate vested interests groups that can create strong obstacles to meaningful reform.

5. A Snapshot of China's Stock Market

From a very low level, China's stock market has experienced rapid growth in the past two decades. By 31 December 2008, 1625 companies were listed on the two exchanges. The combined market capitalization reached RMB12.13 trillion (approximately $1.8 trillion), 19.6 per cent of the NYSE. It also boasts more than 107 securities companies, over 100 000 practitioners, and over 152 million investors' accounts (CSRC 2008 Annual Report).

6. A Stock Market with Chinese Characteristics

The party-state's determination to remain in control of large SOEs and use the stock market to finance them resulted in a stock market with Chinese characteristics.

6.1 A stock market dominated by state-owned listed companies

The Chinese stock market is dominated by state-owned companies. At the end of 2000, 90 per cent of listed companies were originally SOEs (Tam, 2002). A 2003 study showed that approximately 84 per cent of listed companies were, viewed solely from the standpoint of equity ownership and not taking consideration of informal mechanisms of influence, directly and indirectly under state control (Liu and Sun, 2003). This figure is roughly consistent with the conclusions of other analysts (Walter and Howie, 2003; Wall Street Journal, 10 September 2002). By contrast, most profitable private firms have hitherto been denied access to the stock market. Standard & Poor's counted that only 35 listed companies were private out of a total number of 1300 listed companies in 2003, and it further pointed out that a good number of these so-called 'private' listed companies are in fact controlled by local government and even the military (The Economist, 6 February 2003).

6.2 A stock market with two-thirds of shares non-tradable

In the West, equity shares are defined in terms of the specific rights attributed to a holder in the ownership of a company. With the primary objective of preserving the state's ownership of assets contributed to newly corporatized companies, in 1992, the 'Standard Opinion for

Companies Limited by Shares' (*Gufen Gongsi Guifan Yijian*)[29] created two broad classes of shares, one tradable and the other non-tradable. Furthermore, the Standard Opinion created two sub-classes of non-tradable shares based on the distance of the entity contributing assets from the state: state shares and legal person shares. State shares and legal person shares are not allowed to be traded in the market. The Standard Opinion was superseded by the 1993 Company Law, however, since neither the 1993 Company Law nor the later 1998 Securities Law made mention of the share types created by the Standard Opinion, the Standard Opinion remained as the foundation document of the securities industry until at least 2005. Typically, a restructured SOE was required to have one-third of the shares as state shares, one-third as legal person shares, and another one-third would go to the public. As a consequence, two-thirds of shares are not tradable in the market. By the end of 2004, 64 per cent of the total 7149 billion shares were non-tradable, among which 74 per cent were state owned (CSRC, 2008 China Capital Market Development Report).[30] The percentage of non-tradable shares is even higher for some listed companies with large capitalization.

6.3   A stock market artificially segmented

China's stock market is artificially segmented and with shares of the same company being traded in three different markets at different prices. First, as noted, non-tradable shares are not allowed to trade in the stock market. They can only be transferred between legal persons through negotiation, with the approval of the exchange where the company is listed. The negotiated transfer price is heavily discounted, ranging from 54 per cent to 91 per cent of the company's prevailing A-share price, with the average discount being 81 per cent (Walter and Howie, 2003, p. 185).

Second, the market for tradable shares is segmented as well. Tradable shares include A, B, H, N, L and S shares. A-shares are listed on domestic stock exchanges and were originally intended for ownership only by Chinese nationals. Recently, the A-share market has been opened to specially approved foreign institutional investors, termed as Qualified

---

[29]   Issued by the State Committee for the Restructuring of the Economic System (SCRES).

[30]   Hereinafter, the Development Report. Although a reform policy started in 2005 allowing the listed companies to convert their state and legal person shares into tradable ones, it takes time for this to be completed. By the end of 2009, tradable shares only accounted for 28.4 per cent of the total shares outstanding. See also the Development Report. This does not affect the present discussion.

Foreign Institutional Investors (QFII).[31] B shares are also listed on domestic stock exchanges. However, it was not until 2001 that they could only be purchased by foreigners using foreign currency.[32] They may be now purchased by domestic investors as well with foreign currency. H shares are shares listed in the Hong Kong Stock Exchange (HKSE),[33] N shares are shares represented by American Depositary Receipt (ADR) listed in the NYSE,[34] and L shares are listed in the LSE, S shares are listed in the Singapore Stock Exchange (SGX). All these shares have the same rights and obligations, the only differences being the type of investors permitted to own and trade them and the currency used for trading and cash dividends. As a consequence of financial repression policy, China's investors face extremely limited investment options. In addition, the supply of A-shares is tightly controlled by the government. Thus, A-shares are traded at a much higher price than foreign shares. The A-shares market is isolated from overseas stock markets and operates independently.

6.4 A stock market with state ownership

It is not unusual for the state to intervene in the stock market, or even replace private contracting, as observed in many civil law countries (La Porta et al., 2008). Nevertheless, in these cases, the state still remains as a regulator and does not directly participate in transactions. By contrast, in China's stock market, the state is not just the regulator, it is also the most important player. The stock exchanges, securities companies, fund management and trust companies and listed companies are all owned by the state. 'In the entire system, the only matters that do not belong to the state, probably, are the actual money, or capital, put up by presumably individual investors' (Walter and Howie, 2003, p. 4). Thus, we could almost call it a stock market with state ownership!

The direct participation of the state in the stock market is a double-edged sword. As will be discussed in Chapter 4, under a very weak

---

[31] The QFII scheme is borrowed from Taiwan's experience during the earlier years of the island's capital markets development when the conditions for full financial liberalization were not mature. Since November 2002, foreign institutional investors that have obtained the joint approval by the CSRC, the central bank and the State Administration of Foreign Exchange can trade A-shares with an allotted quota of funds.

[32] They are settled in US dollars on the SHSE or in HK dollars on the SZSE.

[33] H shares are traded directly in share form in Hong Kong.

[34] N shares can only be traded in the guise of ADRs in order to control outward capital flows from mainland China.

enforcement environment, without implicit guarantees and assurances provided by the state, China's stock market might have collapsed a long time ago and there is no chance that it could grow to today's scale. On the other hand, the state's participation has stifled the market's ability to grow endogenously and has fundamentally undermined the foundation of various enforcement mechanisms, cultivated a distorted market which is labelled as 'Casino without rules'.[35] Even worse, the poor quality of public governance in China turns the stock market into a perfect channel through which the elites could easily grab public wealth.

III. LISTED COMPANIES

1. Ownership Structure

A typical Chinese listed company has a mixed ownership structure with the state shares, legal person shares, and domestic individuals as the three predominant groups of shareholders. Each of the three holds about 30 per cent of total outstanding shares. The remaining 10 per cent goes to foreigners and employee shares (Xu and Wang, 1999).

State shares are held by the central and local governments,[36] which are now represented by the SASAC and regional asset management bureaus. State shares can also be held by the parent of the listed company, typically, a corporatized solely state-owned enterprise. In many of the public companies, the state is the largest or majority shareholder.

Legal person shares are held by domestic institutions. A legal person is defined as a non-individual legal entity or institution. These domestic institutions include stock companies, non-bank financial institutions, and SOEs that have at least one non-state owner (Xu and Wang, 1999). Securities companies, trust and investment companies, finance companies, and mutual funds are major non-bank financial institutions. These institutions could be further classified according to their ownership

---

[35] Wu made this famous claim in January 2001 when interviewed by the China Central Television (CCTV) programme, *30 Minutes Economy* (*Jingji Banxiaoshi*). It triggered a famous debate over the Chinese stock market in 2001. For details of the debate, see Wu (2005, pp. 247–250).

[36] Before the establishment of the SASAC in 2004, the central government only granted local governments the rights to manage daily operation of local SOEs, with the ownership rights still held by the central government. With the establishment of SASAC and the subsequent reform of the state assets management system it has been undertaking, local governments have been granted the ownership of local SOEs.

structure as SOEs, state-owned non-profit organizations, collectively or privately owned enterprises, joint stock companies and foreign-funded companies. Like state shares, legal person shares are not tradable at the two exchanges.[37]

It would be a misunderstanding to simply equate legal person shareholder to institutional investors in free market economies. It is not only because legal person shares are non-tradable, more importantly, legal persons that hold shares are often industrial SOEs as opposed to private firms, which means they are ultimately controlled by the state (Tenev et al., 2002; Tian, 2001; Sun and Tong, 2003). The similarity between legal person shares and state shares could be further seen from the fact that state-owned legal person shares (the official sub-classification of non-tradable shares of many listed firms) were considered to be a subset of state shares prior to 2003, but after that date were reclassified as legal person shares.[38] As a result, a legal person shareholder is very different from institutional investors in terms of the motivation and objectives that they have.

Tradable A-shares are held and traded by domestic individuals and institutions. The stereotype image of the Chinese stock market is that it is dominated by small investors (Xu and Wang, 1999; Wong et al., 2004; Ho et al., 2003). Institutional share holding according to the Western definition is rare. This belief, however, is misleading. This will be discussed in detail in Chapter 4.

Employee shares are offered to workers and managers of a listed company, usually at a substantial discount, at the time of going public. Employee shares are registered under the title of the labour union of the company, which also represents shareholding employees to exercise their rights. These shares have to be held for six to 12 months after an IPO, and can then be sold on the stock exchange following approval by the regulatory authorities. In 1998 the regulatory authorities issued a circular in relation to discontinuing the issuance of employee shares. As a result, the number of employee shares is gradually falling (Tenev et al., 2002).

---

[37] It worth noting that a large portion of outstanding shares of private or foreign-controlled listed companies also fall into the category of legal person shares, and are thus not tradable.

[38] There are a number of ambiguities in the official classification system. For example, a legal person can hold both state shares and legal person shares; legal person shares can be held by both private and state-controlled entities and both domestic and foreign entities. State shares can be held by both corporatized SOEs and government bureaus.

Tian (2001) reports that average managerial ownership is only 0.005 per cent of the total number of shares outstanding.

Since 2005 the policy in relation to managerial ownership has started to change. In 2005 the CSRC issued 'Measures for Administration of Stock Incentive Plan at Listed Companies';[39] later, in 2006, the SASAC- and MOF-jointly issued 'Trial Measures for Administration of Stock Incentive Plan at State-controlled Listed Companies'[40] introduced a stock incentive plan into listed companies. By May 2009 a total of 116 companies announced stock incentive plans (SHSE, 2009). Nevertheless, the overall percentage of managerial ownership is still very low.

Foreign shares mainly include B, H, N, L and S shares that are supposed to be held exclusively by foreign individual and institutional investors, at least before the B-share market opened to domestic investors in 2001. They are traded against foreign currency. A company may issue shares of all the above types, but in reality, neither dual listing nor multiple listing is common for Chinese firms as the average proportion of companies issuing H or B shares is about 10 per cent (Liu, 2006).

2.   Concentration of Ownership

In Chinese listed companies, overall and within the non-tradable share block, ownership concentration is high; in addition, in most cases, the largest shareholder is the state. Ownership in China's listed companies is highly concentrated. Lou and Yuan (2002) report that as of May 2001, 177 out of 1206 listed companies (15 per cent) were more than 66 per cent owned by a single shareholder; 510 (42 per cent) were more than 50 per cent owned; 742 (62 per cent) were more than 37.5 per cent owned; and 888 (74 per cent) were more than 30 per cent owned. Tian and Lau (2001) find that the five largest shareholders hold just over 60 per cent of the outstanding shares of Chinese listed companies, as compared with 25.4 per cent in the United States and 33.1 per cent in Japan. Xu (2004) reports that, on average, across all listed firms, the largest shareholder

[39]   The CSRC: Measures for Administration of Incentive Plan at Listed Companies (*Shangshi Gongsi Guquanjili Guanlibanfa*), 31 December 2005, available at CSRC website http://www.csrc.gov.cn/n575458/n776436/n804965/n3300690/n3300837/n3330750/11232701.html.

[40]   The SASAC and the MOF, 'Trial Measures for Administration of Incentive Plan at State-controlled Listed Companies' (*Guoyou Konggu Shangshi Gongsi Shishi Guquan Jili Shixing Banfa*) available at SASAC website: http://www.sasac.gov.cn/n1180/n1566/n259655/n260209/1858259.html.

owns 46 per cent of a firm, while the second largest shareholder owns 7 per cent.

The ownership structure of Chinese listed companies is concentrated, but when compared with that in some Western European and East Asian countries and the United States, China is in the middle, at levels similar to those in most Western European countries (Tenev et al., 2002). What really distinguishes China's ownership structure is the identity of the controlling shareholder. In the majority of Chinese listed companies, the controlling shareholder is the state. Tenev et al. (2002), based on a survey of SHSE, estimated that in 1999, in more than 95 per cent of cases, the state is directly and indirectly (through industrial SOEs) in control of listed companies. Recently, Liu and Sun (2003), in the vein of the La Porta et al. (1999) principle of ultimate ownership, surveyed 1160 listed firms in China in 2001. The government ultimately controlled 84 per cent of them, of which 8.5 per cent directly and 75.6 per cent indirectly by 'pyramid shareholding schemes'.[41] A study conducted in 2002 by the CSRC and the SETC found that of 1015 controlling shareholders in the 1175 listed companies studied, 77 per cent could be considered as state organs, while in 390 companies a single state shareholder held over half of the shares.[42]

CONCLUDING REMARKS

This chapter described the historical background and characteristics of the Chinese stock market. The sustained losses of SOEs forced the government to seek new sources of funds; meanwhile, it had to ensure its control over SOEs, which are crucial to its political survival. As a result, China's capital market expanded rapidly, but was subject to strict constraints. The market is dominated by state-owned listed companies, two-thirds of shares are not free floating, the shares of the same company trade in different markets at different prices, and most market participants are owned or controlled by the party-state. Most Chinese listed companies are now partially privatized, but still controlled by the party-state.

Being aware of its background and characteristics is critical to answering our research question, how the Chinese stock market developed. On

---

[41] Ren (2004) reported that by the end of June 2002, state-owned shares (include state shares and legal person shares owned by the state-owned entities) accounted for at least 70 per cent of the outstanding shares of over half of the largest 112 listed companies.

[42] Reported in *Economic Daily*, 30 January 2003.

the one hand, as will be shown in Chapter 3, they significantly changed the incentive of the market players and thereby undermined all kinds of enforcement mechanisms. On the other hand, as shown in Chapter 4, they played a decisive role in prompting the development of the Chinese stock market.

3. Enforcement in China's capital market

INTRODUCTION

This chapter provides a systematic examination of enforcement in China's stock market. It contains five sections. Section 1 looks at the self-enforcement mechanisms including hostage, collateral and hands-tying. Particular attention will be paid to the effectiveness of cross-listing. Section 2 explores the effectiveness of bilateral relationship in enforcement. It first gives a detailed examination of the function of large creditors – SCBs. Second, it looks at the function of large shareholders. Related issues such as the shareholders' general meeting, the board of directors, board of supervisors and legal protection of minority share-holders will also be briefly examined here. Section 3 focuses on the reputation mechanism. It looks at the conditions on which the reputation mechanism functions: the incentive to build reputation, the disclosure of information and credible punishment. Section 4 moves to non-state third-party enforcement. It starts with a general discussion regarding China's social structure which is believed to be crucial to non-state third-party enforcement. Then it explores the function of stock exchanges and investment banks in detail, and auditors and other gatekeepers briefly. Special attention is paid to the media, which has remarkably outperformed other enforcers in the past decade. Section 5 examines the role of formal enforcement. It first introduces North et al.'s (2009) new conceptual framework of state and applies it to China. It points out that formal enforcement will be inherently weak in a 'natural state' like China. Apart from this ultimate cause, it also examines the particular factors that affect the function of public enforcement and private enforcement of law. In the former, major factors include multiple objectives, the conflicting role of the state and judicial corruption. In the latter, Chinese legal tradition, lack of judicial independence and authority, under-development of civil law, the ambiguous concept of rights, judicial corruption and competence are considered. Evidence is also provided of the weakness in public enforcement and private enforcement of law.

I. SELF-ENFORCEMENT MECHANISM

1. Hostage

As discussed in Chapter 1, hostage is very difficult to arrange in a corporate context. Thus, we cannot find any case in China's stock market of using hostage to improve corporate governance of firms towards outside investors.

2. Collateral

Collateral is probably the most important and prevalent mechanism between firms and creditors. Creditors usually require the firm to provide some assets, such as property, or equipment as collateral. If the firm defaults, the creditor can realize its debts by selling the collateral in the market or making use of it.

However, as we will see below, the main creditors of Chinese listed companies are state-owned banks. These banks are heavily influenced by the governments at various levels, who in turn control the listed companies. Thus, under the interference of the government, listed companies often receive loans without providing collateral. By the same token, even if there is collateral, it is hard to realize.

3. Hands-tying

A company can reinforce investors' confidence through costly advertising such as cross-listing on overseas securities exchanges or employing a world-class accountant or investment bankers. These commitments are normally considered credible because otherwise the expenditure will be wasted. In return, the market will reward the company with lower costs of capital. All these measures mentioned above, cross-listing, employing world-class accountants and investment bankers, have been introduced in Chinese listed companies to a varying extent. However, they have only achieved limited effect. In this section, we focus on cross-listing and leave the employing of international accountants and investment bankers to the discussion of gatekeepers.

Since 1993 the listing of Qingdao Brewery (600600) on the HKSE, Chinese companies have begun going overseas to raise capital. As noted before, the major destinations for Chinese overseas listing include the HKSE, NYSE, LSE, SGX, and National Association of Securities Dealers' Automated Quotations (NASDAQ). The major components of overseas listing companies are large SOEs, usually in strategic sectors such as telecommunications, energy, finance and transportation, which the party-state determines to grasp.[1] In regard to these companies, the *primary* objective of cross-listing is not to raise capital, but to piggy-back on the overseas market to improve corporate governance; in Premier Wen Jiabao's term, it is 'paying for management' (*Huaqian mai Guanli*).

3.1 Failure to change incentive

Nevertheless, even a quick glance would cast doubts on the effectiveness of the cross-listing strategy by the Chinese government. The idea underlying hands-tying is that it increases the costs of controllers' opportunistic behaviour. It only works when it is the controllers themselves who bear the costs of hands-tying. In China's case, the cost of cross-listing is not borne by the controllers, but by Chinese taxpayers. Thus, it has little impact on the controllers' incentives. If these SOEs' controllers could take the costs that Chinese people paid for the companies into account, there would not be a need for overseas listing in the first place.

3.2 Failure to resist political intervention

Despite the costs of cross-listing, if the discipline of the overseas capital market could force these large SOEs to improve their governance quality, it is still worthwhile. However, to what extent the overseas capital market could make changes to the two fundamental problems – soft budget constraint and multiple objectives – inherent in state ownership is an open question.

Take the two energy giants PetroChina Company Limited (PetroChina) and China Petroleum & Chemical Company (Sinopec) for instance. Sinopec was set up by China Petrochemical Corporation (Sinopec Group) in 1998 and PetroChina was established by China National Petroleum Corporation (CNPC) in 1999. Both enjoyed the preferential treatment of multiple listing on the HKSE, NYSE and LSE as early as 2000.[2] At the

---

[1] Until recently, overseas listing has been a privilege mainly reserved for these large SOEs. In order to overcome the regulatory barrier and list in overseas markets, a large number of companies (mostly privately owned) operate in China, but are incorporated abroad. These companies are called 'red chip' companies in the Hong Kong market. The effect of overseas listing has a different impact on these companies, but it is beyond the scope of this book.

[2] Sinopec listed on HKSE, NYSE, LSE; PetroChina listed on HKSE, NYSE. They both listed on the SHSE in 2001 and 2006 respectively.

time of writing, international investors own 19.35 per cent shares in Sinopec,[3] 11.79 per cent in PetroChina.[4]

First, we look at the employment issue. Chinese SOEs have long been plagued by the employment burden. In 2004, four years after its overseas listing, it is reported that PetroChina ranked first among oil companies worldwide in term of employment: it hired 417 000 employees, compared to 103 000 in British Petroleum (BP) (the then largest oil company). This contrast is even more remarkable when we consider the fact that BP's annual sales reached US$250 billion and total assets worth US$191 billion, 4.2 and 2.65 times those of PetroChina respectively (Financial Times Chinese, 10 January 2006).

Second, we consider price distortion. Fuel price has always been tightly controlled by the Chinese government. In October 2007, when international wholesale petrol prices were an average of US$102, China's prices were still equivalent to only about US$76 a barrel, even after a 10 per cent adjustment. The global oil prices and strict government controls caused huge losses for PetroChina and Sinopec, who must pay more for oil but cannot raise prices at the pump (Financial Times Chinese, 5 November 2007). Clearly, overseas investors are unable to prevent the company from being used to serve political objectives that are detrimental to their interests.

Then a question arises, if overseas investors are incapable of protecting their interests from political intervention, why do they still invest in these companies? Ironically, a partial answer to this question is found in another drawback of state ownership – soft budget constraint. For instance, Sinopec received a fiscal subsidiary of 12.3 billion yuan (Financial Times Chinese, 14 April 2008) from the central government as compensation for its losses in refining business in 2007, regardless of its overall net profits reaching 54.947 billion yuan (CNPC news, 9 April 2008). Sinopec is by no means an exception, fiscal subsidies and various forms of bail-out are the norm for these large state-owned companies. Since these costs are assumed by Chinese taxpayers, soft budget constraints are actually in the overseas investors' favour: there is no reason to expect that they would like to harden them. The likelihood that the Chinese government would bail out these enterprises offsets the losses caused by its intervention.

---

[3]   Data from Sinopec website: http://www.sinopecgroup.com/english/Pages/guanyu_gsjs.aspx.
[4]   Data from PetroChina website: http://www.petrochina.com.cn/Ptr/Investor_Relations/.

Another reason is Chinese overseas listing companies treat overseas investors very generously. For instance, it is reported that up to 2007, PetroChina paid out total dividends of 305.5 billion yuan to its overseas investors (Chinese Securities Journal, 25 October 2007). Considering the combined capital it raised in the HKSE and NYSE was only around RMB 40 billion,[5] it is a generous reward indeed.

Probably the most important factor attracting overseas investors is that many of these companies, such as Sinopec, PetroChina and China Telecom are monopolies in their respective industries in China. These firms' monopoly position in the world's biggest market seems to be sufficient to guarantee investors reasonable returns and ease their concern about operational inefficiency. Investing in these monopolists means sharing their monopoly rents.

3.3 Limited impact on internal control

The discussion above suggests that the overseas capital market is unable to overcome the inherent problems associated with state ownership. Then, is it able to impose effective discipline on the controllers' behaviour? This does not seem to be encouraging either. There is no doubt that cross-listing has brought many changes to these Chinese listed companies. In many respects, they look very much like their Western counterparts. However, it has limited impact on the key issue, insider control.

First, overseas shareholders have little influence on the personnel decisions of management. This is not only because of the absolute controlling status of the Chinese state; more importantly, it is the result of the so-called 'party supervises the cadre' (*Dang Guan Ganbu*) rule. According to this rule, in ordinary SOEs, it is the Chinese Communist Party (CCP), not the board of directors that appoints top managers. Internal management appointments, career advancement and disciplinary actions are all strictly controlled by party agencies. The overseas-listed Chinese companies are by no means an exception to this rule. In fact, some of them are ministerial units and their top managers, whose appointment is directly decided by the Politburo, enjoy ministerial rank.

The powerlessness of overseas investors on personnel issues is best illustrated by the reshuffling of top managers of the listed telecom companies in 2004. The changes of senior management in the telecom industry included moving China United's chairman and chief executive,

---

[5] This figure was revealed in its prospectus in 2007 available at: http://www.petrochina.com.cn/resource/img/zgsms/gg071102C2.pdf.

Wang Jianzhou, into the top spot at the country's wireless operator. The government also shifted China Mobile's chairman, Wang Xiaochu, into the equivalent position at fixed-line operator, China Telecommunications Corp, while China United was assigned a new chairman, Chang Xiaobing, currently a vice-president of China Telecom. Despite the fact that all the three companies have publicly listed units that trade in Hong Kong and New York, the restructuring occurred overnight, without any advance notice having been given, and did not go through any board approval procedures at all (Asian Wall Street Journal, 2 November 2004).

Next we look at the extent to which these established governance organs, general shareholders' meeting and the board of directors could deter malfeasance by corporate insiders. China Aviation Oil (CAO) provides us with a perfect example. CAO was listed in SGX in 2001 as a subsidiary of the monopoly oil giant, China Aviation Oil Holding Corp (CAOHC). CAOHC holds 75 per cent of its shares and the remaining 25 per cent are dispersed among 19 others (including Singapore subsidiaries of Citibank and HSBC). Before its drastic fall, it was praised as 'the best governed company' and 'the most transparent listed company' in Singapore, and its former leader, Chen Junlin, was ranked among the 'new economic leaders in Asia' by the World Economic Forum in 2003 (Financial Times, 21 January 2005).

On 29 November 2004 CAO shocked its investors with the announcement that it had suffered losses of US$550 million in oil derivatives trading and sought bankruptcy protection from its creditors in Singapore. Singapore's Securities Investor Association (SIAS) called the event a corporate governance disaster comparable to an earthquake registering 7 to 8 on the Richter scale and likened the incident to the collapse of Barings (SIAS, 1 December 2004). What is really striking here is the weak internal control of this 'best governed company' on the key person, Chen Junlin, who bore the principal responsibility for the firm's reckless gambling in the futures market. Later investigation revealed that as a 'layman' in future market transactions, Chen made all critical trade decisions by himself without consulting either the board or his supervisors at the parent company. The corporate stipulation that deals should be suspended if any of the company's ten traders assumed a loss of more than US$500 000 was completely disregarded. 'CAO is by no means an isolated exception, but a typical example of these Chinese overseas listing companies' (Leng, 2004, p. 312).

3.4   The limits of extraterritorial law enforcement

There are also some doubts as to the enforcement capability of overseas stock exchanges and the legal regime against cross-listing companies.

First, exchanges and domestic laws often have different rules for foreign firms. In the United States, the SEC allows foreign companies to have different corporate governance and often applies different disclosure standards to them (Licht, 2003). Under US law, because disclosure requirements are less stringent for foreign firms, they are not bound in the same way that American issuers are. For instance, the SEC requires foreign private issuers to disclose interim reporting only on the basis of home country and stock exchange practice rather than quarterly reports.[6] Foreign private issuers are therefore exempted from the proxy rules and the section 16 provisions regarding insider reporting and short swing profit recovery.[7] The disclosure rules that foreign issuers can avoid seem to be precisely those that would be particularly useful for the market to be able to monitor the issuers for agency problems and minority shareholder expropriation (Cai, 2007, pp. 109–110).

Second, competition among stock exchanges might compromise their willingness to enforce. In recent years, competition between stock exchanges to attract listings has been increasingly intensive. The Chinese government, which controls hundreds of SOEs and decides in which stock exchange they will list, has great bargaining power. It reports that about 78 Chinese companies were listed on foreign exchanges around the world including 20 on the NYSE as of 2007, and some estimate that Chinese IPOs will soon become the second most important source of IPO investment banking fees worldwide after the United States (SGX, 2005 Annual Report).[8] With so much at stake, foreign stock exchanges might tend to overlook uncomfortable features of Chinese corporate governance and try to be more cooperative with the Chinese government as SGX did in the CAO case.

Last but not least, it is quite problematic for foreign authorities to take action against the Chinese parent company. An overwhelming majority of these Chinese cross-listed companies have a parent company in mainland China with its senior managers also serving on the boards of listed companies. More important, as mentioned before, they are often high-ranking administrative cadres. This thus raises the question of how they could be sanctioned by foreign authorities when listed companies are embroiled in corporate governance scandals? The answer is, without the cooperation or at least tacit approval from the Chinese government, it is

---

[6]   SEC, 'International Reporting and Disclosure Issues in the Division of Corporation Finance' (1 October 2003) available at: http://www.sec.gov. See also General Instructions for SEC Form 20-F and Form 10-K

[7]   Ibid.

[8]   Quoted from Milhaupt and Pistor (2008, p. 135).

simply impossible. A case in point is the response to the fraud scandal that embroiled the Bank of China's New York branch in 2004. The manager of the New York branch office received a 12 years' sentence of imprisonment for embezzlement and accepting bribes. Other local representatives of the bank in New York were indicted in a federal court in Manhattan, but no company officials at the Chinese parent company were implicated (China Daily, 15 February 2005). It thus raises the concern that 'weak corporate governance practices of the home country are exported to the foreign listing environment. Rather than receiving additional protections, minority investors are victimized by a distant parent company operating according to very different rules' (Milhaupt and Pistor, 2008, p. 134).

In sum, in recent years, cross-listing seems to have become a favoured strategy by the Chinese government to realize its 'grasp big' policy. However, the role that cross-listing can play in enhancing operational efficiency and corporate governance is limited. It cannot substitute for ownership transformation and formal enforcement in the home country.

II. BILATERAL RELATIONSHIP

1.   Large Creditors

A long-term relationship is often to be found between the firm and its large creditors. By threatening to cut off the relationship and stop financing the firm in the future, the creditors could protect themselves from opportunistic activity of the company. However, the Asian financial crisis also highlighted the costs of relational banking. We have briefly mentioned the NPLs problem of the Chinese banking system above. It is clearly suggested that the Chinese banks failed to protect themselves from the borrowers' default. We look at the banking problem in more detail here.

1.1   The dominance of the 'Big Four'
After the foundation of the People's Republic of China (PRC) in 1949, all of the pre-1949 capitalist companies and institutions were nationalized by 1950. Between 1950 and 1978, China's financial system consisted of a single bank – the People's Bank of China (PBOC), a central government-owned and -controlled bank under the Ministry of Finance (MOF), which served as both the central bank and a commercial bank, controlling about 93 per cent of the total financial assets of the country and handling almost all financial transactions.

By the end of 1979, the PBOC departed from the MOF and became a separate entity while three state-owned banks were established to take over some of its commercial banking businesses. The Bank of China (BOC) was spun off from PBOC to specialize in transactions related to foreign trade and investment; the China Construction Bank (CCB) was set up to specialize in financing investment in fixed assets; the Agriculture Bank of China (ABC) was to be restored to specialize in rural banking. In 1983, the State Council decided that the PBOC was to focus on its function as the central bank and transfer all saving and loan businesses to the newly established Industrial and Commercial Bank of China (ICBC).[9] Before 2004, the Big Four were wholly state owned. To improve the commercialization of the banking industry in the 1980s, the Big Four were allowed to expand into commercial banking businesses beyond those in which they had specialized.

As well as this, new commercial banks and non-bank financial institutions were also established, beginning in the late 1980s, to develop a more diversified financial system. These included joint stock commercial banks with nationwide banking licences and urban commercial banks with licences to engage in commercial banking activities within their designated geographic areas. In 1994, three policy development banks, the China Development Bank, the Export-Import Bank of China and the Agricultural Development Bank of China, were established to take over the policy lending functions of the Big Four. Foreign banks were permitted into the Chinese market to conduct limited banking operations as well.[10] Virtually all these banks are owned by state-affiliated entities and local governments, or SOEs. The first truly private financial institution, Min Sheng Bank, was established in 2003.

Although the insurance industry[11] and the stock market have quickly developed since 1980, China's formal financial sector is still dominated by state-owned banks. Nearly 90 per cent of household savings are held in deposits with state-owned banks (Financial Times, 29 December 2004). In terms of financial assets, the banks account for 73 per cent of

---

[9]   They are referred to as the Big Four.

[10]   Prior to China becoming a member of the World Trade Organization (WTO), foreign banks had been allowed to set up representative offices in China since 1979, and foreign banks were approved to establish branches in 1981. In December 1996 and August 1998, qualified branches of foreign banks were allowed to offer RMB products.

[11]   In 1980, the People's Insurance Company of China (PICC) restored its domestic insurance operations after 20 years' interruption; later Shenzhen Ping An Insurance Company (Ping An) was established in 1988.

the total financial assets in China (Barth and Caprio, 2007). The Big Four in turn dominate the banking sector. In 1986, they controlled 83 per cent of the deposits and accounted for 90 per cent of the outstanding loans (Pei, 1998). By 2004, even though they had lost considerable market share due to the emergence of other financial institutions, they still accounted for 65 per cent of the total deposits and 60 per cent of the outstanding loans (Barth and Caprio, 2007). The dominance of the Big Four has fundamental implications for the entire financial system, and more broadly, the economy.

1.2   The miserable failure of the banking system

The performance of the banking system in the past three decades could be described as a miserable failure. The most glaring problem was the huge number of NPLs. The official figures regarding NPLs first became available in 1998.[12] They revealed that during the period 2000–2002, China had the largest number of NPLs among major Asian countries, measured either as a fraction of total new loans made by all banks or as a fraction of GDP in a given year. This comparison includes the period during which Asian countries recovered from the 1997 financial crisis, and the period during which the Japanese banking system was disturbed by the prolonged NPLs problem. For example, measured as a fraction of GDP, China's NPLs were as high as 24.9 per cent and 22.7 per cent of GDP in 2000 and 2001. The level of NPLs in Japan, which is second to China in the same group, peaked in 2001 and was 15.3 per cent of GDP. The level of NPLs in South Korea exceeded 12 per cent of GDP in 1999, but reduced to below 3 per cent two years later (The Asian Banker, 2003).

However, it is widely believed that the official data largely understated the problem. Compared to the official statistics, findings by independent studies are far more gloomy. Lardy (1998, p. 95) believed that judging by standard accounting criteria, all the major state banks were technically insolvent in the mid-1990s. Even after transferring to AMCs in 2001, NPLs were still reporting at least 30 per cent of loans (Cull and Xu, 2003).[13]

---

[12]   It is believed the scarcity and deficiency in bank data can be viewed as a strategic disclosure decision of the government.

[13]   According to the estimate of the Union Bank of Switzerland (UBS), even after the writing-off of bad loans and transfer of NPLs, the average NPL ratio at the Big Four still stood at a stunning 40 per cent at the end of 2003. See Caijing English Newsletter, 5 November 2003.

Given their dominant position in the banking system, the four SCBs are undoubtedly accountable for the lion's share of the NPLs. Previously, we briefly mentioned the bail-out by transferring NPLs of the Big Four to the four AMCs in 2000, but it was neither the first nor the last one. Earlier, in 1998, the MOF had issued 270 billion yuan in special treasury bonds to shore up the capital base of the Big Four. Only three years after the NPLs transfer, the government had to launch another round of bail-out by injecting foreign currency reserves. At the end of 2003, with the establishment of the Central Huijin Investment Company (Huijin), the PBOC injected US$22.5 billion of reserves into each of the BOC and CCB, while ICBC received US$30 billion in 2005 (Asia Wall Street Journal, 23 December 2004).

1.3 Reasons for the banks' failure

What accounts for the miserable failure of the Chinese banking sector? I believe that the party-state's control over the economy, cronyism and weak internal control are major reasons.

1.3.1 Party-state control over the economy The determination of the party-state to remain in control of the economy has resulted in two major problems in the banking sector – one is the bad lending decisions; another is the severe moral hazard problem associated with state owner-ship of banks.

1.3.1.1 BAD LENDING PATTERN Even a quick look at the lending pat-tern of the SCBs would tell us why the banks perform so terribly. It reveals that as much as 90 per cent of SCBs' loans went to SOEs (Cull and Xu, 2000; Financial Times, 10 May 2005). Considering the poor performance of SOEs, the huge number of NPLs is no surprise at all. Clearly, although they are called 'commercial' banks, their lending decisions are hardly based on risk and return. Instead, they tend to use the government and party line to allocate loans. In addition, when borrowers and lenders belong to the same owner, the creditors lose their basic enforcement weapon – threatening to cut off finance in the future. Thus, the SCBs are unable to force their SOE clients to improve their performance to the extent that German banks sometimes do.[14]

---

[14] In addition, Art 143 of the Commercial Banking Law prohibits banks from investing in non-banking financial institutions and enterprises, making it impossible for bank loans to be transformed into equity in cases of default. Thus, the German-style universal banking system is not able to be transplanted into China.

1.3.1.2 MORAL HAZARD The state ownership of the banks results in a severe moral hazard problem. It has long been known that financial intermediaries whose liabilities are guaranteed by the government pose a serious problem of moral hazard. Moral hazard in this context means depositors have no incentive to police the lending of the banks in which they place their money, and the bankers have every incentive to play a game of heads I win, tails the taxpayer loses (Krugman, 1998). The moral hazard problem has played an important role in many crises, from the US savings and loan debacle to the Asian financial crisis, and the latest credit crunch.

Moral hazard is a serious problem even for privately owned banks and it becomes many times worse in state-owned banks. When banks are privately owned, the guarantee of government is at most implicit. For state-owned banks, the government should assume the liability by definition and thus it becomes an institutionalized moral hazard problem. All the major players, the central government, and the local governments and banks, encounter moral hazard problems to varying degrees. The central government has an incentive to deploy the banks to realize its various policy goals, for instance the Western Development plan and the recent stunning stimulus package; the banks have a strong incentive to undertake excessively risky investments that could yield high returns if lucky, for instance their deep involvement in the current real estate bubble; the local governments have the strongest incentive to misuse bank loans because the gains would accrue to the local fiscal budget while the losses will be borne by the central fiscal budget.

According to Zhou Xiaochuan, the governor of the central bank, direct administrative orders and intervention at various levels of Chinese government, primarily the local governments, were responsible for 30 per cent of NPLs; another 30 per cent was caused by banks' routine lending practice of supporting SOEs; local legal and administrative environments explained a portion of 10 per cent; another 10 per cent was the result of the adjustment of China's industrial structure organized by the central government during the country's transition and 20 per cent can be attributed to banks' own mismanagement and business losses (Economics Monthly, October 2004).

1.3.2 Cronyism State-directed lending often disguises the fact that many of these lending decisions are made under the influence of politicians. Similar to what happened in East Asian countries, Chinese politicians often use their influence to direct loans to their favoured companies that are operated by their family members, friends and the like. Observers are calling attention to the danger that China is heading towards cronyism capitalism (Wu, 2005; Xu, 2010). No available data could tell us about the specific scale of NPLs resulting from cronyism, but some reported cases can offer us a glimpse of it.

1.3.2.1 THE RISE AND FALL OF ZHOU ZHENGYI Zhou Zhengyi is a former Shanghai tycoon, whose rise and fall is closely related to Chen Liangyu, the former party secretary of Shanghai and Politburo member. Relying on the close ties with Chen,[15] Zhou easily received multi-billion loans from banks and valuable downtown land. With Chen's help, in less than ten years, Zhou became the richest man in Shanghai. In early 2002, Zhou gained loans of HKD 2.1 billion from the Hong Kong branch of BOC to finance his back listing plan of Jian Liantong (a Hong Kong listed company). Ridiculously, what Zhou used as collateral for the loans were the stocks of Jian Liantong that he had not yet acquired. Finally, this problem loan triggered an investigation by the Hong Kong Independent Commission against Corruption (HKICAC) and Zhou escaped to the mainland.[16] Meanwhile, Liu Jinbao, the head of BOC (HK), and another responsible manager, were called back to Beijing for investigation. Liu had served as the head of the Shanghai branch of BOC from 1994 to 1997, the exact period during which Zhou's business empire took off. Zhou was arrested in 2003. However, despite the widespread suspicion of Zhou's involvement in serious financial fraud, under Chen Liangyu's protection he was only charged with 'manipulating stock prices and misreporting registered capital' for which he received a three-year jail sentence.[17] It was also unclear how much of his 12 billion yuan borrowing from six banks became NPLs. Dramatically, in August 2006, only three months after his release, he was 'asked to assist investigation' and this time, was less lucky because his patron, Chen Liangyu, was also under investigation. Zhou received a 16-year jail sentence in November 2007 for five charges.[18]

---

[15]   Zhou's business partner, Chen Liangjun, is Chen Liangyu's younger brother. Zhou's wife, Mao Yuping called Chen's wife Huang Yiling '*Gan ma*' (a woman whose position is roughly equivalent to a foster mother and godmother without religious or legal complications). Huang also held shares in Zhou's company.

[16]   At the time of writing, Zhou is still on the wanted list of HKICAC.

[17]   In jail, Zhou was reported to have enjoyed privileges, including using the warden's office daily to continue running his business operations outside the prison.

[18]   For details of Zhou Zhengyi's case, see Caijing, 20 June 2003.

1.3.3   Weak internal control   By international standards, Chinese banks have very weak internal control, which results in rampant corruption and embezzlement of funds. A landmark study by two leading Chinese financial economists in 2002–2003 documented the magnitude of corruption in China's banking system. The director of research at the PBOC, Xie Ping and his colleague, Lu Lei, surveyed 3561 bank employees, enterprise managers, and private entrepreneurs in 29 cities in 2002. In response to their question on whether 'financial institutions use their power of credit/capital allocation to engage in corrupt transactions', 37 per cent of the respondents thought such a practice was 'prevalent', and an additional 45.2 per cent believe it happened 'quite often'. Forty-five per cent also said that they must 'give some goodies' as the 'extra costs of obtaining credit' (Xie and Lu, 2003).

Researchers have documented systematic looting and abuse by insiders in the banking sector in the 1980s and 1990s (Ding, 2000). A large number of senior bank executives, including the presidents of BOC, Wang Xuebing (Xinhua Net, 10 December 2003)[19] and CCB, Zhang Enzhao, have been sentenced to jail (Xinhua Net, 3 November 2006). In 2003 and 2004, four of the five senior executives of BOC Hong Kong branch, including Liu Jinbao, also received criminal penalties (Yang Cheng Evening News, 13 August 2005).[20]

In January, 2005, it was revealed that at BOC Heilongjiang branch, former manager Gao Shan stole deposits of more than 1 billion yuan and fled overseas days before the case was brought to light (Caijing, 24 January 2005). In the worst case of insider looting, managers of the BOC local branch in Kaiping, Guangdong Province stole bank funds worth at least US$483 million during the period 1992–2002. The three managers in question had absconded overseas with embezzled money days before an investigation by BOC's headquarters discovered their theft in October 2001 (Caijing, 5 May 2004).

This brief overview of the reasons for the failure of the banking sector has shown that it has important implications for banking reform: any reform that cannot overcome the problem of moral hazard, cronyism and

---

[19]   In December 2003, Wang was sentenced to 12 years in prison for accepting bribes worth 1.15 million yuan and numerous improper gifts. In March 2005, the former chairman of CCB, Zhang, was sentenced to 15 years in jail for taking bribes worth 4 million yuan. It is worth noting that both cases were first revealed in the US; otherwise, it is doubtful that they would have received such penalties.

[20]   Liu Jinbao was sentenced to death penalty with a suspension of execution; two were sentenced to jail for 13 years; another for 8 years.

weak internal control will not be successful. The answers to the first two questions, however, are beyond economics. There is a requirement for fundamental constitutional reform that imposes credible constraint on the party-state's power.

1.4   The significance of banking reform for the stock market

The success or failure of banking reform has significant implications for the stock market. First, as pointed out before, China's stock market is dominated by state-owned companies. One of the factors that weakened capital market discipline is the persistence of soft budget constraints. Banking finance is one of the major sources of soft budget constraints. Statistics show that by the end of 2006, bank loans constituted an overwhelming 84.9 per cent of external financing for non-financial institutions in China, compared to a paltry 3.9 per cent share for equities (CSRC, the Development Report). Unless SCBs could operate as real commercial banks and harden the budget constraints, managers of listed companies will not be forced to subject themselves to market discipline and have a proper incentive to improve governance efficiency.

Second, with the listing of ABC on the A-share market (the last one of the Big Four), by 15 July 2010, the combined market capitalization of the listing banks constituted about 25 per cent of the A-share market.[21] Thus, the performance of the banking sectors has a direct, significant impact on the stock market.

Third, SCBs, in particular the Big Four, derive virtually all of their income from the net interest margin, for instance, in CCB, non-interest revenue constitutes only 6.7 per cent of their total income (Barth and Caprio, 2007). In order to survive these SCBs (and indirectly SOEs), the official deposit interest rate has long been maintained at such a low level that the real interest rate was sometimes negative (Wu, 2005). As will be shown in the next chapter, the low interest rate and the lack of alternative investment channels are partially accountable for retail investors' excessive speculation in the stock market.

Fourth, the weak internal control of banks often led to a large amount of bank lending shifting into the stock market, which became a major financing source of market manipulation. On one hand, it inflates the bubble in the stock market. On the other hand, it endangers the safety of banks.

---

[21]   Source: Wind information.

1.5   The limits of latest round reform

After years of frustrating attempts, the central government realized it was unable to discipline the SCBs and decided to recruit overseas stock markets in corporate governance, starting with CCB's IPO in HKSE on 27 October 2005, and in 2006 BOC and ICBC also completed their IPOs in both HKSE and SHSE.[22] The limits of overseas listing strategy have already been discussed and the limitation is particularly clear in the listing of Big Four.

Before their IPOs, foreign strategic investors were invited to join in the banks' shareholding. However, there are very strict limits on foreign bank ownership.[23] In fact, their role is more of portfolio investors than strategic ones. None of them took any managerial responsibility and their role in governance is limited to appointment of an independent director on the bank's board. The role of strategic investors is further reduced by the fact that they were not given an opportunity to conduct proper due diligence prior to their buy-in.[24] Instead, their contracts during the pre-IPO period guaranteed them compensation should the book value of the bank decline below a certain historical value (International Monetary Fund,[25] 2006).

The day-to-day management still remains firmly in the hands of managers who are appointed and monitored by the Chinese shareholders, that is to say, by the CCP (Huang and Orr, 2007; OECD, 2005). There is little reason to believe that the CCP would be willing to take its hands off and stop using banks to serve its policies, especially on rainy days. There is also little reason to believe listing on overseas markets would enable bankers to resist the demand of powerful officials to allocate credit to favoured companies since their career is largely decided by them. The ongoing financial crisis quickly revealed the true face of the listed Big Four.

When the Politburo sat down to formulate a response to the financial crisis in December 2008, it decided on a gigantic stimulus of 4000 billion

---

[22]   ICBC's IPO is the world's largest ever.

[23]   A single foreign investor is limited to a 20 per cent stake and all foreign investors are limited to 25 per cent and there is no plan to lift these limits.

[24]   For instance, HSBC was stunned in 2006 when Zhang Jianguo, the president of Bank of Communication in which it had taken a 20 per cent stake, turned up as president of a key competitor, China Construction Bank, the country's second largest financial institution. There was no consultation, nor even notification of the move. See The Economist, 6 February 2010.

[25]   Hereinafter IMF.

yuan, to be delivered through the banking system. Despite deep mis-givings about the Politburo's plan, the central bank, bank regulators and bankers had no choice but to comply.[26] It does not really matter what foreign investors think (let alone domestic investors) once the Politburo issues an order. Just in the first five months of 2009, lenders advanced 5840 billion yuan of new loans which almost tripled the amount of a year earlier. While risk management procedures that were put in place before and after the bank's IPOs have improved their oversight, the 2008 credit binge reversed a lot of gains. 'To win mandates on plum infrastructure projects such as public housing and transport, lenders have relaxed standards. An unknowable amount of this cash has ended up on the blackjack tables of Macou, or that other casino – the SHSE' (Financial Times, 9 July 2009). Many analysts express concern that new NPLs will accumulate and the banks might need another bail-out (Financial Times, 14 May 2010).

2. Large Shareholders

Companies with large shareholders have less concern about managerial abuse because large shareholders have both the incentive and capability to discipline managers. The main enforcement issue is, instead, how to constrain large shareholders from engaging in opportunistic activities that damage minority shareholders.

We have documented that a majority of Chinese listed companies have a large shareholder and that is often the state. With the state as controlling shareholder, minority shareholders find themselves falling into the worst position: the large shareholder is weak in monitoring managers, but strong in expropriating minority shareholders.

2.1 Weak in monitoring

2.1.1 Weak incentive In private companies, the strong incentive of large shareholders to monitor managers comes from their cash flow rights that align their interests with those of the company. In most Chinese listed companies, the controlling shareholder is the state and the state has to rely on its agents to fulfil the monitoring function. The agents, whether they represent the SASAC, or the state-owned parent companies, have no cash flow rights of the company that they supervise. They do not directly benefit or suffer from the performance of the company. Thus, it would be

---

[26] As one banker says, 'The Chinese banks are pure utilities. The State Council tells them to lend and they lend.' See The Economist, 6 February 2010.

unrealistic to expect them to have the same incentive to gain information or maintain ongoing supervision like private owners.

Of course, it could be argued that the agents might be strongly motivated to monitor if they are to be held accountable for the failure of the supervisees. However, first, it is very difficult to establish the causality between a company's poor performance and the monitor's failure in order to hold them accountable; second, it will encourage the agents to over-monitor and that might impede managers' discretion, which is necessary for the operation of the business.

2.1.2 Weak capability Even if we assume the agents had the proper incentive, they often lack the knowledge and skills necessary for effective monitoring. This is particularly problematic when the controller is an official of the SASAC and the knowledge problem is exacerbated by the fact that the officials have to look after the state's shareholdings in many firms and these firms are in a diverse set of industries.

Another factor constraining large shareholders' monitoring capability is that they do not have the power to appoint or remove managers of major companies, which belong to the Party's organization department at various levels. For instance, as mentioned before, at the central level, some top managers of large state-owned companies are ministerial cadres whose appointments are directly decided by the Politburo, not by the SASAC. As a result, although formally these companies are under supervision of the SASAC, in reality, the SASAC has only limited control over them. At local level, SASAC branches are often subject to the influence of local governments. Their supervision capability is thereby compromised because the managers of listed companies are normally backed by the local governments.[27]

2.1.3 Legal person shareholder Compared with the state organ shareholder, the legal person shareholder seems to be a better monitor in terms of incentive and capability. The interest of the legal person shareholder is more closely related with that of the company and they usually have better knowledge of the industry in which the company operates. That explains the positive correlation between legal person shares and performance of companies documented in some previous studies (Qi, et al., 2000; Xu and Wang, 1999; Gul and Zhao, 2001). However, the same reason that makes the legal person shareholder a better monitor could also make it stronger in expropriation. More importantly, when the large

---

[27]   Most managers also have corresponding administrative rank.

shareholder is a parent company, the management of listed companies is often strongly identified with that of the parent company, which results in collusion between the large shareholder and management. Thus, the net effect of the legal person shareholder is very unclear and evidence is mixed (Fan et al., 2000).

Overall, the large shareholders of Chinese listed companies are weak in monitoring. As a result, insiders end up with substantial control rights and use them to benefit themselves at the expense of shareholders.

2.2 Strong in exploitation

2.2.1 Strong incentive The incentive of large shareholders to exploit minority shareholders arises from the divergence of their cash flow rights and control rights. The divergence between cash flow rights and control rights enables the large shareholders to consume private benefits at the expense of minority shareholders (Jensen and Meckling, 1976). The greater their control rights in excess of their cash flow rights, the stronger their incentive and capacity to capture private benefits of control.

The above argument could equally apply to large shareholders of Chinese listed companies. But in China's case, there is another significant reason accounting for expropriation by large shareholders. It must be recalled that the primary purpose of the Chinese stock market is to raise funds for financially distressed SOEs, in other words, the listed company was actually designed to tunnel funds to its parent company from the stock market.[28] This belief remained unchallenged for at least the first decade and still has a deep impact on listed companies, parent companies and the regulator. Unless the party-state relinquishes its control over the economy and stops using the stock market to finance SOEs, the conflicts between large shareholders and minority shareholders cannot be relieved.

Besides, three additional factors render Chinese listed companies particularly keen to pursue private benefits of control:

2.2.1.1 CONTROL PATTERN There are a number of mechanisms that the large shareholder could use to achieve control, including multiple classes of shares, pyramids and cross-holdings. The mismatch of cash flow rights and control rights is particularly severe in pyramid structures[29] and large

---

[28] Bai et al. (2004) concluded that on average, a Chinese listed firm is able to tunnel wealth equivalent to 31.8 per cent of the firm value.

[29] In a pyramid structure one entity, for instance, owns 51 per cent of a second firm, which in turn owns 51 per cent of the third firm and so on. As a result, the owner at the top of the pyramid achieves effective control of all the

shareholders who control through pyramids have a stronger incentive to grab private benefits of control. In China, multiple classes of shares are not available for listed companies because under China's company law, joint stock companies can only issue one class of shares: common shares. Cross-holding is also not popular. The prevailing control pattern is through the pyramid structures. Fan, Wong and Zhang (2005) document that more than 70 per cent of government-controlled listed firms have two or more pyramidal layers and almost all entrepreneur-controlled firms have more than two pyramidal layers. In many large groups, for instance Sinopec, 'even the management of the enterprises have no idea how many offspring their enterprises have in total. At most, they know only the number of second-tier enterprises directly under them and the total number of enterprises in the third tier' (Wu, 2005, p. 162).

2.2.1.2 NON-TRADABLE SHARES Cash flow rights are the key to aligning interests of large shareholders with those of minority shareholders. In Chinese listed companies, however, the state shares and legal person shares were not allowed to trade in the stock market until 2006, which means the large shareholder cannot gain from the increase of value of the company. This institutional arrangement artificially separates interests of large shareholders from those of minority shareholders and aggravates the conflicts between the two. Since large shareholders cannot share the increased value of the company, it can only benefit itself through grabbing private benefits of control.

2.2.1.3 PACKAGE FOR LISTING In order to meet the listing criteria set by the Company Law, most SOEs adopted the 'package for listing' (*Baozhuang Shangshi*) strategy. Selected profitable business units of an SOE are carved out and they form an independent entity for public listing. The original SOE becomes the parent company and retains most, if not all, unprofitable units and liabilities as well as the least productive workforce (Chen, 2003; Wang et al., 2004). This arrangement sharply increases the operating pressure on the parent SOEs and strengthens its incentive to divert revenues out of the listed companies.

---

firms in the pyramid, with an increasingly small investment in each firm down the line. La Porta et al. (1999) suggest that pyramids are the most common method by which controlling shareholders achieve control rights that exceed their cash flow rights.

2.2.2 Strong capability Large shareholders of Chinese listed companies not only have a strong incentive to expropriate, they also have a strong capability to do so. This capability comes from their dominance of the shareholders' general meeting, board of directors and supervisory board and weak legal protection of minority shareholders.

2.2.2.1 DOMINANCE OF LARGE SHAREHOLDERS

Shareholders' general meeting Compared with practices in other markets, the shareholders' general meeting in China has an extraordinarily wide range of powers. It has the power of passing resolutions on mergers, division, dissolution and liquidation, electing and removing directors and supervisors, and amending the articles of association of the company. Beyond that, the shareholders' meeting also has decision-making powers on a range of financial matters.[30] This unusual arrangement is evidently designed to maintain the state's control over the company and thus raises the concern as to the independence of listed companies. Under the 'one share one vote' principle of company law, the large shareholder, given its fixed majority shareholding, could always get whatever it wants.

Board of directors Under the Chinese Company Law, the board of directors is elected by shareholders' meeting. Given the concentrated ownership, the state is in absolute control of the board of directors. In the 1990s, around 70 per cent of directors and board chairmen were appointed by the state and legal person shareholders. In contrast, A-share holders, having ownership of 30 per cent, only appointed 4 per cent of the board seats. It is even worse than for employees who, though owning 2 per cent of the shares, appoint up to 3 per cent of the board seats (Tenev et al., 2002).[31] Apparently, the board of directors represents the interests of the controlling shareholders.

---

[30] Such as deciding policies on the business operation and investment plan of the company; reviewing and approving the annual financial budget, the final accounts, and the plan of profits distribution; and deciding on the increase or reduction of the registered capital of the company and the issuance of debentures by the company.

[31] Chen et al. (2004) documented that politicians and stated controlling owners occupy most board seats. They reported that almost 50 per cent of the directors are appointed by the state, and another 30 per cent are affiliated with various layers of governmental agencies. There are few professionals and almost no representation of minority shareholders.

<u>Board of supervisors</u>   The Chinese Company Law adopted a two-tiered board structure after the German model. However, a closer look shows that the supervisory board is more decorative than functional. In Germany, the role of supervisory board is to oversee the management of the company and that mainly comes from its power to appoint and dismiss members of the managing board and the power to represent the company in its dealings with members of the management.[32] In contrast, the supervisory board in China lacks teeth. The Chinese Company Law simply stipulates that the supervisory board will perform a supervisory role, but does not grant it any authority to control the appointment or business decision making of the management board.

Moreover, under the Chinese Company Law, the board of supervisors shall be elected by shareholders,[33] and the same interests that dominate director voting also dominate supervisor voting. Accordingly, the supervisory boards of Chinese listed firms are often served by party/government officials, trade union members or close friends and allies of the CEO of the company, although the law provides that up to one-third of the supervisors shall be elected by the employees of the company.[34] Considering the employee supervisors report to the top management who decide their promotion and remuneration package, they are not likely to be effective monitors.

Xiao et al. (2004) studied the supervisory boards of 21 listed companies in China. It was found that the supervisors are generally regarded as 'honoured guests' or 'friendly advisors'. As one of the surveyed financial controllers stated: 'our supervisory board basically does nothing. They only meet twice a year ... each meeting lasts for half an hour. It is merely a formality ... it is the secretary of the BOD who drafts the supervisory board report' (Xiao et al., 2004, p. 53).

2.2.2.2   WEAK LEGAL PROTECTION OF MINORITY SHAREHOLDERS   Large shareholders are strong in expropriation also because of the weak legal protection of minority shareholders. Before the revised 2005 Company Law, there was little legal constraint on large shareholders' power except the system of independent directors imposed by the CSRC in 2001. The revised Company Law creates better rules about shareholders' meetings; it regulates related party transactions; it provides minority shareholders some remedies if they are abused; it ensures information rights for

---

[32]   Aktiengesetz [Law on Stock Corporations] s 111(1), translated in Commercial Laws on the World: Germany [rev. edn 1995].

[33]   2005 Company Law Art 52.

[34]   2005 Company Law Art 52.

minority shareholders; and it reinforces the power of the board of supervisors or other supervisory authorities. However, the effectiveness of the new rules largely remains on paper and the status of minority shareholders has yet to be substantively improved.

Independent directors   On 31 May 2001 the CSRC released the 'Guidelines for Introducing Independent Directors to the Board of Directors of Listed Companies', which requires that at least one-third of directors should be independent.[35] At the end of 2005, 1377 listed companies had employed 4640 independent directors (Qiu, 2008). However, as the chief policy advocated by the CSRC, the effectiveness of independent directors turned out to be very disappointing and often joked as 'vase' directors. There are many reasons for this and a few will be mentioned briefly.

First and foremost, lack of independence. The CSRC imposes no restrictions on the power of the controlling shareholders to nominate independent directors, and grants no special privilege to minority shareholders. As a result, the directors are hardly independent of controlling shareholders and do not represent the interests of minority shareholders. According to a survey by the SZSE 2006,[36] 16 per cent of independent directors are directly nominated by controlling shareholders, 73 per cent are nominated by the board of directors (i.e. indirectly by controlling shareholders), and minority shareholders participated in nomination in only seven out of 868 surveyed companies. Thus, it is not surprising to see the following results: in a survey, 65 per cent of the independent directors indicated that they never said no in the meetings of the board of directors; all of them indicated that they did, at least 'occasionally', vote yes when they should have voted no based on the merit of the proposal (China Securities Journal, 28 July 2005).

Second, lack of necessary power. Even if some independent directors do want to perform their duty, they find themselves rather powerless. (1) The guidelines require that the proportion of independent directors should not be less than one-third.[37] In practice, most companies choose to follow the bottom line, which means, even if all the independent directors act collectively, they are still unable to challenge the majority shareholder. (2) The votes of independent directors in Chinese corporate law have no special significance. For instance, it is provided that a

---

[35]   It has now been included in the 2005 Company Law, Art 123.

[36]   The survey was not made public. Data quoted from Qiu (2008).

[37]   The CSRC 2001 Guidelines for Introducing Independent Directors to the Board of Directors of Listed Companies (Guidelines) (*Jianli Dulidongshi Zhudu de Zhidaoyijian*) Art 3.

material transaction between a firm and an affiliate should be approved by independent directors before being submitted to the board of directors.[38] However, a material transaction without independent directors' approval cannot be nullified, nor can the lack of approval of independent directors grant shareholders a basis to sue (Clarke, 2006). Independent directors are also empowered to employ external auditors or advisors,[39] nevertheless, since independent directors do not have the necessary financial resources, they can do nothing but make suggestions to the board of directors.[40] Even worse, the independent directors who attempted to challenge the controlling shareholders often lost their jobs. For instance, one independent director of Yili (600887) and four of Lotus Gourmet (600186) were ousted after calling for external auditors (independent financial advisors) (Shanghai Morning Post, 18 June 2004).

Third, lack of accountability. The inaction of majority independent directors has caused fierce criticism. Lack of accountability is another major reason. The guidelines do not specify the consequence of violation, except that an independent director shall be removed if he fails to attend the board's meeting in person three consecutive times.[41] Of course, an independent director is also subject to the legal liabilities imposed by the Company Law on any director who violates his duty of good faith and loyalty.[42] Nevertheless, the responsibility of independent directors thus far largely remains on paper. Among more than 70 independent directors who were publicly censured by stock exchanges, only one received a fine for three consecutive failures to attend board meetings of 100 000 yuan by the CSRC, the rest did not receive any corresponding penalty, either administrative, civil or criminal (Qiu, 2008).

Cumulative voting   Art 106 of the 2005 Company Law sets out provisions enabling public companies to adopt cumulative voting. Cumulative voting allows shareholders to multiply their votes by the number of

---

[38]   Guidelines, Art 5(1).

[39]   Guidelines, Art 5(5).

[40]   For example, on 28 April 2004, four independent directors of Lotus Gourmet (600186) made a joint statement in which they strongly condemned the fund appropriation by the major shareholder (total of 949 million yuan) and suggested the company should employ independent financial advisors to resolve the problem. However, the suggestion ended up with nothing because both Lotus Gourmet and the parent group (the parent group Lotus Gourmet Group is a wholly state-owned company, thus, the Xiangchen municipal government is the de facto controller) simply ignored it. For details, see Sina.com, 3 August 2005.

[41]   Guidelines, Art 4(5).

[42]   2005 Company Law Arts 147–153.

directors and supervisors to be elected and thus is described by many shareholder activists as a form of proportional representation. However, the law does not make it mandatory. Rather, it leaves it to the companies to choose. Under current circumstances, it is hard to imagine that controlling shareholders would voluntarily opt in to such a system, which is apparently not in their interests.

Constraints on large shareholders' voting   The 2005 Company Law imposes some constraints on the large shareholders' voting. For instance, Art 16 provides that guarantees or investment made by a company in related entities must be subject to the approval of the shareholders' meeting, in which the related parties are not eligible to vote. Art 125 states that directors of listed companies are ineligible to vote on matters in which they have an interest. However, excluding large shareholders or their representatives from voting does not mean their influence could also be eliminated. As noted above, large shareholders have a great impact on independent directors; institutional investors normally tend to avoid standing up against the state which would do no good for them; retail shareholders usually have short time horizons and have little interest in voting.

Private securities litigation   The 2005 Company Law Art 152 formally establishes a system of PSL; before, minority shareholders could only bring civil litigation based on civil law. However, in order to make civil actions an effective weapon, many obstacles have to be overcome, for instance the independence of the courts. But we will leave the discussion regarding PSL to section 5. The point is, there is a long way to go before PSL becomes a meaningful enforcement weapon.

III. REPUTATION

Even in the absence of external force, corporate controllers may still treat investors well because they want to maintain a good reputation. Previously, we identified the conditions for the reputation mechanism to function: information must be spread accurately and timely, punishment must be credible, and the game must be played repeatedly. In China's stock market, we found these conditions are not met and the ground for the reputation mechanism to function is very weak.

1.   Lack of Incentive to Build Reputation

When the reputation mechanism was discussed in Chapter 1, it was assumed that corporate controllers have an incentive to establish or maintain a good reputation. In privately owned companies, it might be the case. Large shareholders have an incentive to establish a good reputation because it could reduce their costs of capital in the future. Professional managers also have such incentive because their future career depends on it. The specific positions of managers might change over time, but they never left the labour market where the reputation records count.

In Chinese listed companies, however, controllers have little incentive to build a good reputation. As noted, the majority of Chinese listed companies are state owned and most corporate controllers (directors and managers) are appointed by the party-state. This indicates that, first, they are not professional managers who stay in the labour market, rather, they are often bureaucrats; second, they gain the jobs more for reasons like political loyalty, personal ties (*guanxi*) than good managerial records. Compared to a good relationship with the superiors, a reputation of being a good manager does not help their careers much. It is more helpful for the controllers to please the bureaucrats who have the personnel decision power[43] than to establish a reputation of treating shareholders well.

In addition, the high insecurity over jobs further shortens the controllers' time horizon and encourages them to play a one-shot game. As illustrated by the reshuffling of top managers of listed telecom companies in 2004, senior managers could be removed overnight without reasons being given. Since controllers do not know how long they could stay in the current position, the best strategy for them is to maximize current gains and consider little about future costs. In fact, they might have a perverse incentive: the better they run the company, the more likely that they will lose the job because it will attract more competitors.

In sum, the state ownership of listed companies and the current personnel system largely destroy the force of the reputation mechanism.

---

[43]   Because bureaucrats do not bear the consequence of their selection, they lack proper incentive to find the best qualified people to fill the position. Rather, they often find it in their interests to choose people who have close ties with them (which means they could share private benefit of control via the managers).

2. Serious Information Asymmetries

Information is critical to the functioning of the reputation mechanism. Information asymmetry is a common problem in stock markets. As an emerging market, China is no exception. Even worse, it is widely believed that in China's stock market, there exists systematic falsification and fabrication of financial data.

If we consider the origin of Chinese listed companies, it is no surprise to see this occurs. As noted earlier, the primary purpose of China's stock market is to provide SOEs an alternative finance channel, thus, the preference for public listing is given to SOEs. However, as we already know, SOEs are often non-profitable and debt-ridden. The quota system adopted from 1990 to 2000[44] to allocate IPOs cast further doubts on the quality of listed companies.

Under the quota system, the annul numbers of IPOs were set by the Central Planning Committee in State Council and allocated among provinces and state administrative bureaus. The latter two had the authority to recommend the listing of public offerings and decided the quota shares among their recommended SOEs. Given public listing means cheap financing in China,[45] local governments and administrative bureaus, for their own interests, tended to select either poor-performing SOEs, which need capital most badly so as to lift the fiscal burden off their own shoulders, or SOEs that they had close ties with.[46]

Companies thus selected often failed to meet listing criteria. Consequently, a practice called 'packaging for listing' (*Baozhuang Shangshi*) was widely adopted. Green (2004, p. 79) reported that nearly 80 per cent of all the companies listed before 1997 had falsified their profits or liabilities to some extent. During the process of packaging, with the support of local government and information intermediaries, 'from financial reports to accounting books, and from bank statements to related transaction contracts, everything can be falsified' (Asia Times, 9 May 2003). Stories about how a moribund enterprise magically turned into a

---

[44] The quota system was abolished in 2001, but it actually governed financial markets until the beginning of 2004 because many companies that were selected under the quota system were placed in a queue and were released to the market only over time. The first non-quota IPO did not appear until 2001.

[45] This issue will be explored in next chapter.

[46] Pistor and Xu (2005) argue that local governments tend to select companies of good quality and the quota system acts as a substitute for legal protection. This argument will be addressed in the next chapter.

blue chip are abundant.[47] These packaged companies quickly revealed their true faces after entering the market[48] and partially account for the overall poor performance of listed companies (Chen and Shih, 2003; Sun and Tong, 2003; Wang et al., 2004).

After an IPO, in order to issue seasoned equity offerings, rights issuance, or avoid delisting, the companies have to continue manipulating financial data so as to satisfy profitability requirements. For instance, over years, the minimum condition for seasoned equity offerings as set by CSRC has gone through various changes: the firm's return on equity (ROE)[49] had to be (1) positive in the most recent two years, a policy as of 1993; (2) as of 1994, above 10 per cent based on the most recent three years' average; (3) as of 1996, above 10 per cent in each of the most recent three years; (4) as of 1999, above 10 per cent based on the most recent three years' average, but at least 6 per cent for each of the most recent three years; (5) as of 2001, above 6 per cent based on some weighted average for the most recent three years. These policy changes have each time caused publicly listed firms to adapt their accounting manipulation schemes. Lang and Wang (2002) find that for each year before 1994, many public firms strangely had their ROE just slightly above 10 per cent; then between 1994 and 1999, more than half of the public firms had an ROE lying slightly above 10 per cent but below 12 per cent; from 2000 onwards (in particular since 2001), most of the firms had an ROE between 6 per cent and 8 per cent. Liu (2006, pp. 440–441) showed a similar tendency. These studies provided 'strong evidence for market-wide earnings manipulation, implying that Chinese investors have been systematically defrauded' (Chen, 2003, p. 11).

In 2001, *Caijing* (7 August 2001) published an extensive investigation on Yin Guangxia (000557). It found that from 1998 to 2001 Yin Guangxia fabricated sales receipts (with hundreds of millions worth of exports to Germany) and lied about various production facilities that

---

[47]   For instance, Yuan (2004), with his personal experience, told a ridiculous story about how a dying Hainan company whose only cash flows came from sauna business before IPO was packaged into a high-tech company and successfully listed on the SZSE traded at a rather high price. Stories of this kind are everywhere.

[48]   The performance of listed companies after IPO is summarized by Chinese analysts as: Merit in the first year, Balance in the second year and Red in the third year (*Yinianying, Ernianping, Sanninakui*). In the most drastic case, Hongguang Industrial (600083) reported a net loss of 0.863 yuan per share during its first year of listing.

[49]   ROE=Net Income/Shareholders' Equity.

actually never existed. The total amount of faked sales was over 1 billion yuan, which resulted in a non-existent profit of 770 million yuan. The Yin Guangxia scandal is shocking but by no means unique. Before and after Yin Guangxia, Lan Tian (600709), Mai Kete (000150) and Zheng Baiwen (600898), were all revealed to have commited similar frauds. In a Chinese Managers Survey, 57.11 per cent of surveyed managers believed that there were 200–500 listed companies like Yin Guangxia (Caijing, 5 November 2001).

Evidently, it is very difficult for the reputation mechanism to function in such an environment. In fact, the serious information asymmetry has resulted in a market with adverse selection (the market for lemons).[50] As investors found themselves unable to distinguish well-performing companies, which are a minority group in the stock market, from poorly run companies, which are the majority, they tend to trade them at the same prices. According to a study by Morck et al. (2000), in 1996 the United States had on average 57 per cent of the stocks moving in the same direction, and Poland had the highest co-movement level of 82 per cent. It was found that in 2005, China still had 91.3 per cent of the stocks moving in the same direction (Chen, 2006, p. 38).

Better-performing companies whose shares traded at prices lower than they should would rather go to overseas capital markets for listings,[51] even though their shares are usually sold at a considerable discount, with an average level of 13 to 14 per cent, as compared to comparable foreign counterparts listed in the same market (Leng, 2004, p. 289).[52] Accordingly, the Chinese stock market is most tempting to those companies bad at performing but good at cheating. It raises the question that, if China's stock market is as bad as has just been described, why does it not replicate the collapse of the Czech Republic's stock market? This question will be answered in the next chapter.

---

[50] The concept 'market for lemons' was introduced by Akerlof (1970) to describe a special case of adverse selection in which the bad products tend to drive out the good ones.

[51] They normally first set up offshore companies, then seek listing on overseas stock exchanges like the NYSE.

[52] The information asymmetry is so serious that the good companies find it even impossible to signal themselves by adopting costly measures like high dividends because that might be considered as the tricks of manipulators.

3. Lack of Punishment

The function of the reputation mechanism also relies on the capability of shareholders as a whole to execute credible punishment against dishonest companies. In China's stock market, shareholders have weak incentive to do so.

It is well known that Chinese investors are speculation-driven and they pay little attention to fundamentals of companies. What they are most interested in is various 'concepts' or 'stories' made up by manipulators that usually entail profit opportunities through capital gains. As long as there is a great story, no one cares about the bad record that a company has had in the past. One distinctive characteristic of China's stock market is some junk stocks trade at abnormally high prices, for instance, special treatment stocks (ST stocks).

In 1998, the CSRC introduced a special delisting mechanism.[53] Companies will be designated as special treatment firms (ST firms) if there are any of certain abnormalities in their financial status or other aspects, resulting in investors' difficulty in judging the company's prospects, to the detriment of investors' benefits or interests. Typically, a listed firm becomes an ST firm if any of the following four conditions holds: (1) it has negative net profits for two consecutive years; (2) the shareholders' equity is lower than the registered capital (the par value of the shares); (3) on auditing the firm's financial report, the auditors issue negative opinions or declare that they are unable to issue opinions; (4) the firm's operations have been stopped and there is no hope of their being restored within three months, due to a natural disaster or serious accident, or the firm is involved in a damaging lawsuit or arbitration. In sum, stocks labelled as ST are either poor-performing or in serious trouble.

If shareholders care about companies' reputations, ST shares would be abandoned or trade at low prices. However, the reality is that ST shares often out-perform non-ST stocks. For instance, according to 2009 annual reports, there are 29 ST firms that have had negative net assets for three

---

[53]   In China, a firm has to be designated ST before it can be eventually delisted. The special treatment means, for example, that the stocks are traded with a 5 per cent price-change limit each day vs 10 per cent for normal stock. Its mid-term reports must be audited. Also, if an ST firm continues to suffer loss for one more year, it will be designated as a particular transfer (PT) firm. PT firm stocks can only be traded on Friday, with a maximum 5 per cent upside limit to last Friday's close, but no restriction on the downside. PT firms will be delisted if they cannot turn profitable within one year. The PT system was abolished in 2001.

consecutive years. However, among these 29 firms, on 6 May 2010, with the exception of ST Baoshuo (600155) which closed at 4.70 yuan, the rest of them all closed above 5.00 yuan and eight firms closed at above 10.00 yuan. Even the lowest price of ST Baoshuo is higher than that of ICBC (601398) and BOC (601988) (Dong, 2010).

There are many reasons for the ST phenomenon, but the indifference of shareholders about companies' reputation is surely an important one. In the absence of credible punishment, we cannot expect the reputation mechanism to function well.

In sum, in China's stock market, corporate controllers have no incentive to build a good reputation, information is seriously asymmetric and shareholders have weak incentives to punish dishonest companies. Therefore, the reputation mechanism cannot be relied on to enforce the financial contract between the minority shareholders and corporate controllers.

IV. NON-STATE THIRD-PARTY ENFORCEMENT

1. Non-state Third-party Enforcement and Social Structure

Non-state third-party enforcement is crucial to the stock market. As Coffee (2001a) and Cheffins (2003) have documented, both in the United States and in the United Kingdom, an active, liquid stock market emerged before the legal system providing strong protection to minority shareholders, based on the function of non-state third-party enforcement mechanisms such as the stock exchanges and investment bankers. Although the limit of non-state third-party enforcement eventually necessitates formal enforcement, it does not change the primary role that the non-state third party enforcers play in the stock market. However, to what extent that non-state third-party enforcers could play such an enforcement role is not a simple question. It is closely associated with the social structure.

1.1 Experiences from other jurisdictions

Coffee (2001a, pp. 34–39) explored the successful experience of the NYSE as well as the LSE (2001a, pp. 39–44) and suggested that a pluralistic, decentralized society in which the private sector was relatively autonomous and free from direct state supervision was the key to the success of these two stock markets. Such social structure made possible private law making and the growth of self-regulatory bodies, which in turn facilitated the development of market-based institutions such as stock exchanges. By contrast, he attributed the failure of the Paris Bourse (2001a, pp. 45–51) and German securities markets (2001a, pp. 51–58) to the strong state intervention (favouritism in the former and antagonism in the latter) that suffocated any attempt at proactive self-regulation. The heavy state intervention, in turn, originated from the absolutism and increased centralization of authority that characterized post-feudal Europe from the 13th to 18th centuries (Macfarlane, 2000).

1.2   Social structure of China

If the above argument is accepted, we can jump to a conclusion, without looking at any details, that there will not be any effective non-state third-party enforcement in China given its highly centralized authority tradition.

As a legacy of two millennia of imperial autocracy and the underlying Confucianist ideology, 'the Chinese conviction that all power should reside in the central authority has been one of the most powerful factors in shaping Chinese history' (Pye, 1985, p. 184). In imperial China, Confucianism legitimized bureaucratic and imperial rule by a mandarin elite. Formal government is the sole legitimate basis for power. Those outside of the ranks of officialdom and the ruling class were not acknowledged as having any proper claims to power (Pye, 1985, p. 56). 'To the extent that pressures from society infringed upon the sphere of government, these pressures were seen as manifestations of corruption' (Pye, 1985, p. 87). Thus, there was a strong sense that wealth should not be translated into political power. By the same token, religion did not generally provide an alternative centre of power (Pye, 1985, p. 88). This was in a sharp contrast to other societies, for instance in post-feudal Europe. Regardless of the increasing tendency towards centralization, there still remained some stable and long-lived alternative centres, such as the landed nobility, the church and the city merchant guilds, that wielded legitimate power. In China 'they were treated as though they did not, or should not, exist. Merely to suggest that landlords, for example, had local power was to imply corruption' (Pye, 1985, p. 57).

To stress that in China all legitimate power comes from above, from the centre, is not to say that there were no other forms of power in practice. Of course there were. Power existed in county offices, in village councils, in clan organizations and in gentry families. And above all these, the provincial governments always stood in the middle level; some of them ruled over populations larger than those of some European countries (Pye, 1985, p. 187). Nevertheless, 'all of these forms of power were so subservient to the centre that whatever autonomy they sought was seen as illegitimate' (Pye, 1985, p. 187).

The tradition of centralization not only persists into modern China, it has been reinforced by the experience of the 20th century. In any case, the era of the warlords, which did give China a period of pluralistic, competitive politics involving provincial power bases, 'was treated as such a humiliation to the Chinese that it drove them once again to centralized politics' (Pye, 1985, p. 188). Thereafter, the problem of accepting diverse and decentralized authority became more difficult. Both the Guo Min Dang (GMD) and the CCP felt the need to keep in line all provincial authorities and dissident voices (Pye, 1985, p. 189), and the latter pushed centralization to its unprecedented high. Under the communist regime, all the potential competitors to state monopoly of power were either destroyed or severely undermined, even families were purposely attacked.

On the eve of the 1978 economic reform, the Cultural Revolution and the miserable fiscal conditions severely weakened the capacity of the central government to control. As a result, local governments, villages and other organizations attained some autonomy. This autonomy was the key to China's economic growth.[54] Undoubtedly, the 30 years' economic reform has greatly increased diversification of Chinese society and economic decisions are now made on a much more decentralized base. Nevertheless, it has yet to change the centralization tradition.

Within the government, although local cadres have gained considerable decision-making power, their authority is still based upon their identification with the central authority and the central government remains in firm control over local authorities through appointments (nomenklatura).[55] Outside the government, any attempt to claim autonomy or power sharing by groups, whether based on economic, political or religious grounds, will be taken as a sign of dangerous centrifugal forces. Various social organizations do exist and increase in number, but the senior CCP leaders have made it clear that this is no free-for-all for society to organize itself to articulate its interests. Rather they prefer that

---

[54] TVEs, private enterprises, emerged from the margin of central control and become the real engine of economic growth.

[55] The thousand-years-old strategy of frequent rotation is employed to prevent local cadres from identifying with local interests. It is noticeable that the firm control does not indicate that there is no defection of local governments. In reality, there is a severe agency problem between central and local governments. But, the de facto autonomy of local governments has no legitimate ground and is often condemned as 'localism'.

the sector be developed within a highly restrictive legislative and organizational framework that ensures the party-state's control (White et al., 1996; Saich, 2000).[56]

---

[56]   Two main strategies are employed by the party-state to control social organizations. Repression is employed against groups the state sees as a threat or does not wish to see develop further. But for the majority of social groups, it adopts the tactics called corporatism. Corporatism can be defined as a system of interest representation in which the constituent units are organized into a limited number of singular, compulsory, non-competitive, hierarchically ordered and functionally differentiated categories, recognized or licensed (if not created) by the state and granted a deliberate monopoly within their respective categories in exchange for observing certain controls on their selection of leaders and articulation of demands and supports. See Schmitter (1974). The 1998 'Regulations for Registration and Management of Social Organizations' provides a clear example of such a strategy. Under the 1998 Regulations, first, all social organizations must find a professional management unit (*Yewu Zhuguan Danwei*) that will act as sponsor, and is usually referred to as the sponsoring unit (*Guakao Danwei*). After finding the sponsor and gaining its approval, the paperwork for the social organization is sent to the Ministry of Civil Affairs or its relevant department. This sets up a two-tier registration system where affiliation precedes registration. The sponsor is expected to examine whether the social organization corresponds to an actual need and check that it will not overlap with other organizations and that its members have the capacity to run the organization. In addition, the sponsors should ensure the social organization abides by the law and is itself held responsible for the organization's actions. There is no right to appeal against rejection at any stage. Second, similar organizations are not allowed to co-exist at the various administrative levels. This helps to control representation to a smaller number of manageable units and has been used to deny registration for some groups. It ensures that the 'mass organizations' such as the All China Federation of Trade Unions enjoy monopoly representation and cannot be challenged by independent groups seeking to represent the interests of workers. Third, social organizations must register with the appropriate civil affairs department from the county level upwards. This makes it impossible for local groups to control members from different areas, thus limiting the potential for the spread of grass-roots organizations that could develop national or horizontal representation. The Regulations expressly prohibit national organizations from establishing any kind of regional branch. The total intent of this legislation is to mimic the compartmentalization of government departments and limit horizontal linkage. This favours those groups with close government ties and discourages bottom-up initiatives. It keeps people with different opinions on the same issue from setting up opposing interest groups. Other aspects of the Regulations further hamper bottom-up initiatives or those by the disadvantaged and poorer sectors of society. The need to have substantial assets and the paperwork necessary to register make it difficult for those groups that lack good

1.3 Implications for non-state third-party enforcement

The highly centralized social structure has significant implication for non-state third-party enforcement in the stock market. As discussed before, the strength of non-state third-party enforcers mainly lies in their information advantage and better incentive, both arising from their status as market participants. Although the ultimate consequence of their activities might be in favour of public interests, they are first and foremost private bodies that pursue their own interests. For them to function well, the primary condition is to admit their autonomy (including their independent interests, rule-making and dispute-resolving power) that might fall out of direct control of the state. However, for the reason just discussed, this condition is hard, if not impossible, to meet in China. As will be seen below, the autonomy of these non-state third-party enforcers has been seriously constrained. They are either directly owned by the state, or treated in the same way as their traditional counterparts, the merchant guilds, so that 'their role could be described as an extra-bureaucratic group fulfilling regulatory functions beyond the normal reach of the bureaucracy. They were, in effect, *pouvoirs subsidiares* whose authority derived from and complemented that of the state' (Fewsmith, 1983, p. 618). I believe the lack of autonomy is one of the most important factors that constrains the effectiveness of non-state third-party enforcement and it is not likely to be changed in the near future.

2. The Stock Exchanges

The precondition for the NYSE arising to play the role of guardian of public investors in the 19th century was its status as a member-run, self-regulatory organization (SRO). As a SRO, from its inception, the NYSE 'operated a miniature legal system, with its own rules governing securities trading and its own mechanism for resolving trade-related disputes' (Banner, 1998, p. 271). Suppose the NYSE had no power to develop and implement its preferred rules, to decide listing and delisting of firms – it could offer investors no additional protection even if it desired to do so. The self-regulatory capacity of the NYSE can be traced back to the 'centuries-old Anglo-American tradition of self-regulation by mercantile groups' (Banner, 1998, p. 271).

---

connections and a relatively sophisticated organizational apparatus. For details, see Saich (2000, pp. 129–132).

By contrast, given the traditional tendency towards centralization, self-regulation was an idea alien to Chinese society. As just mentioned, traditionally, Chinese merchant guilds never constituted a separate structure of authority and their authority was thought of as having been delegated by the bureaucracy. They were limited to performing an extra-bureaucratic function that the state was ill-disposed to deal with (Fewsmith, 1983). The following study of the Chinese stock exchanges will show how strong this tradition is and how little China has moved away from it.

2.1 The status of exchanges

On paper, the SHSE and SZSE are often referred to as a member-run, not-for-profit self-regulatory legal person. For instance, The Constitution of SHSE Art 3[57] describes the exchanges as 'self-regulatory member-run legal person'. The Regulation on the Administration of Stock Exchanges[58] Art 3 prescribes the exchanges as 'self-regulatory legal person'; the 2005 Securities Law[59] Art 102 defines exchanges as 'self-regulatory legal person'. Notwithstanding this, a close look suggests that this is simply misleading.

Unlike the NYSE, the Chinese stock exchanges were not established by their members. Instead, the exchanges came first, thereafter the securities companies were accepted as 'members' by the exchanges.[60] The two exchanges were established by the Shanghai and Shenzhen municipal governments with the approval of the State Council. The setting up of SHSE was primarily promoted by Zhu Rongji[61] (the then Shanghai party secretary) and a three-person working group spearheaded the preparatory work staffed by the chairman of the BOC, the governor of the PBOC Shanghai branch, and the director of the SCRES. Hence, from the inception, Chinese stock exchanges are distinctively different from the NYSE, which is a private body set up and managed by

---

[57]   First version enacted in 1990, amended in 1999.

[58]   First version enacted in 1996 (1996 Regulation), amended in 2001 (2001 Regulation).

[59]   The 1998 Securities Law defines exchanges as 'not-for-profit legal person', Art 95; amended in 2005.

[60]   Securities companies include underwriters, brokers, dealers, and investment management companies. Securities companies are generally members of a stock exchange. 2005 Securities Law: Arts 112, 123, 125. Only a member of a stock exchange may engage in aggregated trading of securities on the exchange: 2005 Securities Law Art 110.

[61]   Zhu was backed by Deng Xiaoping who told him to go ahead, see Li (2000).

members, Chinese stock exchanges are quasi-administrative organs established and overseen by state agencies (Fang, 2007).

During 1990–1992, the stock exchanges were mainly overseen by the Shanghai and Shenzhen municipal governments and branches of the PBOC.[62] Since 1992, the CSRC has gradually increased its influence,[63] and in 1996 it finally won the exclusive authority to supervise and administer the exchanges.[64] Whether supervised by local governments or the CSRC, the stock exchanges never had separate authority and operated as a real SRO. Their regulatory authority is delegated by the state and they perform the functions delineated by the state, although the scope of functions may vary from time to time.

Since 1997, the CSRC has exercised excessive control that left little autonomy to exchanges. A stock exchange is required to adopt a constitution, and the CSRC must approve the constitution and any alteration;[65] the CSRC has the power to appoint and remove major stock exchange personnel,[66] including the general manager;[67] the CSRC approves the listing of securities on the exchanges and effectively retains exclusive authority to delist firms;[68] stock exchanges are required to timely report any abnormal trading to the CSRC[69] and to seek CSRC approval to form rules of listing, trading and membership;[70] the CSRC has the authority to investigate misconduct of listed companies and to determine the action to be taken;[71] each stock exchange department is directly and closely managed by a corresponding department of the

---

[62] The authority of PBOC is still a proxy for control by municipal leaders, since before 1998, the local branches of the PBOC operated under the management authority of the local leader.

[63] During 1992–1996, the CSRC was in a rather weak position, especially in Shanghai, whose leader is a member of the Politburo. It was still the municipal governments that played the principal role during this period. See Green (2004, pp. 137–155).

[64] The Regulation on the Administration of Stock Exchanges (1996) delegated the authority to the CSRC alone. But it was resisted by the PBOC, until 1999, when the Securities Law brought the dispute to a final close.

[65] 1998 Securities Law, Art 96; 2005 Securities Law, Art 103.

[66] 2001 Regulation, Art 25: The CSRC also appoints the directors of the exchange's finance and personnel department, in addition, the exchange must report the appointment of middle-level managers.

[67] 1998 Securities Law, Art 100; 2005 Securities Law, Art 107.

[68] 1998 Securities Law, Arts 55, 56.

[69] 1998 Securities Law, Art 110; 2005 Securities Law, Art 115.

[70] 2005 Securities Law, Art 118.

[71] 1998 Securities Law, Arts 168, 172; 2005 Securities Law, Art 180.

CSRC (Green, 2004, p. 115); the CSRC controls all aspects of market development, including not only the introduction, but also research into new financial instruments (Green, 2004, p. 203); the CSRC is also responsible for governance and operation of listed firms, and so on. In sum, by taking over most of the functions that are usually undertaken by exchanges in other jurisdictions, the CSRC has made exchanges more like its micro-organs. As expressed in an industry joke: the exchanges have become 'the son of the CSRC', the 'trading departments' of the CSRC, or the 'housemaids' of the CSRC (Green, 2004, p. 117).

The 2005 Securities Law attempted to shift the balance and delegate more authority to the exchanges. For instance, it gives exchanges the power to temporarily suspend trading in securities[72] and to delist companies.[73] It also states that administrative review of decisions to suspend trading or to delist companies shall be handled by a body established by the exchanges, no longer subject to review by the CSRC.[74] However, it has not brought about any meaningful change by far.

Given the limited autonomy, Chinese stock exchanges only play a marginal role in enforcement. The experience of the Chinese stock exchanges is clearly a continuity of the old tradition and we have many reasons to suspect this could be changed in the foreseeable future. Even if the CSRC relaxes its control and delegates more authority to the exchanges one day, Chinese stock exchanges might never play the same role as the NYSE.

2.2   Competition between the exchanges

Even if the stock exchanges gained more autonomy, it does not necessarily mean that they will play a desired role in enforcement. Bear in mind that the exchanges have their own interests which are not necessarily consistent with those of public investors. One of the key factors for the NYSE to take on the investors' guardian role is the competitive pressure it confronted. If the NYSE was a monopoly, it would have little incentive to invest heavily in good reputation.

Chinese stock exchanges face much less competition. Before the establishment of the SHSE and SZSE, there were some regional trading centres in cities like Shenyang and Beijing, but they were all ordered to close down by 1999. The central government also shut down two NASDAQ-like automated systems, the Securities Trading Automated

---

[72]   Art 55.
[73]   Art 56.
[74]   Art 62.

Quotations (STAQ) system[75] and the National Electronic Trading System (NETS),[76] both concentrated on legal person shares trading. In addition, the central government sternly cracked down on local over-the-counter markets that emerged spontaneously.[77] As a result, the SHSE and SZSE face no domestic competition. In addition, the stock exchanges are shielded from international competition by the financial repression policy.

In addition, the competition between the SHSE and SZSE is also limited, especially since 1997. First, as mentioned above, exchanges have little rule-making power and their listing rules and trading rules must be subject to approval by the CSRC. The CSRC consolidated the listing rules of the SHSE and SZSE, and those rules are largely similar to the Securities Law's general requirements. Thus, neither of them is capable of offering different rules and enhancing investors' protection on its own. Second, the CSRC has exclusive authority over listings. Once the CSRC has authorized a firm for issuance, it allocates it to either the SHSE or SZSE. Neither the company nor the exchange has competence to oppose this choice. Third, the competition has been further reduced since autumn 2000 when the central government decided that the SZSE should suspend all new listings, in anticipation of the SZSE establishing the Growth Enterprises Board, and the planned transfer of the SZSE's A-shares to SHSE. Until February 2004, all new A-shares were listed at the SHSE. Although firms are allowed to list on the SZSE once again, it is now developing into a small-cap market, as part of the State Council's stated policy of developing a 'multi-level' capital market. The weak competition may demotivate the exchanges to play an active role in enforcement.

---

[75] The STAQ was supported by 17 major Chinese entities as founding members of the new exchange. It opened on 5 December 1990 and closed on 9 September 1999.

[76] The NETS was established in January 1991 with direct sponsorship of the PBOC and was operated by its majority-controlled company, China Securities Trading System Corp. Ltd.

[77] Among them, the most well known is the *Hongmiaozi* market in Chengdu city. It operated during 1991–1993 and impressed people with its good order. At its peak, it attracted about 80 000 traders per day and more than 20 types of products were traded. For details, see Yang (1996).

3. Gatekeepers

Gatekeepers are major enforcers in the stock market. They are professional players who interact with equity markets repeatedly. When gatekeepers function well, they can effectively reduce information asymmetry and prevent problems before they become crises. However, the whole gatekeeper theory is based on the very assumption of gatekeepers' reputational capital: there is demand for gatekeepers' reputation and reputation is crucial to gatekeepers' survival. If this assumption does not hold, then the whole gatekeeper institution will collapse. As will be shown below, in China's stock market, there is a lack of demand for gatekeepers' reputation and gatekeepers do not rely on reputation to live on. As a consequence, gatekeepers not only fail to play their designated enforcer role, they are also actively involved in various misconduct and become part of the problem.

3.1 Investment banks

When a company raises capital by issuing equities in the stock market, it faces the difficulty of how to convince the prospective investors about its true value. Because ordinary investors usually lack the resources to gain, and the knowledge to evaluate, the information about the issuer, they choose not to buy the stocks or only purchase at low prices. In other words, the issuer faces high risk in the IPO market. This risk could be reduced by employing a reputable underwriter. The investment banker represents to the market that it has evaluated the issuer's quality and that it is prepared to stake its reputation on the value of the issuer. Investors have more confidence in underwriters because they are repeat players in the market. If the stocks that they underwrite proved to be of bad quality, investors could reduce the value of stocks they underwrite in the future, which in turn will reduce prospective issuers' demand for their service (Gilson and Kraakman, 1984; Booth and Smith, 1986). Since reputation is crucial to underwriters' income, they have a strong incentive to protect it through scrutinizing and declining to underwrite the issuer's securities if they find the issuer's disclosure is materially deficient. By so doing, they fulfil their role of third-party enforcer.

However, if the issuers face no risk in the IPO market, there will be little demand for the investment bankers' reputation; if the investors have little concern about the long-term performance of issuers, they will have less incentive to punish dishonest investment bankers. If the investment bankers gain business for factors other than good reputation, they will be diverted from the role of reputational intermediary or third-party enforcer. This is what occurs in China's stock market.[78]

3.1.1 Lack of demand for reputation The demand for investment bankers' reputation originates from issuers' concern about IPO failure. However, thanks to the government's strict restriction, there is almost no risk in China's IPO market. As noted before, the primary purpose of China's stock market is to raise funds for SOEs. In order to reach this goal, the government has to ensure the success of IPOs and it realizes this by strictly controlling the supply of IPO stocks. Before 2000, it used a quota system for new shares issuance. After 2000, it abolished the quota system and adopted an 'examination and review system (*Hezhun zhi)*', and after 2004, a sponsorship (*Baojianren*) system. Whether under the quota system or sponsorship system, the ultimate control power has invariably remained with the CSRC. It is the CSRC who decides whether or not to approve the IPO and the number of listing shares. The restricted control of IPO supply combined with the fact that two-thirds of shares are not tradable results in shortage of new shares supply. On the other hand, given the lack of alternative investment channels, there is a high demand for IPO. In addition, the extraordinarily high return of IPO shares[79] generated by the price bubble in secondary market[80] further stimulates the demand for new shares. The new shares are such scarce resources that they have to be allocated by a lottery system. The odds of winning the lottery are very low, for instance, during 1999–2002, the average winning probability was 1.06 per cent, and in 2002 it was only 0.17 per cent (Liu, 2003, p. 8).[81]

---

[78] In China, investment banks are also referred to as securities companies. The terms investment banks, securities companies, underwriters will be used interchangeably in this book. As mentioned previously, in China, like the US, commercial and investment banking function separately.

[79] The extraordinarily high initial return has been documented by previous studies. For instance, Su and Fleisher (1999) found that the average initial return of 308 IPOs in China during 1990–1995 was 948.59 per cent. Datar and Mao (1998) found the average initial return of 226 A-share issues in China during 1990–1996 was 388.0 per cent.

[80] Studies show that the theories based on information asymmetry fail to explain China's IPO under-pricing (e.g. the high return of IPO), and it should be attributed to government regulation and the bubble price in the secondary market. See, for instance, Liu (2003), Liu and Xiong (2005).

[81] The high risk-free return of IPO shares attracts huge amount of funds that concentrate on new shares subscription. The average amount of money used for one IPO in China was 155.28 billion yuan (Liu, 2003, p. 8).

The CSRC not only controls the supply amount of IPOs, for most of the time in the short history of China's stock market, it has also controlled the pricing of IPOs. The CSRC requires issuing firms to price IPO shares by multiplying net earnings per share by a fixed multiplier, which is always fixed far below prevailing market price-earnings ratios (P/E). Although average P/E in secondary market is over 30 most of the time, the multiplier is set between 15 and 20. The specific multiplier is chosen by the issuer, but under a cap set by the regulator.[82]

Taken together, the serious imbalance of supply and demand and IPO price control created a risk-free IPO market (Liu, 2003; Chi and Padgett, 2005).[83] Since there is no risk in marketing new shares, the issuers have no need to rely on investment bankers' reputation, which is designed exactly to mitigate such risk.

3.1.2 Lack of punishment from investors   Investment bankers are paid by the issuers, their willingness to protect investors primarily due to investors' capacity to punish them in the case that they fail to do so. Investors could penalize investment bankers by declining to buy the stocks that they underwrite in the future or heavily discounting them. Nonetheless, as discussed above, in China's stock market, new stocks almost guaranteed investors high returns in the secondary market and the chances of getting them are very low. There is no reason to expect that the investors would give up subscribing new stocks only because of the underwriter's wrongdoing in the past. As in this case, giving up buying new stocks is giving up big profits, which is apparently irrational. In addition, as will be discussed in the next chapter, Chinese investors are highly speculative and seek short-term returns from price fluctuations.[84] They are not very interested in the long-term performance of issuers and thereby have little incentive to punish the investment bankers who underwrote stocks of bad quality. Facing little deterrence from the investors, China's investment bankers tend to stand with their clients and give little consideration to investors' interests.

---

[82]   Since 2005, the CSRC has introduced book-building, which gives investment banks more power in price setting. However, where the supply of IPO is still strictly controlled, marketization of pricing only further pushes up the already high P/E ratios and creates even bigger bubbles in the secondary market.

[83]   In China, it is called the 'New Stocks Never Lose Myth' (*Xingu Bubai Shenhua*).

[84]   Of course, they have good reason to do so, see the discussion in the next chapter.

3.1.3 What to compete? Although the investment bankers do not play the reputational intermediaries role, they do play an important role in IPO, which is 'packaging'. As mentioned before, since the majority of listed companies are transformed SOEs that are usually in financial difficulty, in order to meet the listing requirement, they have a high demand for 'packaging' services. In order to gain clients, investment bankers compete with each other in offering packaging services such as providing bridging finance, helping the issuers to falsify application documents, or disclosing false information. In almost every IPO scandal, we can find the involvement of underwriters. Some of the biggest investment bankers, such as Shenyi Wangguo, Nanfang Securities and Guotai Junan were all found to deeply engage in the most notorious IPO frauds like Daqing Lianyi (600065),[85] Dongfang Boiler (600786), Mai Kete (000150), Hongguang Industrial (600083) and Tonghai High Tech (000991).

More importantly, since the CSRC remains the IPO approval power, the extent to which the investment bankers can influence the CSRC becomes the key to their competitive capacity. The capacity to influence the CSRC has something to do with the size and performance of the investment banks, but more depends on their background and connections *(guanxi)* with the CSRC.

Chinese investment banks are SOEs that are owned by the state finance ministries, state-owned banks, SOEs, or state asset management companies. Private and foreign shareholdings still remain small. According to 2002 data, in 88 out of the total 113 securities companies, the state is the first large shareholder.[86] Thus, some major investment banks and their senior managers also hold a corresponding bureaucratic rank. For instance, China International Capital Corporation (CICC) is a ministry-ranking unit that is parallel to the CSRC; Shenyin Wanguo is a bureau-level unit. The administrative status of the securities companies

---

[85]   Take Daqing Lianyi (600065) for instance. Daqing Lianyi (600065) is a petroleum company from Heilongjiang Province which was approved as a stock-holding company in late 1996. In order to help it satisfy the listing requirements that a company should have at least three years of operations and 10 per cent annual return on assets, the Heilongjiang SCORES faked its business licence to read late 1993. The false accounts were submitted by its underwriter, Shenyin Wangguo. See Chen et al. (2005, p. 485).

[86]   This data quoted from Wang (2006). For instance, before the 2004 crisis, Galaxy Security was wholly owned by the MOF; in Guotai Junan, 30 per cent of shares were held by Shanghai state-asset-management company, 14 per cent shares were held by Shen Zhen Investment Bank; the latter also hold 70 per cent of shares of Guo Xin Securities.

and that of their shareholders has some clear impact on the CSRC's decisions. Again take CICC – due to its strong background, the CSRC has never disapproved or delayed any IPO underwritten by it. It undoubtedly grants CICC a great competitive advantage and helps it quickly to become China's largest underwriter.

Another strategy to enhance competitive capacity is to nurture a good connection (*guanxi*) with the CSRC officials. Since 1998, some underwriters have started employing former CSRC officials as managers and that evidently increased their shares in the underwriting market. For example, Guoxin Securities had little underwriting business before 1996, but with the joining of four former CSRC officials, it overtook most competitors almost overnight and jumped up to the top three underwriters since 1998 (Economic Observer, 18 November 2001).

3.1.4 Other factors affecting reputation supply Chinese   investment bankers' incentive for reputation supply is further compromised by the following factors: state ownership, lack of autonomy, and weak formal enforcement. Corporate controllers in these state-owned investment banks cannot fully reap the gains from the enhanced reputation as those in private companies can. Accordingly, they have less incentive to provide it. State ownership also gives rise to serious governance problems, which led to an industry-wide bankruptcy around 2004.[87]

The Chinese securities industry also lacks autonomy. In a mature market, investment banks are primarily disciplined by industry self-regulatory bodies. As noted, the self-regulation body has an evident advantage in flexibility and information that cannot be easily replaced by formal enforcement. In China, the Securities Association is operated under the administrative control of the CSRC. Its president and vice-presidents are nominated by the CSRC.[88] Its representatives 'have been actively involved neither in rule making nor in significant lobbying on behalf of the industry' (Green, 2004, p. 201).

Before 2002, it served as little more than a score keeper for the industry – producing securities company ratings in its annual industry yearbook. From July 2002, the CSRC was moved to activate the Association and has begun to transfer certain of its own functions to it, including the training and certification of industry professionals. To date, the most important role it has assumed is that of supervising the operation of the Third Board (Green, 2004). Overall the Association

---

[87]   This will be discussed in the next chapter.

[88]   The Constitution of Securities Association (2007) Art 35.

functions as the 'second CSRC' rather than a SRO. In the absence of self-regulation, the burden of disciplining investment banks largely falls on the shoulders of the CSRC. For the reason just mentioned, formal enforcement alone is by no means effective.

In a market where investment banks are not punished by investors, the state could incentivize them to value reputation by directly imposing costs on opportunistic behaviour. In so doing, the state might facilitate reputational intermediaries to grow. However, in the absence of market demand, the extent to which such effort could be effective is a question. As pointed out before, even if we assume formal enforcers had the best incentives, they could not overcome the limitation of formal enforcement imposed by information and costs. Consequently, only a small fraction of misconduct could be detected and punished by the state and companies could always find a collaborator. In reality, formal enforcement in China is very weak. As we will see below, private enforcement plays almost no role, and public enforcement is weak in general, and particularly weak against investment bankers, given their state ownership, strong background and complex links with the CSRC.

3.1.5 International investment banks According to its WTO commitment, China has gradually opened up its securities industry to foreign securities companies. International giants like Morgan Stanley, Goldman Sachs and Credit Suisse have started entering into China's IPO market through setting up joint ventures with Chinese partners since 2002. At the beginning, some people expected these international players could bring positive changes to the IPO market. As compared to domestic underwriters, they have better expertise and more valuable reputational capital. However, as revealed in the current credit crunch, even in a developed market where they face much rigorous discipline, these world-class investment bankers often play a disgraceful role. There is little reason to expect that they will suddenly become innocent angels in an emerging market.

Indeed, these international investment bankers quickly learned how to play the game and take advantage of the ill-disciplined Chinese stock market. They enrolled many members of the 'princelings' (*Taizidang*) – the offspring of senior CCP officials – and relied on their connections (*Guanxi*) to win the deals. To name but a few, Wilson Feng, the son-in-law of Wu Bangguo, officially second in the party hierarchy, worked for Merrill Lynch and was the key to securing Merrill's position in ICBC's IPO (Financial Times, 29 March 2010); Citigroup lured Margaret Ren, daughter-in-law of former Chinese Premier Zhao

Ziyang.[89] Ren brought Citi a slew of deals, including China Netcom, Minsheng Bank, and China Life (Forbes, 2 August 2007).[90] But of course, the most striking is Morgan Stanley, which co-founded CICC with the CCB. Thanks to Levin Zhu, the son of former premier Zhu Rongji, CICC won almost all the major deals, such as ICBC, PetroChina, China Mobile, Sinopec, China Life and Air China.

Some of these investment banks had already attracted criticism for their suspicious activities in IPO, M&A and Private Equity (PE) investment in China. For instance, UBS was suspected of being involved in insider trading during the A-shares IPO of PetroChina in 2007 (its subsidiary, UBS Investment Bank undertook the leading underwriter) (21st Century Economic Report, 24 December 2007). Goldman Sachs attracted criticism for its controversial PE investment in Western Mining (21st Century Economic Report, 20 April 2010). It does not seem likely that the international players will change the domestic market. Rather, it is more likely that the domestic market will assimilate them. In sum, in China, the investment banks do not act as reputational intermediary and they are unable to perform the third-party enforcer role.

3.2 Auditors

Auditors are another significant third-party enforcer in a stock market. However, like the investment bankers, Chinese auditors have failed to perform their enforcer role and have engaged in most scandals. In November 2001, The National Audit Office randomly selected 32 audit reports completed by 16 auditor firms. It found 'gravely inaccurate errors' in 23 of them, involving 14 auditor firms, 41 Certificated Public Accountants (CPA), and fraudulent funds amounting to 7 billion yuan (National Audit Office, 23 January 2003). Things became so bad that the then premier, Zhu Rongji, called for foreign auditing firms to conduct supplemental audits of all listed firms in China (Financial Times, 28 January 2002).[91]

---

[89]   Her father is Ren Zhongyi, also a very influential official in the reform era.

[90]   Ren had been forced out by Citigroup in 2004, after a probe by the SEC that was dropped in autumn 2006. Citigroup has not recovered since the incident. The bank has been an also-ran in the new issue market, costing it a fortune. See The Economist, 8 February 2007.

[91]   Under pressure from auditing firms and the MOF, also affected by the failure of Andersen in the Enron scandal, in 'Notice on Implementing Supplemental Audits In A-share Firms (*Guanyu A-gu Gongsi Zuohao Buchong Shenji Gongzuo de Tongzhi*),' the CSRC restricted the firms that need to conduct

The reasons for the failure of accountants are similar to those for investment banks. First and foremost is that there is no demand for independence of auditors. As discussed above, the risk-free IPO market renders hiring an accounting firm with good reputation of independence to signal its value unnecessary; what companies need is an auditor who is willing to conspire. After IPO, given the concentrated ownership, the controlling shareholder has little demand for independent auditing because they are able to directly control and monitor managers. Only minority shareholders might prefer credible financial information and thus theoretically provide the basis for a demand for independent auditing. However, in reality, minority shareholders are highly speculative and pay little attention to fundamentals. Even if they indeed had an interest in doing so, they have no means to assure an independent auditor since the board of directors and board of supervisors are both dominated by the large shareholders. As study shows, in the absence of market demand for independent auditing, the firms that acted more independently lost a considerable market share in terms of both clients and assets audited to those more willing to acquiesce (Defond et al., 1999).[92]

The second key factor accounting for the failure of auditors is weak formal enforcement. For example, despite the fact that its clients Kangsai Group (600745), Xinghua Shareholding (600886), Xingfa Group (600141) and Xingfu Industries (600743 had either received notice of criticism, or public criticism for providing false accounts, Hubei Lihua accounting firm and the relevant auditors did not receive any penalty for the misconduct in these cases (China Securities Journal, 20 August 2001).[93] It was not until 2000 that Zhong Tianqin, the auditor of Yin Guangxia became the first accounting firm to suffer from the consequences of its actions (Caijing, 20 December 2001).[94]

---

supplemental audits to those issuing more than 300 million stocks in a single issuance. Since firms of this kind are very rare, it actually made the requirement irrelevant to most firms. In 2007, this requirement was officially removed.

[92] Defond et al. (1999) reported that large auditors that were more independent lost 22 per cent of their share of clients to small auditor firms that were less independent, and they lost more than 50 per cent of their share of IPO clients.

[93] Lihua accounting firm was merged with Beijing Zhongshen accounting firm in 2011 and became the latter's local branch.

[94] Zhong Tianqin was one of the biggest accounting firms in China, and had about 60 listed company clients. For details of the fall of Zhong Tianqin, see Caijing, 20 December 2001.

Facing little legal risk, even the Big Four[95] tend to behave opportunistically.[96] In recent years, the Big Four have been involved in a series of corporate scandals and a study found that they do not perform significantly different from domestic firms (Liu and Zhou, 2007). For instance, in 2005 it was uncovered in an investigation by the CSRC of Kelong (000921) that from 2002 to 2004, 477.18 million yuan profits were fabricated. As its auditor during this period, Deloitte failed to disclose this information (China Securities Journal, 23 November 2005).[97] In 2005, PwC was required to make a rectification by the MOF for its auditing errors in Huangshan Travel (600054) and Jing Dongfang (000725) (Sina.com, 9 August 2005). KPMG's client Jinzhou Port (600190) received public criticism from the SHSE in 2003 for accounting errors (Liu and Zhou, 2007).[98]

The small size of Chinese accounting firms also affects their independence. According to a study in 2004, only five domestic accounting firms had annual revenue beyond 100 million yuan (Hu and Jiang, 2005), a sharp contrast with the Big Four. Small size means that it is more costly for firms to lose a big client and thus they are more willing to acquiesce.

Moreover, the Chinese accounting industry lacks autonomy and is heavily affected by the governments at various levels. It was not until 1998 that accounting firms separated from the government and operated as independent entities. Before 1998, an accounting firm was a subordinate organ under the local finance bureau or audit bureau and affiliated with the finance department. After 1998, auditing firms are still directly administered by the MOF and its local branches. The close ties between the accounting firms and local governments persist. In the process of helping local firms to go public and retain listing status, local governments often demand assistance from accounting firms. It is

---

[95]   The Big Four include Ernst and Young (EY), Deloitte Touche Tohmatsu (Deloitte), Klynveld Peat Marwick Goerdeler (KPMG) and Pricewaterhouse-Coopers (PwC).

[96]   In fact, given the strong background of the Big Four's Chinese partners (early partners including the MOF, Shanghai Finance Department) and their lobbying capacity and international reputation, they actually enjoy 'super national treatment' and they face even lower legal risk than Chinese counterparts.

[97]   The CSRC has not yet made any penalty decision after holding a hearing 4 years ago (usually, the decision should be made 2 months after the hearing); this is an illustration of the Big Four's super national treatment. Interestingly, a study shows that after the Kelong Incident, the market share of Deloitte did not decrease, instead, it experienced considerable increase, confirming my argument that there is no demand for intermediaries' reputation. See Yin (2007).

[98]   However, there was no penalty against KPMG.

difficult for the firms to decline because that will offend the local government, apart from losing the client.

Last but not least, Chinese accounting firms normally register as limited liability companies. Only a small fraction of them register as partnerships. Limited liability undoubtedly reduces the risk facing auditors and thereby encourages them to focus on current gains.

3.3 Other gatekeepers

Other gatekeepers include attorneys, securities analysts and rating agencies. Facing the same institutional constraints, their enforcement roles are similarly undermined. In order to avoid duplication, these will not be discussed in any detail but a few words will be added.

Attorneys and securities analysts are both new industries in China. They emerged in the mid-1980s. Sophisticated securities attorneys and analysts are very rare. The overall low standard undoubtedly affects the quality of their services. In addition, China's stock market is speculative in nature and the professional manipulators (*Zhuang Jia*) often employ securities analysts to help in trapping retail investors. For instance, the best known manipulator, Lüliang, often published false stories under his pseudonym 'Mr. K' in the respected *Securities Market Weekly* to support his trading strategy (Caijing, 7 February 2001). More recently, Wang Jianzhong, the legal representative and manager of the well-known Beijng Shouchuang Investment Consultation Limited was revealed to have manipulated the market through recommending to public investors the stocks that he bought beforehand. As one of the very unlucky few, Wang got caught, but most of his peers remain at large (Xinmin Weekly, 28 July 2010). Credit rating agencies in China are still at an early age and unable to play any meaningful role in the stock market.

4.   Media

In the past two decades, the media remarkably outperformed the problematic gatekeepers in respect of enforcement. *Caijing*, the leading financial magazine in China since 1998, has published numerous critical reports and disclosed a series of scandals involving almost every aspect of the stock market. Some reports not only heavily influenced the stock market, but also shocked the whole country. To name but a few, The Black Funds Scandal (*Jijin Heimu*) (8 October 2000), Ying Guangxia Falls into Trough (*Yinguangxia Xianjing*) (7 August 2001), The Market Manipulator Lüliang (*Zhuangjia Luliang*) (7 February 2001), The Predicament of CPA (*CPA Kunju*) (20 December 2001). These reports directly resulted in the fall of Yin Guangxia, and its auditor, the Zhong

Tianqin accounting firm. They also put huge pressure on the CSRC and therefore partially contributed to the 'supervision storm' in 2001. *Caijing* indisputably highlighted the value of media in enforcement in an emerging market. However, the success of *Caijing* is an exception, rather than the norm. In China, the media confronts serious handicaps to realize its potential in enforcement.

4.1 Lack of autonomy

A distinctive characteristic of Chinese social control is that the state not only controls human conduct, but also controls thought. The socially harmonious state, as the ultimate goal of social control, means both behavioural conformity and thought uniformity (Ren, 1997, p. 1). Such a model has been carried on for generations by the Chinese rulers, regardless of their philosophical beliefs and political demands.[99] Therefore, ever since the creation of the popular press in the late 19th century, the Chinese governments tended to place the media under its control;[100] however, only the CCP regime really realized complete control of the media.

Since the 1950s, the Propaganda Department of the Central Committee of the Communist Party (CPD) has been responsible for overall management of culture, including mass media. Most major papers are formally linked to the CCP and many central party organizations publish their own newspapers or magazines. This model is replicated at the provincial and local levels. For instance, at central level, *People's Daily*[101] is published by The Central Committee of the CCP. At provincial level, the *Southern Daily* is the official paper of the Guangdong Province Communist Party

---

[99] This tradition can be traced back as far as 220 BC, when the Qin emperor ordered the burning of all social, political and humanitarian books and literature and buried alive more than 460 Confucian followers, thus marking the first use of legal sanction against political and intellectual dissidents in Chinese history (Ren, 1997, p. 38). Thought control reached its historical peak under the CCP regime. In the anti-Rightist Movement alone, by the end of 1957, over 300 000 intellectuals had been branded 'rightists' and were sent to labour camps, prison, or to punitive exile in the countryside for the rest of their lives.

[100] For a discussion of the efforts to control the media at end of Qing Dynasty and government control of the media during the Republican period, see Lynch (1999).

[101] Anyone who knows about Chinese politics would be familiar with People's Daily. As official newspaper of central committee, it is a real political bell-weather. Thus, People's Daily editorial is a very powerful tool that the central government uses to intervene in the stock market.

Committee (Liebman, 2005, pp. 18–19). In addition, numerous government departments and institutions also publish their own newspapers and magazines. For example, *People's Court News* is published by the Supreme People's Court (SPC). These publications are subject to overall regulation by the propaganda department in addition to direct supervision by their parent government departments or institutions (Lynch, 1999, p. 41). Television and radio stations are generally linked to a government entity, either to the State Administration of Radio, Film and Television (SARFT), or to the corresponding provincial radio, film, and television bureau. They are also subject to a degree of CPD regulation and oversight equivalent to the print media (Liebman, 2005, p. 20).

These media also have administrative ranks corresponding to the administrative rank of the department or party organization with responsibility for the publication or station (Fu and Cullen, 1996). For instance, *People's Daily* has ministerial rank, which derives from its link to the Central Committee.

Commercialization of the Chinese media started in the late 1970s and continued and accelerated in the 1990s. Many media outlets have become financially self-sufficient without government subsidy.[102] A number of leading media outlets were thus transformed into state-owned corporate groups with a wide range of commercial interests, generally including both a major party newspaper and other more commercially focused newspapers and publications (Liebman, 2005, pp. 23–25).[103,104] Although commercialization has increased the importance of attracting readers or viewers and redirected the focus of many media outlets from delivering

---

[102] Before, they mainly relied on mandatory subscription for survival.

[103] For instance, the Central Party's flagship paper, *People's Daily*, now publishes a total of 20 newspapers and magazines, including commercialized, mass-market subsidiaries *Huanqiu Shibao* and *Securities Times*. The Southern Daily Group, whose flagship *Southern Daily* is the official paper of the Guangdong Province Communist Party Committee, also publishes the mass-market *Southern Metropolitan Daily* and a weekly paper *Southern Weekend*, which is widely regarded as one of China's most forthright and outspoken papers (Liebman, 2005, p. 25).

[104] An interesting question is about the ownership of these media conglomerates. Although the Party has always controlled the media, there has been a common assumption that it is the Chinese state, rather than the CCP, that has the ownership rights over the media. However, in a secret document jointly issued by the CPD, the SPPA and the SARFT in August 2002, the Party claimed proprietary rights over these media groups. According to this document, China's media conglomerates are owned by the CPD at various levels, while state agencies such as SARFT, SPPA and their counterparts at local levels are

and gathering information on behalf of the party-state to meeting audience demands, it has little influence on the party's media policy. Tight control remains.

4.1.1 Licensing system   In the newspaper sector, during the process of commercialization, the Party has relied on the licensing system to ensure its control over the press structure.[105] Under the licensing system, no newspaper can be set up as an independent business. All prospective newspaper enterprises must be registered under a recognized institutional publisher or sponsor that includes party committees, government bureaucracies, mass organizations, and other institutions of above county level official standing.[106] Individuals or other social organizations are prohibited from owning media.[107]

Among these authorised publishers, only Party committees can publish general interest papers based on the presumption that they are capable of standing above different social groups and representing the 'general interest' of the population. All other publishers must confine their papers either to a special social group (youth, women, workers and so forth) or to an area of specialization (culture, business, sports and so on) (Zhao, 2004, p. 189).

4.1.2 Content control   China's media operate subject to a web of formal and informal regulations that inform, or dictate in some cases, how and what the media report. The CPD provides overall guidance and the propaganda bureaus of provincial and local party branches are responsible for implementing such policies at their respective levels. Party guidance range from details regarding how to cover major news stories, to requirements that the media use only officially prepared texts for certain stories, to instructions to the media to focus, or remain silent, on particular issues. In addition, since each propaganda department has the authority to issue directives, the media faces different degrees of regulation depending on their administrative ranking and the particular

---

Party-delegated administrators of these media conglomerates. The explicit ownership claim by the Party was explosive in China (thus the secret nature of the document). See Zhao (2004, p. 196).

[105]   The licensing system is enforced by the State Press and Publication Administration (SPPA).

[106]   State Council, Publication Regulation, enacted in 1997, Art 10(2), amended in 2002, Art 11(2).

[107]   In practice, individuals and other social organizations do invest in media, but there is no legal ground for their ownership.

propaganda department with direct authority over the publication or station (Liebman, 2005, pp. 43–44).[108]

Informal norms also set boundaries on the topics on which the media may and may not report, in particular relating to coverage of alleged official misconduct, unfair official decisions, or other potentially sensitive topics. The most important informal rules concern the targets and subject matter of reports. Most critical reports expose low-ranking officials, particularly officials at the county level and below.[109] In addition, critical media reports generally expose misdeeds either at a lower administrative rank or in a jurisdiction other than that in which the report will be published or aired. It is rare for the media to target problems at the same level of government as the media itself. Critical reports regarding the politically important cities of Beijing and Shanghai by any media are infrequent. The same applies to criticism of the central government or national ministries. In fact, CPD rules explicitly ban media from reporting on crimes committed by any officials at or above the rank of deputy minister; in such cases, the media are only permitted to use reports prepared by Xinhua Agency or *People's Daily*. Critical reports regarding provincial governments are also uncommon. When they do occur, they usually come from media with central government or party rank (Liebman, 2005, pp. 46–48).

Informal norms also govern subject matter, making some topics easier to report than others. Certain topics are clearly off limits, such as reports about national leadership, criticism of the military, reports on protests by overtaxed farmers or laid-off state enterprise workers.[110]

The media that try to challenge the boundaries will find themselves in serious trouble. This might lead to the removal of outspoken journalists, the closure and forced reorganization of media outlets, and even imprisonment of journalists. Take Southern Daily Group, for instance, which is

---

[108]   Media with national rank obey directives of the CPD; provincial media must obey both the CPD instructions and those of their respective provincial propaganda departments; and municipal-level media must obey central, provincial and municipal propaganda directives. See Liebman (2005, p. 44).

[109]   CPD notices have explicitly told the media that critical reports should limit their targets to county-level and lower-ranking officials, although some national media journalists state that they are also able to criticize some municipal leaders, including deputy mayors and municipal bureau heads (Liebman, 2005, p. 47).

[110]   Ordinary Chinese who provided details of these protests to the Chinese National People's Congress and the international media have received jail sentences as long as 10 years. See Zhang (1999), quoted from Zhao (2004, p. 185).

widely regarded as China's most forthright and outspoken media group. In the late 1990s, the chief editor of one of its subsidiaries, the *Southern Weekend*, was removed for various violations of the Party's Propaganda disciplines. In March 2003 another subsidiary, *21st Century World Report* was shut down after it published an interview with a senior Party intellectual who called for greater political openness (Zhao, 2004, p. 183). After exposing the beating to death of a college graduate wrongfully detained as a vagrant in Guangzhou[111] and the cover-up of the severe acute respiratory syndrome (SARS) epidemic in the city in 2003, the paper's two top editors were accused and later convicted of taking bribes by local authorities.[112]

4.2 Other difficulties facing the media

Besides entry barriers and contents control, local authorities often attempt to silence the media by various measures such as regulation, force or litigation. Some local governments pass regulations requiring reporters to obtain permission in advance of publishing critical reports or conducting interviews (China Youth Daily, 14 January 2002) and some regulations go so far as to forbid the publication of bad news altogether (Southern Weekend, 3 March 2003). Other local governments also use extralegal measures to suppress negative news. Numerous publications reported the abuses journalists suffered such as beatings at the hands of local police. Even journalists from powerful central media have been detained and beaten (Jinghua Times, 30 March 2002; Procuratorate Daily, 17 January 2002). In other cases, newspapers carrying critical reports disappear or are destroyed before they can be sold in the area covered in

---

[111] This is the well-known Sun Zhigang case which finally brought the notorious 'Custody and Repatriation (*Shourong Shencha*)' system to an end.

[112] Yu Huafeng and Li Minying were sentenced to 8 and 11 years in jail respectively. Another editor, Cheng Yizhong, was expelled from the CCP and also accused of corruption, but the charge was dropped in October 2004. For details of the Southern Metropolitan case (known as 'Nandu An' in China), see Caijing, 20 March 2004; 5 June 2004. In the latest issue, *Caijing* revealed the dominant role played by Wang Huayuan, the former vice party secretary and secretary of the Discipline Inspection Committee of Guangdong Province, in the Southern Metropolitan case. Wang felt these critical reports were a challenge to his personal authority and therefore determined to punish Yu and Li, disregarding the fierce criticism in China and overseas. See Caijing, 3 August 2010. It must be noted that *Caijing*'s report on Wang Huayuan was possible only after Wang's fall. In August 2009 Wang was expelled from the CCP and accused of taking bribes in July 2010. Ironically, his own trial, as usual, remained secret and Xinhua Agency was the only media permitted to report.

a critical report (China Youth Daily, 22 September 2003).[113] Even where local governments do not use force or threats, they may rely on connection to higher-level officials to block critical reports (People's Court News, 23 May 2002; People's Procuracy, 27 August 2000).[114] In addition, in recent years, local officials and local powerful persons have increasingly used defamation litigation to silence the media. The economic risks arising from critical reporting are now as significant as the risk of sanction by propaganda departments (Wei, 1999; Liebman, 2005, p. 54).

4.3 Media corruption

The professional ethics of China's media are also an important factor that restricts its effectiveness. Corruption permeates China's media (Zhao, 1998). Reporters often receive offers of cash or have their travel expenses paid by one party in the dispute, to report on a particular matter. The phenomenon of reporters 'reporting for payment', or writing (or threatening to write) biased stories in return for payments by concerned parties, is common (Procuratorate Daily, 19 December 2001).

4.4 The uniqueness of Caijing and the end of an era

Relatively speaking, the media enjoy more leeway to report on wrongdoing in the financial sector than in many other areas. However, given the close ties between listed companies and governments at various levels, the administrative rank of many corporate managers, and the strong background of those who are able to have access to inside information or mobilize huge amount of funds to manipulate stock prices, the media often encounter great difficulties. A recent event provided a vivid illustration of this.

On 5 and 22 June 2010, the respected newspaper *Economic Observer* published a series of critical reports on a listed company Kaien Gufen (002012) with headquarters in Suijiang county, Zhejiang Province. These reports questioned the company regarding issues like state assets draining

---

[113] It reported on confiscation of a *People's Daily* edition in the county that was the target of the critical report.

[114] *People's Court News*, 23 May 2002, reported a line of persons at CCTV seeking to block coverage by *Focus* (a nightly news and commentary programme on CCTV). *People's Procuracy* (27 August 2000) reported the number of reports prepared for *Focus* have been blocked prior to being broadcast, and discussed similar activities at local level. Liebman (2005, p. 54) documented that approximately one-third of the critical reports that journalists at *Focus* prepare are never aired, often because of intervention by interested parties.

and related transactions. On 23 July Qiu Ziming, the reporter, found himself accused of 'damaging the company's business reputation' and wanted by the local police. Later, on 27 July Qiu disclosed that the company tried to silence him by offering cash and a laptop before the publication of the reports. The offer having been rejected by him, it turned to bribe the press by offering enormous advertising fees (Caijing, 28 July 2010; Economic Observer, 28 July 2010). Under huge social pressure, the Suijiang county police was forced to revoke the arrest warrant and apologize to Qiu on 29 July. Throughout the incident, all Zhejiang-based media remained silent.

The experience of Qiu is by no means unique, but a typical story of China's financial media. Against this background, the success of *Caijing* is particularly outstanding. The success of *Caijing* should primarily be attributed to the support and protection of its sponsor organization – The Stock Exchange Executive Council (SEEC) (*Lian ban*). The SEEC was established in March 1988 and affiliated with the SCRES in 1991. The SEEC encompassed a group of people who played a significant role in the establishment of China's stock market – Wang Boming, Gao Xiqing, Wang Wei,[115] Wang Qishan[116] and Zhou Xiaochuan[117] to name but a few. The SEEC provided *Caijing* access to inside stories and protected it from censorship and trouble. In addition, the background and competence of the leading editor, Hu Shuli, is also crucial to the success of *Caijing*. Hu was born in a reporters' family and her grandfather, Hu Yuzhi, was former vice-chairman of the Standing Committee of the National Congress. Hu Shuli is known for her courage to challenge powerful elites and thereby regarded as 'the conscience of China's media'.[118] The SEEC's

---

[115] Wang Boming, the current director-general of SEEC, the president of *Caijing*. Gao Xiqing, former vice-president of the CSRC during 1999–2003. The establishment of China's stock market is intimately bound up with the personal efforts of Wang Boming, Gao Xiqing and Wang Wei. On their return to China from the US in 1988, they wrote a report entitled 'Policy Suggestions for Promoting the Legalization and Standardization of China's Securities Markets'. Later on, Wang Boming and Gao Xiqing joined the eight-person working team of the PBOC and became part of the official push for securities and exchanges.

[116] At the time of writing, Vice Prime Minister.

[117] Former president of the CSRC during 2000–2002, currently governor of the PBOC.

[118] She has also won herself an international reputation. For instance, in 2001, she was selected by *Business Weekly* as one of the 50 Asia Stars, and was called 'the most dangerous woman in China'. In 2006, the *Financial Times* named her as the most influential Chinese columnist.

protection together with Hu's charisma created the legend of *Caijing* and that cannot be easily replicated.

Nevertheless, even *Caijing*'s autonomy is fairly limited and faces insurmountable obstacles. For instance, in 2003, its 20 June edition was banned from distribution by the CPD for including sensitive subjects[119] (Reuters, 23 June 2003). In 2007, large numbers of its 6 January editions were purchased by unknown people in Beijing and Jinan,[120] and the coverage article 'Whose Luneng' (*Shuide Luneng*) was removed from all domestic websites, including *Caijing*'s own website.[121]

In recent years, the CPD has increasingly tightened control over the media and not even *Caijing* would be spared. The SEEC has changed its hands-off policy and engaged in regular review of editions. *Caijing*'s legal reporting team was almost forced to dissolve after reporting the clash in Xinjiang. In 2009, Hu Shuli's insistence that two sensitive reports as 17 August and 31 August edition coverage articles should be used regardless of the SEEC's objection eventually led to the breaking up of this ten-years marriage. Hu Shuli and her team (i.e. 70 per cent of *Caijing*'s personnel) resigned on 9 November. It is widely considered as the end of an era (Southern Weekend, 16 November 2009).

In sum, although the media has the potential to play a significant role in enforcement in the stock market, it faces insurmountable obstacles to

---

[119] It included articles on the impact of SARS, the thickening banking scandal in Shanghai (Zhou Zhengyi) and moves by Communist Party leaders to amend the constitution.

[120] Jinan is the capital of Shangdong Province, headquarters of the Luneng Group.

[121] 'Whose Luneng' is probably the biggest bomb that *Caijing* ever dropped. It uncovered an astounding story about the secret privatization of Luneng Group, the biggest state-owned conglomerate in Shandong Province. It found that through a series of complicated transactions, by May 2006, two mysterious Beijing-based companies had acquired 91.6 per cent of Luneng's shares at a cost of only 3.73 billion yuan (the total assets of Luneng being worth 73.8 billion yuan). The whole process remained highly secretive; neither the SASAC nor Luneng's superior unit was informed. Only after *Caijing*'s report of 26 January 2007 were three Luneng-controlled listed companies forced to disclose the changing of large shareholders. The ending of the Luneng story is also dramatic. On 4 February 2008 Luneng was renationalized by Shangdong Power group and other two SOEs at a cost of 8.95 billion yuan. No one was held accountable for the strange privatization (or more accurately, bold looting), nor was the de facto controller of the two Beijing companies disclosed. It can only be assumed that the people who were behind the privatization are far beyond the reach of any media.

realize such potential in China, and there is no sign that this could be changed in the near future.

V. ENFORCEMENT BY THE STATE

In all countries through much of their history, formal enforcement was very costly, slow, unreliable, biased, corrupt, weak or simply absent. In most countries this situation still prevails (Dixit, 2004, p. 3). It has only been in recent times in advanced countries that effective, low-cost state enforcement has become available. Certainly, factors like financial resources and staffing affect the efficiency of state enforcement, but I believe the immense difference in the degree to which people can rely upon formal contract enforcement between developed countries and developing countries has a more fundamental reason that directly relates to the nature of the state. There exist fundamental differences between developing and developed countries in the way that the state structures and operates and such differences in turn decide to what degree formal enforcement could be relied upon. The state is a proper starting point to study formal enforcement.

1.   The State and Formal Enforcement

1.1   Theory of states

North, Wallis and Weingast (2009) presented a new conceptual frame-work to look at the state which I find has particular explanatory power for China. In previous studies, the state has usually been treated as a single actor with a monopoly on the legitimate use of violence (Weber, 1947, p. 156). In different models, it could be a revenue-maximizing monarch, a stationary bandit, or representative agent.[122] By contrast, North et al. (2009) took a different approach and treated the state as an *organization* of organizations. They start with the problem of violence and ask the fundamental question: how did the state achieve a monopoly on violence?

Because individuals always have the option of competing with one another for resources or status through violence, a necessary corollary to limiting the use of violence within a social group is placing limits on competition. There have been three different ways of dealing with

---

[122]   Brennan and Buchanan's (1980) state as Leviathan, North's (1981) neoclassical theory of the state, and Olson's (1993) roving and stationary bandits, are three well-known examples.

violence in human history. In small groups characteristics of hunter-gatherer societies, violence is managed through personal knowledge and repeated personal interaction[123] (North et al. call the resulting social order 'foraging order'). In large groups, no individual has personal knowledge of all the members of the group or society, and so personal relationships alone cannot be used to control violence. Some form of social institution must arise to control violence (North, et al., 2009, pp. 14–15).

For most of the last ten thousand years, large societies secured physical order and managed violence through forming a coalition whose members possess special privileges. By limiting access to valuable resources[124] to members of the dominant coalition, rents are created that provide the glue to hold the coalition together. Because elites know that violence will reduce their own rents, they have a credible incentive to cooperate rather than fight among themselves. Among the most valuable sources of elite rents is the privilege of forming organizations that the state will support.[125] The resulting social order is called 'limiting access order' or 'natural state' (North, et al., 2009, pp. 18, 30).

North et al. (2009, p. 17) stress that:

> systematic rent-creation through limited access in a natural state is not simply a method of lining the pockets of the dominant coalition; it is the essential means of controlling violence. Rent-creation, limits on competition, and access to organizations are central to the nature of the state, its institutions, and the society's performance. Limiting the ability to form contractual organizations only to members of the coalition ties the interests of powerful elites directly to the survival of the coalition, thus ensuring their continued cooperation within the coalition.

---

[123] Individuals in a society of small groups learn to trust one another by acquiring detailed personal knowledge. This includes the proclivity of each individual to be violent, and the belief that through repeated interaction the ongoing relationships create an interest: North, et al. (2009).

[124] It limits access to valuable resources like land, labour and capital and control of valuable activities – such as trade, worship and education – to elite groups.

[125] Fukuyama (1995) places special emphasis on organizations in his definition of social capital. In his view, the ability to form organizations explains both the development of modern politics and economies. The importance of groups and organizations to the operation of modern liberal democracies has been a mainstay of enormous literature on civil societies. A rich and varied network of groups and organizations provides both a check on the activities of government and an environment in which individual values of tolerance, participation and civil virtue can be nurtured.

In most natural states, some protections are also available to non-elites through patronage or clientage networks. 'The heads of patron-client networks are powerful elites who dispense patronage to clients, provide protection for some aspects of their clients' property and persons, and negotiate arrangements among elite networks that limit violence if the negotiations are successful' (North et al., 2009, p. 35). 'Personal relationships and rent-creation provide the incentive systems that contain violence and allow cooperation in a natural state. The inherently personal nature of all relationships in a natural state expresses the fundamental logic underlying the limited access social order' (North et al., 2009, p. 37).

Until two hundred years ago, there were no open access orders. Even today, 80 per cent of the world population lives in limited access order (North et al., 2009, p. 13). Open access order controls violence through a different logic than the natural state. In open access order, the government holds a monopoly on the legitimate use of violence. Control of the government, in turn, is contestable and is subject to clear and well-understood rules. The danger of the state using violence for its own ends is constrained by opening access to *all* citizens to form organizations that can engage in a wide variety of economic, political, and social activities without the consent of the state. The ability to form organizations at will assures non-violent competition in the polity, economy and indeed in every area of society with open access. The ability of political actors to use organized military or police power to coerce individuals is thus constrained by the ability of economic and other actors to compete for political control. When embedded in a constitutional setting with institutions that provide credible incentives that protect various rights, open access and democratic competition prevent illegitimate uses of violence (North, ct al., 2009, pp. 21–25).

1.2   China as a natural state

China seems to perfectly fit the natural state framework. Scholars outside political science often neglect the fact that the real foundation of the CCP regime is its control over the People's Liberation Army (PLA). The control of the PLA is far from consolidated, but dispersed among elites[126]

---

[126]   Even Mao Zedong and Deng Xiaoping had to rely on their mountaintop (*Shantou*) in the PLA. For instance, Mao awarded most of the chief positions (in the management of the Party Central Military Commission, the Defence Ministry, the Headquarters of the General Staff, the General Political Department and the General Logistics Department) to those who came from the Fourth Red Army in the late 1920s, and the First Front Army in the early 1930s. Deng Xiaoping,

and the influence over the PLA directly decides the distribution of political power.[127] Peace and social order relies on the balance of interests among CCP leaders.[128] The personalized nature of Chinese politics has long been noticed by observers and factionalism[129] is regarded as the central model to Chinese political behaviour (Nathan, 1973; Tsou, 1976; Pye, 1981; Dittmer, 1995). Particularly in the post-Deng era, with the erosion of ideology and the lack of clearly defined nationalistic ideals, 'state authority is going to depend more than ever on the personal power and status of a self-perpetuating elite' (Pye, 1995, p. 52).

1.3 Formal enforcement in the natural state

Previous studies often highlight the inefficiency of formal enforcement in most countries. However, looking at the problem in North et al's (2009) framework, we find it is a corollary of the logic of the natural state.

In the natural state, social order relies on the balance of interests among elites. The behaviour of powerful elites is not constrained by laws but only by the powers of others. Powerful elites are normally immune from punishment by the state. In some cases that indeed happen, it is often primarily the result of political struggle. In addition, elites' protections also extend to some non-elites through patron–client networks. Connected non-elites face a much lower possibility of being

---

after his political return in 1977, promoted into key army positions a large number of high-ranking cadres who had served in the 129th Division of the Eight Route Army (1928–1945), the PLA second Field Army (1945–1949), and the Southwest Military Region (1949–1953), all of which he had led. In 1982, when the PLA was reorganized, most of the key positions in the PLA departments and 11 military regions were controlled by Deng's former subordinates. See Guo (2001, p. 80). The deep root in the PLA made Mao and Deng strong leaders, something not available for the third and fourth generation leaders.

[127] The shift of political power is often accompanied by the reorganized and shuffled regional military commanders among the eight military regions. The collapse of Liu Shaoqi, the Gang of Four, Hu Yaobang and Zhao Ziyang should be at least partially attributed to their weak influence in the PLA.

[128] The Cultural Revolutions was, among other things, the result of the struggle between Liu Shaoqi and Mao Zedong. In more recent times, the Tiananmen Square incident is a reflection of the struggle between the Chen Yun clique and the reformists led by Hu Yaobang and Zhao Ziyang. Deng Xiaoping himself acted as either a reformer or as a swing element.

[129] Faction is defined as a vertically organized patron–client network linked by personal connection (*guanxi*) (Dittmer, 1995, p. 2).

punished by the state than the non-connected non-elites. Formal enforcement in the natural state is therefore *inherently* weak. The inefficiency of formal enforcement is deeply rooted in the nature of the state and cannot be substantively changed before the transition from the natural state to open access order is completed.[130]

1.4   Formal enforcement in the Chinese stock market

Formal enforcement in the natural state is generally weak, and particularly weak in the Chinese stock market. As noted, the Chinese stock market is dominated by SOEs. As a result, most corporate controllers are either members of the dominant coalition (i.e. the CCP) or well connected with powerful elites. In addition, in the stock market, public wealth can be easily transferred into private pockets through various market abuses like insider dealing and market manipulation. Numerous elites are therefore tempted to take part in it. The deep and wide involvement of elites makes formal enforcement in the Chinese stock market particularly difficult.

An example at hand is Qiong Minyuan (000508). Qiong Minyuan made its public offering in 1993. On 29 April 1998 the CSRC published findings of a year-long investigation in which it found that the company had fraudulently inflated accounts by 1.2 billion yuan from illegal real estate transactions in Beijing. Criminal charges were filed against the chairman and five directors. However, Qiong Minyuan audaciously refused to help the CSRC find the five directors. The inability of the CSRC to pursue the five directors is suspected to be for political reasons. Two of the largest shareholders of Qiong Minyuan had ties to Deng Xiaoping. Deng Pufang, the son of Deng Xiaoping, heads the China Welfare Fund, which owned 1.45 per cent of the company's shares. Another shareholder, Shenzhen Non-ferrous Metals Finance, was linked to China Non-ferrous Metals Corporation, which until 1998 was controlled by Deng's son-in-law, Wu Jianchang. 'One has to wonder whether such investigation would have occurred at all if Deng had lived'[131] (Anderson, 2000, p. 1935).

---

[130]   Only advanced countries have completed such a transition. According to North et al. (2009), historical transitions occurred within relatively brief periods, typically about 50 years. But no forces inevitably move societies along the continuum from natural state to open access order. Societies appear as capable of regression as progression.

[131]   Deng died on 17 February 1997 and the investigation was launched on 5 March 1997.

Qiong Minyuan is certainly not an isolated case, nor is Deng's family the only patron. In fact, there are many patron–client networks in the stock market. On whom and to what extent the enforcers could impose a penalty primarily depends on the status of the patron. The lower the status of the patron, the higher the chance that they and their clients would be penalized, and vice versa. Powerful patrons and their clients, like the members of the Politburo, are simply beyond reach. The weak formal enforcement is endogenous to the natural state and cannot be rescued through marginal improvements such as increasing financing resources and professional standards of enforcers.

2. Public Enforcement

Besides the fundamental reason that weakens formal enforcement as discussed above, some other factors also affect the efficiency of public enforcement in China's stock market.

2.1 Multiple objectives

The effectiveness of the CSRC is affected by its multiple and sometimes conflicting goals. In the United States, the SEC was created as an agency that was insulated from administrative interference by the executive. The central goal, if not the only goal, of the SEC is to protect investors and it has little interest in the rise or fall of the stock market or any reason to tolerate market abuse. The CSRC, by contrast, although formally established as a non-governmental organ (*Shiye Danwei*),[132] operates directly under the State Council and must follow the dictates of State Council policy. Since the overriding imperative of the State Council is to support SOEs, the primary task of the CSRC is to nurture a bullish stock market so as to issue and list SOEs' shares. However, given the poor quality of listed companies, they have little investment value and the market is mainly driven by speculation. In a speculation-driven market, the key to attracting investors is to create the expectation of high prices. As a result, the CSRC has to tolerate illegal activities as tough enforcement practices would diminish trading turnover and cause a fall in prices.

Of course, this does not imply that the CSRC has no concern about protecting small investors at all. It does, at least to the extent of preventing financial crisis or social instability that might be triggered by the problems in the stock market. The CSRC has to retain a balance

---

[132]   *Shiye Danwei* consist of public universities, government think tanks and so on. The CSRC is given full ministry rank.

between different goals. As a consequence, the public enforcement by the CSRC is characterized as selective, periodic and, ultimately, instrumental. The CSRC enforces rules more intensively during a bull market in order to cool down the frenzy that may eventually lead to a disaster. It is much more tolerant and passive in enforcement during a bear market in order to avoid further depressing the prices.

2.2 Conflicting role of the state

One major governance problem in Chinese listed companies is the conflict of interests between controlling shareholders and minority shareholders. Where both the controlling shareholders and minority shareholders are private entities or individuals, the regulator is more likely to remain impartial and punish the controlling shareholder for expropriating minority shareholders. However, in most Chinese listed companies, the controlling shareholder is the state. That is to say, the state acts as both player and referee. Such conflicting roles inevitably affect the enforcement willingness of the CSRC. Additionally, tough public enforcement will give rise to contradiction between the CSRC and governments at various levels,[133] which the CSRC by no means likes to confront. Consequently, despite its repeated declaration that it will make investor protection a priority, in reality, the CSRC often favours the controlling shareholders,[134] or is hesitant to impose severe punishment on controlling shareholders.

2.3 Regulatory corruption

Substantial power and lack of accountability cast serious doubts on the integrity of the CSRC. In the absence of systematic evidence it is widely believed that the securities regulatory agency is one of the most corrupt organs. For instance, in a landmark research, 90 per cent of the surveyed securities companies stated that the transparency of securities regulation is low; 71.5 per cent of the surveyed securities companies believed that the penalty of the CSRC is elastic (Xie and Lu, 2003, p. 24). In the same survey, 86.6 per cent of surveyed listed companies stated that there are hidden expenditures for shares issuance; 97 per cent of surveyed listed companies confirmed that they had to bribe the CSRC officials around the period of shares issuance (Xie and Lu, 2003, p. 25).

---

[133]   They are the ultimate controllers in most listed companies.

[134]   For instance, although the CSRC has long been aware of the deficiency associated with the independent directors, it has not yet imposed any constraints on the power of controlling shareholders to nominate independent directors.

The CSRC has substantial power ranging from rules-making to delisting. However, it has little accountability. In the United States, the SEC must submit itself to regular inspection and oversight by congressional committees and must operate within the bounds of statutory law laid down in Acts of Congress. In addition, any administrative action or regulation issued by the SEC can be tested against legislation and overturned by the courts if it is found to be illegal. In contrast, the substantial power of the CSRC is not subject to any effective oversight. The suggestion that the National People's Congress (NPC) should form a permanent organ to oversee the CSRC was rejected by the CSRC leadership and their senior party backers (Green, 2004, p. 196). Thus, the NPC has no mandate to supervise the regulator's activities. Similarly, the judiciary has exerted little oversight over the CSRC's regulations and administrative decisions.

Regulatory corruption drew public attention as early as 1992 and directly resulted in the establishment of the CSRC. Before 1992, the regulator was the PBOC. On 9 August 1992, about one million people queued at 303 sales points around Shenzhen to buy 5 million IPO application forms. However, after delays in sales throughout the day, officials announced that all the forms had been sold. As a later investigation found, the majority had been sold on to the black market and stolen by the police, PBOC staff and other government officials. On the following day, 10 August, the angry crowds burst into a riot, the most serious social disturbance in China since the 1989 Tiananmen Square incident (Green, 2004, p. 140). The '8.10 Incident' led to a wholesale reorganization of the regulator.

Despite the widespread suspicion of CSRC corruption, thus far, only seven officials have been caught. Except for two in local offices, the remaining five were from the Department of Public Offering Supervision or Department of Listed Company Supervision. Among them, the most noticeable was Wang Xiaoshi's case. Wang was sentenced to 13 years in prison for selling name lists of the Public Offering Review Committee (PORC) which is responsible for reviewing and approving IPOs. It is reported that Wang set up a firm with a partner in Shenzhen to sell the name lists to the companies whose IPO applications were under review.[135] Each list was sold at 200 000 yuan and Wang had earned a profit of 10 million yuan at the time of being caught (Sanlian Life Weekly, 26 November 2004). Wang's case is most noticeable as it proved

---

[135]   After getting the list, the listing candidates and investment banks will give massive payments to public relations firms to lobby the PORC members.

the longstanding suspicion of IPO corruption. It raised public concern about the severity of the problem since Wang was only a middle-level official and had very limited power in the department. However, as with many corruption cases in China, these cases were handled quietly. There was no further investigation and nor was any senior official in the CSRC held accountable.

A recent case highlighted the corruption of senior officials in the CSRC. Wang Yi was the former vice chairman of the CSRC during 1994–1999. Relying on the network (*Guanxi wang*) webbed in the CSRC, his influence on the CSRC remained until 2008 when he was arrested. It was reported that Wang Yi played a significant role in the controversial Guojin Securities companies (Guojin) (600109) backdoor listing. Guojin was controlled by Yongjin Group whose chairman, Wei Dong, was one of Wang's most intimate friends.[136] Lei Bo, the Chairman of Guojin, was Wang's former secretary in the CSRC and he was also arrested in May 2009 (Caijing, 9 May 2011).

Wang Yi was also allegedly involved in the odd listing of Pacific Securities Company (Pacific) (601099) in 2007. Pacific was formed in 2004. Before its listing in 2007, it suffered two consecutive years' losses in 2004 and 2005 and only started making profits in 2006. Such performance was far from meeting the listing criteria. However, Pacific shocked the market with its sudden listing on the SHSE in 2007. There are two normal ways for listing in China's stock market. One is through IPO, which needs to be approved by the PORC, and the other is through mergers or acquisitions (backdoor listing), which needs the approval of the Review Sub-committee for Mergers, Acquisition and Restructurings. Surprisingly, Pacific did not go through either procedure and completely disregarded the listing rules. The only official document the listing relied on was the 'Reply to Some Questions Regarding the Listing of Pacific Securities Shareholding Company' (*Guanyu Taipingyang Zhengquan Gufenyouxian Gongsi Gupiao Shangshi Youguan Wenti de Pifu*)[137] issued by the General Office of the CSRC which has no power to approve listing. It is now discovered that Wang Yi's younger brother and sister held 1 per cent of shares in Pacific[138] that were worth 300 million yuan after listing (Securities Market Weekly, 1 March 2008). Wang Yi was probably not the only senior official involved in the Pacific listing. Li Delin, the correspondent who first revealed the scandal, implied that

---

[136]   Wei committed suicide before Wang's formal arrest.
[137]   *Zhengjianban han* [2007] 275.
[138]   Indirectly through Tianjin Shunying which is held by them.

other senior CSRC officials also engaged and attempted to prevent the publication of the report (Li, 2008).[139] As a domino effect of Wang Yi's case,[140] Xiao Shiqing, the president of Galaxy Securities Company (also a former CSRC official) and Li Kejun, the party secretary of Hongyuan Securities Company (000562), who both had close ties with Wang, were arrested in 2009.[141] In addition, Fan Xiaowei, executive director of Guotai Junan Hong Kong, the son of Fan Fuchun, who served as vice-chairman of the CSRC during 1997–2009, was also under investigation on suspicion of market manipulation (Caijing, 5 June 2009).[142] The CSRC has thus far remained silent on all these scandals and refused to respond to public questioning.

2.4 Other factors

Another often mentioned factor leading to public enforcement deficiency is that the CSRC lacks investigatory power and has no responsibility for criminal investigation.[143] However, as discussed before, weak enforcement is inherent in the natural state, and it is doubtful whether increasing disciplinary power or resources could bring any substantial change. Furthermore, the corruption problem raises the question of whether it deserves any more power. The 2005 Securities Law grants the CSRC the power to carry out investigations and collect evidence in a place where

---

[139] In his blog, he also claimed that he had some 20 000 words of unpublished materials in hand.

[140] Wang Yi was sentenced to a suspended death penalty for taking bribes during his tenure as vice-president of China Development Bank. All the problems regarding the stock market were filtered and received special treatment in the trial. His agreement not to hire a lawyer in exchange for a lighter sentence indicated that what was made public in the sentence is only the tip of iceberg.

[141] At the time of writing, Xiao Shiqing had received a suspended death penalty for taking bribes and insider trading. See Caijing, 9 May 2011.

[142] However, his case was dropped in June 2010. It was reported that due to his cooperation during the investigation, some minor problems were 'disregarded' (Phoenix Finance, 12 July 2010).

[143] Some also point out financial resources are insufficient, see Zhang (2007). By saying so, they might overlook the fact that the CSRC is a comparatively rich organization, able to pay its staff salaries at roughly 50 per cent more than the standard rate for central government employees, not to mention its provision of far superior housing and other welfare arrangements. In 2000, the fees that the CSRC collected from A-share trading already exceeded 200 million yuan (Green, 2004, p. 151). Although these fees are not attributed to the CSRC, I believe financial resources are not a serious problem in the CSRC. In addition, the CSRC has the best educated staff among governmental organs or institutions. Many of them hold doctoral degree.

any suspected irregularity has happened;[144] to freeze or seal up the capital account, bank account and securities account of any relevant party concerned in, or any entity or individual relating to, a case under investigation.[145] In addition, the CSRC set up a Disciplinary Bureau in 2007 which doubled its enforcement staff. Nonetheless, as I predicted, these institutional changes have not brought any visible improvement in enforcement. By the same token, I suspect empowering the CSRC with responsibility for criminal investigation would make little difference.[146]

2.5   Just how weak it is

2.5.1   Low sanction rate   Weak public enforcement by the CSRC first manifests itself in the low penalty rate.[147] In 2002 there were 1224 companies listed in the SHSE and SZSE, but only 17 enforcement actions were carried out by the CSRC. Even if we ignore the fact that not each enforcement activity represents enforcement against a different company and that enforcement activities were directed not only against issuing companies, but also against intermediaries, this means that on average only one in every 72 companies was subjected to any kind of enforcement initiated by the CSRC.

In the United States, by contrast, the SEC initiated 598 enforcement actions in 2002, of which 518 were targeted at an issuing entity (SEC, 2002 Annual Report). The SEC regulates all companies that are traded on national exchanges which are larger than the roughly 2800 companies currently listed on the NYSE. Nevertheless, a rough approximation using the number of stocks currently listed on the NYSE suggests that every fifth company listed on that exchange has been subject to SEC enforcement proceedings in 2002 (Pistor and Xu, 2004, p. 23). The comparison between the CSRC and SEC enforcement is even more striking if we consider the severity of the governance problem in Chinese listed companies.

We can also look at the low sanction rate for the enforcement of insider trading. Insider trading is one of the most extensive areas of misconduct in the Chinese stock market (Xie and Lu, 2003; Huang,

---

[144]   2005 Securities Law, Art 180(2).

[145]   2005 Securities Law, Art 180(6). Before the adoption of the Securities Law, the CSRC had to apply for a court order before it could seize evidence or freeze bank accounts.

[146]   The responsibility for criminal investigation rests with Public Security Bureaus or Anti-Corruption Bureaus.

[147]   As admitted by a former CSRC official in an interview, although the CSRC have rules, 'they do not enforce the rules' (Tomasic and Fu, 2005).

2007). However, by the end of June 2004, there were only 11 cases reported in China and nine out of the 11 were dealt with by the CSRC. Until March 2003, China did not have any criminal insider trading cases. Regarding market manipulation, thus far, none of the major cases was discovered by the CSRC. They were either revealed by the media – for instance, *Caijing* disclosed Yin Guangxia – or uncovered by the splitting of capital chains – for instance, Zhongke Chuangye (000048) and De Long Group. Even when they are discovered, the CSRC is often slow at taking action. Take Yian Technology (000008). As early as 1999, the SZSE had notified the CSRC of the abnormal price movement and submitted a special report in 2000 (Cheng, 2001). Nevertheless, the CSRC launched an investigation only two years later when the price skyrocketed from 6 yuan to 126 yuan per share. As a result of the slow reaction, the CSRC found nowhere to impose its 490 million yuan fines because the major manipulators had all fled, and small investors suffered huge losses from the following price avalanches.

Table 3.1 shows the CSRC Administrative Sanction Rates from 2002 to 2009.

Table 3.1   CSRC administrative sanction rates 2002–2009

Year	2002	2003	2004	2005	2006	2007	2008	2009
No. of listed companies	1224	1287	1377	1381	1434	1550	1625	1718
No. of CSRC administrative sanction decisions	17	35	49	43	38	35	52	58
No. of CSRC bar from the market decisions	n/a	n/a	18	11	19	13	27	16
Percentage of CSRC sanction decisions/no of listed companies	1.39	2.72	5.01	3.91	3.97	3.10	4.9	4.3

Note: The decisions include sanctions against all market participants.

Source: The CSRC website

2.5.2 Soft sanctions   In the cases where the CSRC does impose sanctions, they tend to be soft and far from sufficient to deter wrongdoers. There are three enforcement tools that the CSRC uses to sanction listed companies. For lesser infractions, the CSRC may issue reprimands or correction orders (*Zeling Gaizheng*), in which a company or individual is told to correct certain behaviour. The CSRC could impose more serious sanctions like warnings or fines. Fines for companies range from 300 000 yuan up to 600 000 yuan;[148] individuals (including the person-in-charge and the directly responsible person) might be fined amounts ranging from 30 000 to 300 000 yuan.[149] Individuals who commit serious misconduct may also be barred from participating in the securities market temporarily or permanently, and from serving as a senior manager or director of a listed company.[150] As to the intermediaries, the CSRC could revoke or suspend their licences.

In reality, the CSRC tends to use soft sanctions like reprimands, warnings or fines, and is less willing to impose more serious ones like revoking licences or permanently barring from the market. Despite the fact that the fines stipulated in the Securities Law are modest at most, the CSRC tends to pursue the lower bound. The fines against companies are normally 300 000 yuan; fines against a chairman of the board normally range from 30 000–50 000 yuan; and fines against directors and senior managers are normally 30 000 yuan (Wang, 2009). Compared to the huge gains from the stock market, such fines are simply laughable.

Consider the following case: Sanjiu Yiyao (000999) is one of China's largest pharmaceutical concerns and is listed on the SZSE. It found that in 1999 and 2000, more than 2.5 billion yuan were channelled to its controlling shareholders, Sanjiu Yaoye, representing 96 per cent of the company's total net assets. The CSRC imposed a fine of 100 000 yuan on the board chairman of Sanjiu Yiyao, less on other individuals. It fined Sanjiu Yiyao 500 000 yuan. Because the controlling shareholder, Sanjiu Yaoye, was not a listed company and thus not under the CSRC's jurisdiction, it was not punished at all.[151]

As mentioned before, sanctions against investment banks are particularly weak. Take Nanfang Securities. Nanfang Securities was once one of the biggest Chinese investment banks. In 2004, its closure shocked the market. Investigation revealed that Nanfang was deeply involved in a

---

[148]   2005 Securities Law Chapter XI: Legal Liabilities.
[149]   Ibid.
[150]   2005 Securities Law, Art 233.
[151]   See the CSRC website: http://www.csrc.gov.cn/n575458/n776436/n3376
288/n3376382/n3418730/n3419021/3442909.html.

series of misconduct such as market manipulation[152] and misappropriation of clients' capital and caused a loss of 21 billion yuan. In 2007, the Nanfang case again shocked the market with its unbelievable 'happy ending'. Criminal charges against two former presidents, Kan Zhidong and Liu Bo, were dropped; another former president, He Yuan, was only barred from serving as a senior manager in investment banks; vice-president Sun Tianzhi, who had direct responsibility for market manipulation, was sentenced to two years in jail, suspended for two years. Two senior managers received 13 and 15 months' jail sentences respectively; the remaining six were all exempted from criminal charges. It was particularly ironic because this occurred against the background of the CSRC calling for 'strengthening enforcement' (Caijing, 14 May 2007).

Figures 3.1 and 3.2 show the CSRC sanctions against accounting firms and accountants from 1993 to 2005. As we can see, even though when compared to securities companies and listed companies, accounting firms are less connected, sanctions against them are still rather soft.

3. Private Enforcement of Law

The role of private enforcement of law in the Chinese stock market could be described as negligible. It was not until 2002 that the first PSL was accepted by the court, 12 years after the establishment of stock exchanges. Apart from the weakness inherent in the natural state, the role of the courts is further constrained by the following factors.

3.1 Chinese legal tradition
The Chinese legal system is often categorized as belonging to the German civil law family. This neglects the fact that China has its own distinctive legal tradition, which still retains a heavy influence on judicial enforcement in general, and private securities litigation in particular.

A distinctive feature of the Chinese legal tradition is that the legal system is not separated from, or independent of, the administrative system. Rather, it has been traditionally regarded as the utilitarian tool of the state, to accomplish political goals (Jones, 2003; Fairbank and Goldman, 2006; Ren, 1997; Potter, 2002; Lubman, 1999). In contrast to the Western notion that the state was founded on law and that the ruler was bound morally and often politically by it, in the traditional Chinese view, government was best conducted by men who behaved like the

---

[152]   The Nanfang clique was one of the major manipulators (*Zhuan Jia*) in the Chinese stock market.

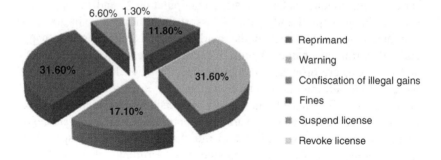

Sources: CSRC website (2001–2005); Zhang and Ma (2006)

Figure 3.1   CSRC sanctions against accounting firms 1993–2005

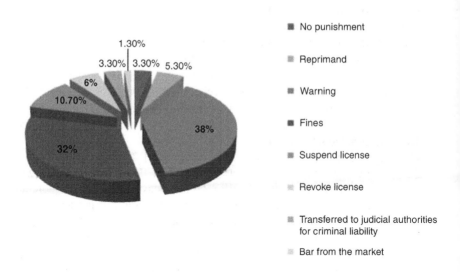

Sources: CSRC website (2001–2005); Zhang and Ma (2006)

Figure 3.2   CSRC sanctions against accountants 1993–2005

ancient sages and set high moral examples for their subjects to follow, which granted the Chinese emperors sacrosanct power over all facets of life, including law making and the judiciary.[153] As a result, unlike the Western legal order, which is 'institutionally autonomous to the extent that its rules are applied by specialized institutions whose main task is adjudication' (Unger, 1976, p. 53), Chinese law was a form of what Unger (1976) has called 'bureaucratic law' and administered by magistrates, who represented the central government and exercised all of the power of the state, including tax collection and public works, and adjudication was simply one of the many administrative duties.

Another striking feature of the Chinese legal tradition is that it is chiefly penal or criminal in nature, a corrective for the untutored (Fairbank and Goldman, 2006; Ren, 1997; Lubman, 1999; Peerenboom, 2002). Chinese law was not only inferior to the will of the ruler, it was also inferior to Confucian moral code, *Li*.[154] By the time of the Han

---

[153] The Chinese emperor is called the 'Son of Heaven' (*Tianzi*) who is the equivalent of what people would call God on earth, the one person who in Western parlance might be termed a god incarnate (Fairbank and Goldman, 2006). Of course, it could be argued that although the emperor was not subject to legal limits, he was subject to normative constraints reflected in the notion of the Way (*Dao*), heavenly principles (*Tianli*), the mandate of heaven (*Tianming*), and practical limits, including the expectation of the people and ministers that the ruler would follow the precedents of earlier rulers. See Peerenboom (2002, p. 41).

[154] *Li* refers to the propriety that regulates 'human desire that has been devised for the protection of the people'. *Li* governs social relationships, including those between the emperor and his ministers, between father and son, between husband and wife, between brothers and between friends. *Li* governs relationships between the ruling and the ruled, the senior and the junior, man and woman, and the blood-related and the acquainted (*Wulun*). Achieving the state of *Li* requires *zheng ming*, 'rectification of names', meaning that a person's position in relation to others – such as a father with his son, or the emperor with his ministers – must be clarified by a ranking system that hinders social expectations and designates behavioural norms and moral responsibilities to others. When people are located in specific social positions with proper titles designating their role behaviour, the society will be orderly and organized because everyone will know what he is or is not expected to do. See Ren (1997, p. 20). *Li* has often been construed as universal ethical principles, as a result, Confucius' *Li* has been depicted as a kind of natural law. However, *Li* is better understood as customary norms that gain favour within a particular historical tradition at a particular time and that constitute not unchanging, determinant rules of behaviour but culturally valued, though negotiable, guidelines for achieving harmony in a particular context. There is nothing sacred about *Li* in the manner of the Ten Commandments. See Peerenboom (2002).

Dynasty (206 BC–AD 220), Confucianism had become the most favourable political ideology[155] and Imperial law had undergone a process of Confucianization, which firmly established the supremacy of *Li* and the subservience of law. Law was identified with retributive punishments and served as a deterrent to others in order to preserve the inviolable status of *Li*.

Chinese legal tradition is also significantly distinct from the Western legal system in the relationship between individuals and the state. In the Western legal system, rights-based theory maintained a sphere within which individual activity was protected from the power of the sovereign and rested on an individualism that is characteristic of the West (Lubman, 1999). There were no such concepts in Chinese thought. The dominant feature of Confucianism was a pervasive hostility to the notion of personal autonomy and individualism. The Chinese individual's identity has been consistently derived from particularistic relationships with

---

[155]   It worth noting that this should be called 'Imperial Confucianism' in order to distinguish it from the original teaching of Confucius. It represented an amalgam of *Confucianism* and *Legalism* (Fairbank and Goldman, 2006, p. 62). *Legalism* is another school that had significant influence on the Chinese political and legal system. Legalist scholars such as Lord Shang and Han Fei were the earliest Chinese jurisprudents who introduced the concept of law to China and constructed China's first imperial legal system. In contrast to (original) Confucianism, which favours achieving social harmony through moral persuasion and thought reform, Legalism insisted that the moral order is inadequate to maintain social order because original human malignity would constantly drive people into trouble. A well-ordered society can be maintained only through a set of formally and publicly announced rules. Rulers of the states had the duty to establish and enforce law with uniformity, certainty, clarity, and severity. Although the difference between Legalism and Confucianism attracted more interest, their agreement on the ruler's absolute authority and instrumental usage of law laid the basic foundation for their amalgamation; neither could be associated with civil liberty and political freedom (Ren, 1997, pp. 21–22, 32). Compared to Confucianism, Legalism aimed at undermining group ties and loyalties in favour of obedience to the state, thus, it was liked by rulers who could use the material inducements of rewards and punishments to keep the common people in order; and Confucianism was liked by bureaucrats (Fairbank and Goldman, 2006, p. 68). More accurately, the Imperial system is one of Confucianism in appearance, Legalism inside (*Wairu, Neifa*). The influence of Legalism persists into modern China, for instance, Mao Zedong was an ardent admirer of Legalism, especially its belief in the iron power of the state and the rigorously repressive function of law and the legal system. Mao and his party's zealous advocacy and exercise of the state's power in all societal affairs were best exemplified through the history of Legalization in the PRC (Ren, 1997, pp. 9–10).

others (Fei, 1947;[156] Liang, 1963;[157] Pye, 1991). Since there was no place for a 'private self' (Munro, 1977), there was no notion of individual rights. Chinese governments have always been paternalistic[158] and the individual's relationship to the state has all along been one of dependence, which made self-sacrifice for the state the highest ideal of citizenship (Pye, 1991).

Since formal law mainly served the interests of the state, private or civil law remained only informally developed in the Chinese legal system. Most disputes were mediated by the clan elders, guild leaders or village heads in accordance with clan or guild regulations and communal practices and norms rather than through litigation[159] (Fairbank and Goldman, 2006; Peerenboom, 2002; Lubman, 1999). This is in sharp contrast with the Roman law tradition, from which Western laws are derived. At the heart of Roman law is civil law and the law developed mostly in response to the occurrence of disputes between private citizens or social groups.

In these respects, nothing much has changed in China. After the collapse of the Qing dynasty in 1911, China was in a state of almost

---

[156] Fei (1947) described the organizational matrix of the social order of traditional rural China as consisting of concentric circles radiating from each individual circle of persons standing in differential degrees of intimacy to that individual. The moral nature of the social relationship between two individuals is determined by their respective locations within this complex differential order.

[157] Liang Shuming (1963), a pioneer in the comparative study of Chinese culture and philosophy in relation to the Western tradition, described Chinese society as 'relationship (*Guanxi*)-oriented' as opposed to being 'group-oriented' or 'individual-oriented'.

[158] Traditionally, the China state was based on the same logic of family, the head of the government was the head of the extended family of the whole nation, governmental officials were called 'parental archons' (*fu mu guan*). The image of father has been and still dominates the political rhetoric of China.

[159] The heavy reliance on informal means to settle disputes is partly a product of Confucian *Li* tradition: many people felt it was a disgrace to be involved in a lawsuit; partly a product of the harshness of the formal legal system: at trial, even plaintiffs were required to kneel throughout the proceeding, and could be subject to torture. See Miyazaki (1980). Although litigation fees were not necessarily out of reach of the average person, extra costs arising from the need to pay off court officials often made litigation an expensive proposition. Extraordinary, too, were the delays and errors. Thus, according to a Chinese saying, 'to enter a court of justice is to enter a tiger's mouth', 'to involve someone in a lawsuit was a way of ruining him'. See Van der Sprenkel (1962); Douglas (1901), both quoted from Lubman (1999, p. 24).

constant war. Thus, despite European-style codes[160] being promulgated by the nationalist government,[161] they had little effect outside the Treaty Ports and some other large cities – which had a good deal of Western law because of extra-territoriality (Jones, 1978), and they were all repealed by the CCP government after 1949. In the 1950s, the CCP had attempted to establish a Western legal system based on the Soviet model but it was soon brought to end by the Anti-Rightist Campaign of 1957. In the Cultural Revolution era (1966–1976), the entire legal system was destroyed and lawlessness was hailed as good, revolutionary.[162] Since 1979, the Chinese authorities have erected a new legal system from scratch and made remarkable achievements. However, in fundamental respects, we still clearly see the persistence of legal tradition and significant gaps remain in China's legal structure governing economic activity.

3.2 China's legal system today

3.2.1 Lack of judicial independence and authority Since 1949, the CCP has replaced the dominant status of emperors and overwhelmed all aspects of society. Like emperors in the past, the CCP has paramount ruling power and is subject to no legal limits. The judicial system continues to be treated as branches of the administrative system,[163] as a tool of governance and control.[164] As Clarke (1996, p. 52) stated:

---

[160]   These codes are modelled on those of Japan, which are in turn modelled, for the most part, on those of Germany.

[161]   The Western influence on Chinese law actually began in the 18th century.

[162]   Probably it is not striking if we consider the actual role of law in the Chinese political system.

[163]   A manifestation of the bureaucratic nature of courts is that they are often called upon to do the kind of tasks Chinese bureaucracies are frequently called upon to do – for example, to help with the latest birth control campaign or tax collection drive (He, 1999).

[164]   For a recent example, Hu Jintao has given new orders that political and legal departments must observe the so-called 'three priorities', meaning the latter must give utmost priority to the party's enterprise, the people's interests, and the constitution and the law. Later on, in a national meeting of judicial and security officials in June 2008, the newly promoted president of the Supreme People's Court (SPC), Wang Shengjun, indicated that 'only by upholding the "three priorities", from beginning to end can the work of the people's courts go along the correct political path'. Echo Hu Jintao's calling for 'building harmonious society', Wang said the goal of the courts is to 'increase harmonious elements and to curtail disharmonious elements to the maximum degree'. In an interview, the president of the Higher People's Court in Jinlin province, Zhang Wenxian

'Chinese courts are not along the Anglo-American model, powerful arbitrators of last resort who can decide important questions involving powerful state leaders. Instead, they are in practice just bureaucracy among many with a limited jurisdiction.' Therefore, there is little judicial independence and authority.

The lack of independence of the courts is first reflected in the control exercised by the CCP over the various aspects of the courts' operations. Each level of the CCP organization has a Party's Political-Legal Committee (PLC),[165] which directly makes decisions on important policies and issues related to the courts and law enforcement. In many cases, the PLC even determines the outcomes of major court cases. In terms of judicial appointments, the Judges Law provides that the NPC at the same level elects the president of the court; vice-presidents and other judges are chosen by the corresponding NPC's standing committee.[166] However, in reality, the NPC only acts as rubber stamp and the appointments of key personnel in the court system are controlled by the Party Organization Department. In order to show their loyalty to the Party so as to climb up the bureaucratic ladder, the majority of judicial personnel would choose to accept or even to seek Party interference. Furthermore, 'if the courts try to go their own way and not to involve the party organization, they may find their judgment unenforceable. A single telephone call from the Party Secretary could bring the execution to a halt' (Clarke, 1996, p. 50).

Interference from government officials is another serious threat to the independence of the courts.[167] Since the courts remain as one bureaucracy among many and have low status in the political system,[168] very

---

(who is also a well-known law professor), stated that 'the courts must uphold the party's leadership so as to keep up their correct political orientation, they must take as their holy task the sustenance of the party's ruling foundation and the consolidation of the CCP's ruling-party status'. See Asia Times, 8 July 2008.

[165] The PLC usually includes the deputy Party secretary in charge of political-legal matters, the president of the Court and Procuratorate and the heads of various ministries or bureaus including public security, state security, justice, civil affairs and supervision. The PLC is one department within the Party answering to the Party Committee at the same level and the PLC at the next highest level. Most PLC members have little formal legal training, having risen up through the Party ranks.

[166] 1995 Judges Law, Art 10; 2005 Judges Law, Art 51.

[167] Although it is difficult to distinguish government interference from Party interference in China given the majority of government officials are Party members.

[168] In the Chinese political system, the rank of the chief officer determines the rank of the institution he/she heads. Although the president of a court at any

often other government agencies may ignore courts with impunity and consider themselves bound only by orders issued by their superiors (Chow, 2003, pp. 223–224). More importantly, the courts heavily rely on governments at the same level for finances, material supplies and other welfare benefits for court officials and their families. Hence, it is very difficult for courts to go against the wishes of local governments even should they wish to do so. The so-called 'local protectionism' is particularly problematic in administrative cases and commercial cases involving locally based SOEs.[169] The courts are often unsympathetic to plaintiffs from other provinces. Civil judgments rendered in other provinces are often refused enforcement (Clarke, 1996, pp. 41–49; Chow, 2003, p. 221; Peerenboom, 2002, pp. 311–312).

In addition, one Chinese view of independence is that it is the judiciary as a whole that is to be independent, not the individual judge (Lubman, 1999, p. 262). Thus, judges often consult with other judges, especially higher-level judges, in reaching decisions. This bureaucratic culture leads to unusual judicial practices: higher courts sometimes act on their own initiative to instruct lower courts how to decide cases without hearing parties or counsel (Chow, 2003, p. 219); major or difficult cases are decided by the adjudicative committee (*Shenpan Weiyuanhui*),[170] which results in the assertion that 'those who try the case do not decide it, and those who decide the case do not try it' (Lubman, 1999, p. 261).

The lack of judicial independence and authority leads to severe obstacles in enforcement. As publicly conceded by the former president of the SPC, Xiao Yang, 'the difficulty of executing civil and commercial judgments has become a major "chronic ailment" often leading to chaos in the enforcement process. There were few solutions to the problem.' 'China's courts lack the authority and stature to command obedience to their decisions, especially where such decisions affect other government branches and officials' (China Law and Governance Review, 2004).

3.2.2 Under-development of civil law Economic reform has created a political space for the development of private law. Since 1978, a large

---

given level of government is not technically subordinate to the head of government at the same level, the court president's official rank is typically just below, and not equal to, that of the head of government.

[169] For instance, a judge in Fujian who executed a judgment against a local enterprise found his daughter transferred the next day by her employer, the county, to an isolated post on a small island (Tang, 1991, p. 391).

[170] The adjudicative committee consists of the president and other high-ranking Party members within the court.

number of civil and commercial laws have been enacted. It is undeniable that China has started to move away from its traditional viewpoint of overwhelmingly focusing on criminal law and ignoring civil law (*Zhongxing Qingmin*). Nonetheless, the long-term tradition is not easy to change. Given the difficulty in enforcement, many of the laws remain only on the books. As before, the overwhelming majority of transactions still occur outside the formal legal system and are governed by informal mechanisms based on relationships and networks of familial, personal and social connections, which is now known as 'Chinese Capitalism' (Redding, 1990; Jones, 1994; Clarke et al., 2006).

Perhaps there is nowhere where we can see more clearly its impact on the contemporary legal system than in the stock market. Although the stock exchanges were established in 1990, the first Company Law and Securities Law were only enacted in 1993 and 1998 respectively, three years and eight years later. In addition, the 1993 Company Law and 1998 Securities Law were both rough and left many gaps and loopholes to be filled (Gao, 2000). Thus, before and after, the stock market has been mainly governed by regulations imposed by the administrative agency. Moreover, both the 1993 Company Law and 1998 Securities Law maintained almost complete silence on civil liability; for instance, only three provisions in the 1998 Securities Law slightly touched civil liability.[171] By contrast, there are about 30 provisions regarding administrative liability and 18 provisions regarding criminal liability. The 2005 Company Law and 2005 Securities Law made some effort to increase civil liability, but the imbalance still largely remains.

3.2.3 The ambiguous concept of rights   During 1949–1978, the CCP regime pushed the cultural hostility against individualism and dependence upon the state to its extreme. Any claim regarding 'self' would encounter fierce attack.[172] Economic growth has not yet brought major change to this ideology and 'rights' is still an alien notion to most Chinese people. Typically,

---

[171]   Art 192; Art 202; Art 207.

[172]   In his autobiography, Liu Binyan (1990), a former high-ranking CCP cadre, well-known correspondent and dissenter documented his slow discovery that the Party's attack of what he called the 'original sin' of individualism was directed at keeping the masses in line so that the leadership would be free to advance its interests, which could be quite personal and not necessarily in the national interest.

rights are conceived of as grants from the state rather than natural rights which individuals possessed by reason of birth. Justified on utilitarian rather than deontological grounds, rights are not anti-majoritarian trumps of collective interests and the social good but another kind of interest, to be weighed against interests of the group and society as a whole (Peerenboom, 2002, p. 43).

Since rights are granted by the state, it is reasonable that for rights provisions to be programmatic, or for the state to grant rights only to those who are friendly or loyal to it or who are its 'members', and to deprive of rights those who are hostile to its purposes, it is also reasonable for the state to have full powers to restrict them as long as it does so in the same way that it grants them – by legislative enactment. In addition, since the state acts legitimately when it restricts rights by law, no law can be invalid because it restricts rights, and no procedure is needed to determine whether particular laws do violate rights (Nathan, 1985, p. 116). Manifested in the judicial system, Chinese courts have the power to refuse to accept cases brought before them, even doing so will violate individuals' rights of action, as will be illustrated by the SPC's decision on private securities litigation.

3.2.4   Other factors affecting the judicial system

3.2.4.1   JUDICIAL CORRUPTION   Judicial corruption is another major obstacle that obstructs the courts from playing a meaningful role in enforcement. Corruption is an endemic problem in the Chinese legal system (Lubman, 1999; Gong, 2004) that continues, if not intensifies, in contemporary China.[173] Reliable statistics of judicial corruption are not available. The successive reports submitted to the NPC in the recent years by Xiao Yang, the former president of the SPC, may provide some indications. In 2005, it was reported that nearly 470 judges were punished for corruption in each of 2003 and 2004 (SPC 2005 Annual Working Report).[174] On 17 March 2010, the former vice president of the

---

[173]   Certainly, given corruption is a pervasive social problem in China, one can hardly expect judges to be honest when government and party officials from top to bottom are busily filling their pockets.

[174]   It must be pointed out here that this number constituted only a small fraction of the judges that got caught; the majority of them received administrative penalties or were punished by Party rules. For instance, in 1998, former SPC president Ren Jianxin claimed that only 376 judges were punished on criminal grounds between 1992 and 1996. However, it reported that 1654 judges received administrative penalties and 637 were punished by Party rules in the single year

SPC, Huang Songyou, was sentenced to jail for life for taking bribes of 4 million yuan and this case also involved four judges in the SPC (Sina.com, 17 March 2010).

3.2.4.2 JUDICIAL COMPETENCE The low level of judicial competence is also a big concern. Prior to the 1995 Judges Law, there were no objective qualifications in terms of legal training that all judges had to have. Judges might come from military officers (particularly during the 1970s and 1980s), from government institutions, or from lower-level personnel within courts, such as bailiffs, with only a minority from law school graduates or legal professors and researchers. The overall low level of competence of the judiciary has resulted in many incorrectly decided cases. In 1999 people's courts supervised and reviewed 96 739 cases, and corrected the judgment in 21 862 cases (SPC 2000 Annual Working Report). Since 1995, the authorities have taken a number of steps to improve judicial competence and professionalism, such as requiring all judges to pass a national examination, raising the academic standards to qualify as a judge.[175] Despite these laudable reforms, the overall level of judicial competence still remains low, and the courts are likely to suffer from poorly trained judges for at least another generation.[176] The low technical competence casts serious doubts on the efficiency of courts in securities litigation which is highly technical and complicated.

3.3 Private securities litigation in China

As discussed earlier in this book, the effectiveness of private enforcement of law relies on a high-standard court. Given what we have found about the Chinese judicial system, it is hard to believe such weak courts could play any meaningful role in PSL. This has been proved by the difficult progress of PSL: it was not until 2002 that the first PSL against a listed company was accepted by the courts.

---

of 1997. See SPC Annual Working Report (1998), (1999). In addition, the judges who received any form of penalties account for a small proportion of the corrupt judges. Thus, the real extent of judicial corruption would be very striking.

[175] The educational qualifications set by the Judges Law do not apply to the judges in office at the time of its passage.

[176] The best example is the current president of the SPC (also, China's Chief Justice) Wang Shengjun. Wang never went to law school, nor does he have any experience as lawyer, judge or prosecutor.

Before 2002, even if investors wanted to sue for damages, they found little ground in the 1993 Company Law or 1998 Securities Law.[177] Despite this, since 1998, Chinese investors have made continued attempts to seek civil compensation. On 4 December 1998 the first civil suit was filed in Shanghai, where a shareholder brought a suit against Hong Guang Industrial (600083) for financial damages due to the defendant's accounting fraud, following a fine and administrative sanction given to the company by the CSRC. After a long delay, in early 2000 the court dismissed the case.

In spite of the failure of the Hong Guang suit, the large numbers of frauds perpetrated by listed companies had caused investors to bring civil actions against a number of companies around the country, including Ying Guangxia (000557), ST Houwang (000535) and Zheng Baiwen (600898). On 20 September 2001 PSL actions against Yian Technology (000008) were filed simultaneously at the Intermediate People's Court in Beijing, Guangzhou and Shanghai. A wave of lawsuits seemed to be in

---

[177] Arguably, shareholders could rely on the PRC General Principles of Civil Law, which provide that victims of torts are entitled to civil compensation. In addition, the 1993 Company Law, Art 111, which provides that 'if the resolution of a shareholders' meeting or board of directors violate laws or administrative regulations and infringe the legitimate rights and interests of shareholders, the shareholders shall have the right to institute proceedings with a people's court requesting the cessation of such illegal activities and acts of infringement'. Some scholars regarded this as providing the grounds for derivative action, but some disagree. Other sections of the 1993 Company Law spell out statutory duties of officers and directors to the company, and Art 63 states that directors, supervisors and managers shall be liable for damages caused to the company by their violation of law, administrative regulations, or the company's articles of association, but it fails to state that shareholders may enforce the liability on the company's behalf if the company fails to do so. The 1998 Securities Law did not contain general provision for civil liability. Art 63 and Art 207 of the 1998 Securities Law stated that companies and their directors should be held liable for making false statements in prospectuses and annual reports. But it did not contain any detailed rules for how such action should be judged. Art 42 provides that gains from short-swing (6-month period) trading by a 5 per cent shareholder shall belong to the company and shall be recovered in an action initiated by the board of directors. It further states that shareholders may request the board to take action if it fails to do so, and that directors responsible for a failure to take action shall be liable for losses thereby caused to the company. However, it fails to spell out that shareholders may step into the shoes of a recalcitrant board and sue in the name of the company. In any case, these provisions remained on the paper since the SPC had no intention of drafting procedural rules to make them enforceable. See Li (2004); Clarke (2008).

formation which apparently panicked the SPC. The next day, the SPC issued Circular No 406, instructing courts nationwide not to accept PSL temporarily on the ground that the legislative and judicial conditions were not ripe yet. Circular No 46 apparently contradicted Art 163 of the 1998 Securities Law, which granted investors the right to civil compensation.

The decision of the SPC caused intense criticism from investors, legal scholars, practitioners and the CSRC. Four months later, on 15 January 2002, the SPC issued the 'Notice Regarding Civil Lawsuits Against Companies on the Grounds of False Statements' (known as 1.15 *Tongzhi*).[178] The notice dictated that lower courts may accept PSL based on false disclosure and material misrepresentation, subject to the condition that administrative penalty has been imposed for the alleged fraud. Although the notice did open the door for PSL, serious problems remained. First, it explicitly excluded PSL based on other types of claim like insider trading and market manipulation which are the most prevalent, serious abuses in China's stock market. Second, the required precondition of an existing enabling government action added an extra condition for bringing civil litigation outside Art 108 of the Civil Procedure Law. By doing so, it substantially compromised shareholders' rights and was against the principle of judicial independence (at least on paper, this principle is guaranteed by the constitution) (Chen, 2003). Third and probably most important, it rejected class action (*Jituan Susong*),[179] which is found in Art 55 of the 1991 Civil Procedure Law (Li, 2004).[180]

Despite these limitations, the 1.15 *Tongzhi* was welcomed by investors and lawyers and followed by increased numbers of PSL filings around China. Immediately after the promulgation of the 1.15 *Tongzhi*, three investors went ahead to file individual suits in Harbin Intermediate People's Court against Daqing Lianyi (600065) and its management for false disclosure and accounting fraud. Soon afterwards, 767 other investors sued the same defendants for the same claim. By the end of 2002, nearly 900 PSL suits against ten companies had been filed, some of which were accepted by the courts (Chen, 2003). However, due to the

---

[178] It contained only 6 articles in total.

[179] An equivalent term in Chinese to class action (*Jituan Susong*) is the term representative litigation (*Daibiaoren Susong*), provided in Art 55 of the Civil Procedure Law, 1991. Academic literature in China often uses *Jituan Susong* to replace *Daibiaoren Susong*, or use the terms interchangeably.

[180] Enacted in 1991, revised in 2007.

lack of detailed rules regarding the calculation of losses and the estab-lishment of a causal link between losses and falsified accounts, the cases were stalled as judges waited for further guidelines from the SPC[181] (Chen, 2003; Li, 2004).

On 9 January 2003 the SPC issued detailed rules on PSL: 'Several Rules on Adjudicating Civil Lawsuits against Listed Companies on the Ground of False Statements' (known as 1.9. *Guiding*). The 1.9 *Guiding* contained 37 articles and is the most detailed legal interpretation of the Securities Law. However, it did not bring changes to the key issues in 1.15 *Tongzhi*: PSL is still limited to false disclosure; the requirement of government action as the precondition remains.[182] Class action is still not permitted. In addition, it imposed new restrictions. Among other things, Art 9 provides that all PSL lawsuits must be filed with the intermediate court of the jurisdiction in which the listed firms is headquartered. This provision is inconsistent with the 1991 Civil Procedure Law which allows the plaintiff to choose jurisdiction between the plaintiff's local court and the defendant's.[183] Given the local protectionism pointed out before, this is apparently in favour of fraudulent listed companies at the cost of shareholders' rights.

Although the 1.9. *Guiding* lays out some useful rules that should enable courts better to handle PSL cases and since early 2003, a few additional cases have been heard, in practice, the courts still remain uncertain about how to apply rules. As a result, by the end of 2003, although a small number of settlements have been reached, not a single case has been resolved through adjudication by the courts (China Securities Journal, 30 December 2003).

The 2005 Company Law finally established a system of PSL. Article 152 formally allows shareholders to directly file a lawsuit in their own name on the condition that they separately or in the aggregate hold 1 per cent or more of the total shares of the company for more than 180 days and must make a demand on the company first. The 2005 Securities Law also extends civil liability to insider trading and market manipulation.[184] However, there is a lack of any procedural guidance that will make them

---

[181]   Several cases have been settled out of court.

[182]   Though it did enlarge the preconditions required to sue listed companies to include criminal verdicts against company directors and administrative sanc-tions given by relevant government organs such as the MOF. Art 6.

[183]   1991 Civil Procedure Law, Art 29.

[184]   Arts 76, 77.

enforceable.[185] After 15 years' debate, the significance of PSL has been widely recognized, thus, this legislative flaw could only be regarded as an intentional omission aimed at restricting PSL that might cause substantial losses to state-owned listed companies along with powerful elites.

Legal obstacles clearly inhibit PSL from playing a useful role in enforcement. From 2000 to 2006, only 99 companies have been suit-eligible as a result of CSRC administrative sanctions. It is estimated that an additional 20 listed companies are suit-eligible as a result of criminal judgments or the MOF sanctions. Thus, the total number of suit-eligible companies appears to be approximately 120 (Liebman and Milhaupt, 2008). Among them, it is suggested that roughly 20 companies have in fact been sued in this period (Shanghai Securities News, 28 April 2006). The rate of filing suit is about 17 per cent, or put differently, approximately 83 per cent of the eligible target companies have not been sued. It looks particularly dismal if we consider that the factual finding of wrongdoing has already been made and plaintiffs simply need to show that they were harmed by the fraud.

In addition, the progress of cases seems to be very slow. For instance, in Daqin Lianyi's case, since the court insisted on individual actions (*Dandu Susong*), the court took two months to accept and heard only 94 out of the 770 suits and took two years to reach judgment. So far, only a handful of cases have resulted in a judgment in favour of plaintiffs; a small number have settled. Comprehensive data on such outcomes is unavailable, but according to a report, up to April 2006, among the 20 cases that were accepted by the courts, only two cases have resulted in court judgments ordering compensation to plaintiffs and another four cases have resulted in settlements (Shanghai Securities News, 28 April 2006). Many of these judgments and settlements have yet to be enforced.[186]

In total, compared to the weak public enforcement, private enforcement of law in China's stock market could be described as negligible. It should not be a surprise to anyone who is familiar with Chinese legal tradition and culture. By the same token, I have serious doubts about any

---

[185] For a detailed discussion on the flaws of Art 152, See Tan and Wang (2007).

[186] For instance, the investors in Daqing Lianyi (600065) received the final judgment from Heilongjiang Provisional Court in December 2004, nearly three years after the case was accepted. But it was not until December 2006 that they actually received compensation (Shanghai Securities News, 5 December 2006).

optimistic claim about PSL.[187] The enhancement of PSL needs fundamental social changes which will take years, even a century, to complete.

CONCLUDING REMARKS

In this chapter, the enforcement mechanisms in China's stock market
have been systematically examined. It has been found that neither
informal nor formal enforcement could be said to be effective. The
dominance of state ownership has significantly undermined the foundation of self-enforcement. State ownership results in a severe split
between controllers' short-term and long-term interests. Neither representatives of large shareholders nor managers have sufficient cash flow
rights that could force them to take future costs of the current gains into
account. In addition, state ownership also leads to the politicization of
managers. Accordingly, market mechanisms that work well for professional managers only have limited effect on the bureaucrat-managers.

Non-state third-party enforcement is also dysfunctional. The primary
reason is the lack of genuinely autonomous third-party enforcers, as a
result of Chinese centralization tradition and the CCP's rigid social
control. Stock exchanges or securities associations all operate as a
macro-organ of the CSRC and have little rule-making or punishment
power. Moreover, the strict control of IPO supply by the CSRC has
created a risk-free IPO market, which fundamentally destroyed the basis
of financial intermediaries. Although the media has played a remarkable
role in enforcement, it is facing insurmountable obstacles created by the
CCP.

Formal enforcement is weak. At the root of the weakness is the nature
of the state. China still remains at the stage of a 'natural state' where
powerful elites are only constrained by the power of others, not by the
rules. Additional reasons for weak public enforcement include multiple
objectives of the regulator, the conflicting role of the state, regulatory
corruption and so on. The negligible role of PSL could be attributed to

---

[187]   It is particularly noticeable that China has experienced a shift away from
the legal reform principles that Chinese authorities have pursued since the 1980s.
As a result of political concerns regarding social stability, Chinese authorities
have shifted away from dispute resolution models emphasizing court adjudication according to legal norms. In their place, Chinese authorities are reviving
dispute resolution models that emphasize Party-led mediation practices according
to flexible norms, and that seek to prevent outbreaks of social unrest and mass
citizen petitioning to higher authorities. For details, See Minzner (2011).

the lack of judicial independence and authority, under-development of civil law, ambiguous concepts of rights, judicial corruption and so forth, which are the legacy of Chinese legal tradition.

The weak enforcement in China's stock market raises a question: how did China's stock market develop in the absence of any form of effective enforcement? Does China present a counter-example to my 'enforcement matters' thesis? What can explain this obvious deviation? This question will be answered in the next chapter.

4. Developing a capital market under weak enforcement

INTRODUCTION

This chapter attempts to provide an explanation for the development of China's stock market which is clearly inconsistent with my 'enforcement matters' thesis. It contains four sections. Section 1 casts some doubts on the often quoted data on China's stock market. It takes a second look at the real size of market capitalization and the number of investors. Section 2 raises a critique of the argument by Pistor and Xu (2005). Pistor and Xu (2005) claimed that the fact that China's stock market avoided the failure of other transition economies should be attributed to its adoption of the quota system to fill the governance vacuum during the initial period. Section 3 provides an alternative explanation. It argues that China's stock market is driven by four factors: state guarantee, rent seeking, speculation and financial repression. Section 4 draws attention to the inefficiency of the stock market. It points out that although China's stock market expanded quickly in the absence of effective enforcement, it displays serious deviation from the macro economy and extreme volatility.

I. A SECOND LOOK AT THE CHINESE STOCK MARKET

In Chapter 1, I established the thesis that enforcement is crucial to the development of a capital market. In the absence of any form of effective enforcement, a capital market will not develop. In Chapter 3, I examined the enforcement mechanisms in the Chinese securities market and found that neither formal nor informal enforcement mechanisms are effective. As a result, an under-developed stock market may be observed in China.

However, the Chinese stock market seems to present a counter-example. By the end of 2008, there were a total of 1625 companies (including both A-share and B-share) listing on China's two stock exchanges with 2 452 284 billion outstanding shares and the combined market capitalization reached 12.13 trillion yuan. Investors' accounts totalled 152 million and 107 securities companies had been set up with total assets of 1.1912 trillion yuan (CSRC 2008 Annual Report). Impressive indeed. Especially compared to China's former socialist counterparts such as the Czech Republic and Russia. A question arises then, does China challenge my thesis that enforcement matters? If not, how do we explain this obvious deviation? In this chapter, I attempt to provide a systematic explanation.

The first step is to take a second look at the Chinese securities market. This reveals that the data shown above is misleading, and the actual size of the Chinese stock market is much smaller than originally suggested.

1. Market Capitalization

The combined market capitalization of 12.13 trillion yuan would have ranked China around fourth in the world by the end of 2008. Nevertheless, such a calculation is very problematic. As previously mentioned, two-thirds of shares in Chinese listed companies are non-tradable which led them to sell at a large discount to tradable shares, sometimes by as much as 90 per cent (Chen and Peng, 2002; Walter and Howie, 2003, p. 186). If this is taken into account, then the realistic valuation would be much lower; for instance, the capitalization of free-floating shares was only 4.52 trillion yuan in 2008 (CSRC 2008 Annual Report).

In addition, when we measure the Chinese stock market by looking at market capitalization as a percentage of GDP, we find it is not only smaller than developed countries, but also smaller than some transition countries. For example, in 2006, the United States showed 148 per cent, Hong Kong showed 904 per cent, and other transition economies such as Poland, Russia and the Czech Republic showed 44 per cent, 107 per cent and 34 per cent respectively. By contrast, China showed only 6 per cent (World Bank, 2006).

2. The Number of Investors

The number of investors is also significantly overestimated. The fact that there are 152 million investors' accounts by no means indicates that there are 152 million investors. First, the majority of investors hold duplicate accounts – one in the SHSE and one in the SZSE. Thus, the figures are double counted. Second, many counterfeit accounts are illegally opened by major market players such as securities companies, fund management companies or wealthy individuals to manipulate share trading.[1] Third, many accounts are opened only for entry into IPO lotteries, since the larger the number of accounts one controls, the greater the chances of gaining the right to buy IPO shares. Fourth, many accounts are dormant and disused after their holders sustained losses and interests in the market. As a consequence, a generous estimate would suggest that active investors represent one-third of 152 million share accounts; some estimate that this fraction is only one-tenth (The SZSE, 2007;[2] Walter and Howie, 2003, p. 148).

In sum, a careful examination reveals that the Chinese stock market is much smaller than some figures suggest. Even so, considering its short history, it is still a remarkable achievement by any measure. How can we explain its growth under weak enforcement?

II.   ARE PISTOR AND XU CORRECT?

Interestingly, in the burgeoning literature on the Chinese stock market, the question of how it developed has rarely been studied. Among the few, Pistor and Xu (2005) presented a systematic explanation to the puzzle.

1.   Pistor and Xu's Argument

Acknowledging the marginal role that formal law and enforcement have played in China's stock market development, Pistor and Xu argued that China avoided the failure of other transition economies as a result of its reliance on the quota system that filled the governance vacuum during the early stage.

As noted previously, during 1993–2000 (de facto until 2004), a quota system was adopted to select companies that issue shares. Pistor and Xu (2005) argued that under the quota system, the owners of the firms, i.e. local governments or central ministries, were assigned the responsibility of collecting and verifying information regarding the firms. In

---

[1]   It is well known that such players use false identification sourced by sending professional runners into the countryside to buy peasant identity cards in bulk. It is normal for them to control thousands of different trading accounts. See Walter and Howie (2003).

[2]   The SZSE shows that during the period of 2005, 2006, and January to August of 2007, total numbers of accounts which actually held shares averaged 11.2 million, 10.6 million, and 11.8 million respectively, representing 33 per cent, 28 per cent and 26 per cent of the total accounts opened with the SZSE during the same periods. See the SZSE Report (2007).

order to compete with other regions in economic performance, which is crucial to their career advancement, regional bureaucrats had an incentive to select more over less viable companies to list since good performance of listing companies could bring more quotas (that is to say, more equity finance) to the region, while delisting or forced bail-out would tarnish their economic performance records. By creating such an incentive structure, the quota system functioned as an alternative to information mechanisms normally relied upon in mature markets and helped mitigate the serious information problem investors and regulators face in transition economies.

2. Critique of Pistor and Xu

In theory, Pistor and Xu's argument sounds reasonable; in reality, however, it is quite problematic. Key to their argument is the assumption that the performance of listed companies is important to economic performance (via bringing more equity finance), which in turn is crucial to regional bureaucrats' career advancement. I believe this assumption is questionable.

First, it clearly overestimated the importance of equity finance to regional economics. As shown in Chapter 3, even today, banking finance still absolutely dominates external finance and equity finance remains insignificant. Thus, the benefit brought by choosing good-quality companies is limited.

Second, it seemed to misunderstand the assigned role of the equity market. As repeatedly mentioned, the fundamental role of the stock market in China is to finance SOEs, particularly in the early stages. Certainly, the central government has an interest in developing a healthy, efficient market, but this is at best secondary and often subordinate to other political goals. A significant fact that has been completely ignored by Pistor and Xu is that, in order to serve Zhu Rongji's 'get large and medium SOEs out of difficulty in three years' plan, in 1997 the CSRC issued a circular in which it stated that the priority of listing would be given to companies that acquired or merged with loss-making SOEs.[3] As a consequence, during 1997–1999, the so-called 'bundled listing' (*Kunbang Shangshi*) became prevalent, which allowed a poorly operated company to be listed through bundling with a good one. In such

---

[3]   The CSRC, Circular Regarding Share Issuance in 1997 (*Guanyu Zuohao 1997 Gupiao Fangxing Gongzuo de Tongzhi*), available at http://www.chinaacc. com/new/63/69/112/1997/9/ad63194301110197991l8530.htm.

circumstances, neither the regulator nor the local officials had the incentive to select good companies as suggested by Pistor and Xu.

Third, the punishment is not credible. It could be argued in order to avoid the embarrassment caused by delisting, local officials would prefer good companies to poor. However, in the Chinese stock market, delisting is far from a simple, economic issue, rather, it involves complicated political bargaining between various parties[4] and therefore rarely occurs. In the 20-years history of the stock market, only a total of 41 companies have been delisted (CSRC, the Development Report). In regard to another punishment, forced bail-out, it would be an oversimplification to emphasize its negative impact on regional economics. First, if the company was already on the verge of bankruptcy before listing, bail-out would cause no additional burden to the local governments. Second, the costs of bail-out could soon be offset by the funds it raised from the market, as long as the local governments could help maintain the precious listing quota.[5]

Last, but probably most important, the argument assumes that local officials have no other personal interests in the selection process, which is simply naïve. In fact, the quota system created a fertile soil for rent seeking and corruption. Companies seeking listing often bribed officials by offering cheap or free shares and the personal gains were too huge to resist. Reported cases revealed the dirty deals between listing companies and government officials. An example is the well-known Kang Sai (600745) case. Kang Sai group was a company located in Huangshi City, Hu Bei Province, which listed in the SHSE in 1996. It was discovered that during 1993–1996, in order to list, it offered bribery in the forms of cheap employee shares and cash to about 100 officials at various levels, including two ministerial officials,[6] deputy provincial governor and deputy secretary of Huangshi municipal Party Commission (Yuan, 2004). Kang Sai is by no means an isolated case: in Hu Bei Province alone, Xing Hua Gufen (600886) and Xing Fu Shiye (600743) broke similar scandals around the same period.[7]

---

[4]   In particular, between local governments and the CSRC.

[5]   As discussed in chapter 2, the funds of listing companies are often tunnelled into their owners, i.e. the local governments.

[6]   They are Xu Penghang, alternate member of the Central Committee and Wu Wenying, the president of China National Textile Council. Like many other cases, they were only dismissed in addition to an inner-Party disciplinary measure and did not receive any criminal penalty. For details, see Yuan (2004).

[7]   Similarly, it was discovered that 17 bureau-level officials and 44 county-level officials bought employee shares in Daqing Lianyi (600065).

The dysfunction of the quota system was reflected in at least two ways. First, they allowed the wrong types of company to be listed. It wrongfully allowed so many processing, commercial and real estate companies to list, which wasted IPO proceeds on unproductive and speculative ventures (Chen, 1997). In 1993, even when the central government had already released guidelines that banned such firms from listing, 16 per cent of listing firms were commercial or real estate companies. Provisional leaders were keen backers of such firms because of their potential for making large profits quickly (Green, 2004, p. 78). Second, as discussed in Chapter 3, not only was the quality of companies coming to market poor, but many firms faked their entire financial histories, presumably with the support of local officials.

To summarize, in my opinion, Pistor and Xu's argument is questionable. Their proposition of relying on administrative measures to fill the governance vacuum is problematic, at least in China where public governance quality is poor.

III. AN ALTERNATIVE EXPLANATION

I attempt to offer an alternative explanation to the China Puzzle. I believe China's stock market is mainly driven by four factors: state guarantee, rent seeking, speculation and financial repression.

1. State Guarantee

Key to the Chinese stock market is the guarantee provided by the state that it will not allow the market to be closed down. In a normal stock market, where the companies are privately owned and the state only plays the role of enforcer, investors face real risks that the market might collapse and their investments would be lost forever, as observed in many countries.[8] Certainly, no state would like to watch its market collapse, but it has neither sufficient incentive nor the capability to prevent it. Things are different in China. As noted before, the state is the biggest player in the market. Apart from the actual money put up by investors, almost everything in the system belongs to the state. The state ownership of the stock market sends investors a signal that the state will not allow the

---

[8] Although there are some companies that are too big to fail, they constitute only a small fraction. The majority of the companies cannot expect bail-out from the government.

market to collapse. Although it is doubtful to what extent the state actually has such capability, especially when the market grows big, what matters is investors believe it. Also, the state has indulged, if not strengthened, such belief by constant bail-out.

1.1 Bail-out of listed companies

Where listed companies are privately owned, investors face a real risk that the company might go bankrupt and their stocks become worthless paper, therefore they might be more cautious about what they invest in. By contrast, in China, investors have less concern about the quality of listed companies since most of them are supported by the government, which will bail them out whenever needed.

The government has many reasons to bail out its companies. For one thing, listed companies are usually important to local economics in terms of taxation and employment, in particular in less developed regions. Second, as noted above, the costs of bail-out could be covered by the funds raised from the stock market as long as this can help the company maintain listing. In addition, government officials also have a strong incentive to bail out companies. Since the news of bail-out usually drives share prices up sharply, it provides those involved in the process an opportunity to make a fortune via insider trading. As a recent example, it is reported that several officials of Gao Chun county were involved in insider trading during the restructuring of ST Gao Chun Ceramics (600502). Among them, Liu Baochun, the director of Nanjing Economic Commission, one of the three key persons in the restructure, was arrested. He made a profit of 7.38 million yuan within one month (Legal Daily, 6 January 2010).

Table 4.1 shows subsidies from government in China's listed companies during 1992–2003.

Constant and prevailing government bail-outs result in some peculiar phenomena in China's stock market. One is the extremely low delisting rate. Only 41 companies have been delisted which is around 2.3 per cent of the total listed companies and the annual listing rate is around 0.1–0.2 per cent. The last delisting in the SZSE occurred in July, 2007. Another is the 'ST puzzle'. As noted in Chapter 3, ST shares are often traded at prices higher than good-performance companies, even where net assets per share are negative. Apart from the reason pointed out before, the most important reason probably is the investors' belief that the government will arrange some sort of rescue that will keep them happy. ST restructure stocks therefore have always been the darling of Chinese

Table 4.1 Subsidies from government in China's listed companies 1992–2003

Year	Number of listed companies	Number of listed companies receiving subsidies from the government	Subsidies as a percentage of operating profits	Percentage of listed companies receiving subsidies from government
1992	52	0	0	0
1993	176	1	29.41	0.57
1994	283	23	21.21	8.13
1995	307	70	14.00	22.80
1996	510	112	12.71	21.96
1997	715	150	11.41	20.98
1998	821	405	22.26	49.33
1999	918	510	17.18	55.56
2000	1054	506	10.98	48.01
2001	1132	567	17.11	50.09
2002	1188	631	13.14	53.11
2003	1263	713	8.84	56.45
Average			14.17	43.81

Source: China Stock Market & Accounting Research Database, quoted from Wong (2006, p. 418)

investors, including the best fund manager, Wang Yawei.[9] This also partly explained the drastic reaction to the State Council's sale of state shares plan in 2001. The concern that the state would withdraw its support along with the dramatic increase in share supply triggered a 4-year bear market and the Shanghai Composite Index dropped from 2245 to 998.23.[10]

In sum, state ownership and its implicit guarantee reduced ownership risk and induced investors to jump into the stock market, although a serious consideration would suggest that this is no more than a transfer of public wealth from taxpayers to shareholders, and shifts the risks from current shareholders to prospective investors.

[9] The manager of Huaxia Fund Management Company.
[10] 2245 on 14 June 2001; 998.23 on 6 June 2005: data source, the SHSE.

1.2   Bail-out of investment banks

Investment banks are major players in the stock market and without them, the market could not function. In 2002, China's investment banks created an industry-wide crisis. If the central government had not intervened, the whole industry would have gone bankrupt and the market might have collapsed.

In fact, before 2002, several major investment banks had experienced serious crises, one after another. Among them, the most shocking was the collapse of the then biggest securities company, Wan Guo Securities Company, which directly led to the closure of the Treasury Bond Futures (TBF) market. TBF 327 was a three-year contract expiring in June 1995. Analysts at Wan Guo expected the price of the contract to fall, thus they sold short. By 23 February 1995, Wan Guo held a short position of some 3 million contracts, six times the maximum set by the SHSE. Liaoning Guo Fa, another state-owned securities company, held a similar position. A MOF-owned company, China Economic Development Trust Investment Company (Zhong Jing Kai), took the opposite position on the 327 contract. It was widely believed that Zhong Jing Kai already had knowledge of what was to happen next.[11] On the evening of 22 February 1995 the MOF announced its Treasury bond issuance volume for 1995, with only one-third of the volume that Wan Guo had been expecting and with higher interest rates. As a result, the price of 327 rose from 148.5 yuan to 151.98 yuan. Facing catastrophic losses, Wan Guo sold 10.6 million 327 contracts in the last eight minutes of trading, which forced the price back down to 147.5 yuan. Such a sudden fall in the price became a disaster for other market players. As the market closed, around 20 financial firms faced bankruptcy with potential losses in excess of 1 billion yuan. Nevertheless, in the evening, the SHSE announced that all TBF trades that had taken place after 4.22 p.m. were cancelled and the market was suspended for the renegotiation of the contracts for three days. This decision saved Zhong Jing Kai and its allies but pushed Wan Guo into the abyss. On 18 May the TBF market was ordered to close down (Xia, 1996; Green, 2004). Wan Guo merged with another major Shanghai securities company, Shen Yin Securities,[12] under the arrangement of their common owner – the Shanghai government. It remains unknown how much it cost the Shanghai government, but considering

[11]   It is hardly a surprise given its Board Chairman was the vice minister of the MOF, Tian Yinong and the first three general managers were all MOF officials. See Caijing, 18 June 2002; Yuan (2004).

[12]   Now known as Shenyin Wanguo.

Wan Guo lost around 2 billion yuan in 327, it would not be less than 1.5 billion yuan.[13]

The 327 incident is significantly important in the history of China's capital market, not only because it caused the collapse of Wan Guo and closure of the TBF market, but, more importantly, it highlighted the danger of the Chinese securities market where someone could peek at their opponents' cards.[14] Worse still, even the winner, Zhong Jing Kai, did not look good. Despite the calculated profits reaching 7 billion yuan, Zhong Jing Kai only received less than 0.1 billion, one-seventh of the total (Caijing, 18 June 2002). Then where did the money go? It went to the insiders. The 327 incident created a good number of millionaires overnight. To name but a few, Wei Dong (then MOF official, the trader of Zhong Jing Kai), Xu Weiguo and Chen Shupeng all made their fortunes in the 327 incident.[15] Moreover, the disposal of Wan Guo set a terrible precedent that spurred other investment banks to bet on risky investments, the consequences of which were to be seen not long after.

As mentioned in Chapter 3, most Chinese investment banks are owned by the state and therefore suffer from similar deficiencies as other SOEs. Weak corporate governance and internal control resulted in blind expansion and wild speculation. Many (if not all) were also found engaging in illegal activities such as market manipulation, misappropriation of clients' capital and insider trading. From 2002 to 2005 there were four consecutive years of losses across the industry. By the end of 2004, the total net assets of the entire industry reduced to only 96 billion yuan, among which 48.74 billion were non-performing assets, more than 51 per cent (Beijing Youth Daily, 25 July 2004). But this was just the tip of the iceberg. The real problem lay in the misappropriation of clients' capital and asset management services.

The CSRC survey revealed that misappropriation of clients' capital amounted to 60 billion yuan (Beijing Youth Daily, 25 July 2004). Conservatively estimated, the overall scale of asset management funds

[13]   Recently, in his autobiography, the then general manager of Shen Yin Securities, Kan Zhidong, disclosed that at the time of merging, the assessed net assets of Wan Guo were 0.66 billion yuan, among which, however, several hundred million were fabricated. See Kan (2010).

[14]   That is the reason why Wu Jinglian claimed it is worse than a casino. Even a big player like Wan Guo ended up in disaster in such a game, let alone retail investors.

[15]   After the 327 incident, Wei Dong left the MOF and set up Guo Jin Securities; Xu Weiguo set up Da Peng Securities; Chen Shupeng established Guo Yuan Securities.

reached 100 billion yuan (Huang, 2004). Most of them operated off balance sheet because securities companies guaranteed clients returns ranging from 6 to 15 per cent, which was explicitly prohibited by the Securities Law.[16] These funds were mainly used by securities companies or third parties for market manipulation. Given the plunge of the stock market, a considerable portion of them would be unable to recover. Taken together, the Chinese securities industry was technically bankrupt.

This time the central government took a stand. On 5 November 2004 the PBOC, the MOF, the CSRC and the China Banking Regulatory Commission (CBRC) jointly issued an 'Opinion on Acquiring Individual Debts and Customers' Securities Transaction Settlement Funds' (*Geren Zhaiquan ji Kehu Jiaoyi Jiesuanjin Shougou Yijian*),[17] which guaranteed to repay customers securities transaction settlement funds in full; to repay individual debts under 0.1 million yuan in full; and to repay 90 per cent of individual debts above 0.1 million yuan. The funds mainly came from the PBOC re-loans, which were estimated to be 60 billion yuan (21st Century Economic Report, 24 November 2004).

In addition, in June 2005, Central Huijin injected 10 billion yuan into Galaxy Securities; in August 2005 Huijin and the MOF jointly set up China Galaxy Financial Holding with total capital of 7 billion yuan, which in turn acquired Galaxy Securities in 2007; in August 2005 it injected 2.5 billion yuan into Shenyin Wanguo, and provided additional loans of 1.5 billion yuan for liquidity support; it injected 1 billion yuan into Guotai Junan, and provided additional loans of 1.5 billion yuan for liquidity support.[18] Its subsidiary, China Jianyin Investment (Jianyin), assumed the responsibility of restructuring local, smaller securities companies. It reported that it injected a total of 10 billion yuan into dozens of companies such as West Southern Securities and Xiang Cai Securities[19] (Economic Observer, 23 October 2005).

Last but not least, the PBOC provided an unknown number of loans to the China Securities Depository and Clearing Corporation (CSDCC) to cover the losses incurred by asset management. Asset management attracted many individuals, but the lion's share came from institutions, in particular SOEs. Since SOEs were prohibited from short-term share

---

[16]   1998 Securities Law, Art 143; 2005 Securities Law, Art 144.

[17]   Available at http://www.chinaclear.cn/main/09/0903/1163805430187.pdf.

[18]   As a return, Huijin received a 78.57 per cent shareholding in Galaxy, 37.23 per cent in Shenyin Wanguo, and 21.28 per cent in Guotai Junan. See the Huijin website at http://www.huijin-inv.cn/investments/investments_2008.html.

[19]   2 billion yuan each.

trading until 2005,[20] the asset management between the SOEs and securities company usually took the form of treasury bonds (TBs) repo. The SOE deposited TBs in the security company, which allowed the latter (or a third-party via security companies) to use the repo funds. Once the security company was in crisis, the TBs would be at stake, which in turn endangered the operation of the CSDCC. Thus, although the PBOC did not assume institutional debts, it had to save the CSDCC. The figure was never made public, but considering the severity of the problem, it would be rather striking.

The intervention of central government saved the security industry and arguably stabilized the market. However, to what extent the bail-out could be justified is questionable. First, unlike commercial banks, the bankruptcy of investment banks will not cause systematic risk, especially considering the small size of the Chinese securities industry. Second, it did not touch the roots of the problem – state ownership and lack of accountability. Simply centralizing control of securities companies was unlikely to enhance governance quality. Most importantly, it aggregated the moral hazard problem that caused the crisis in the first place.

In sum, I believe the presence of state ownership and its implicit guarantee is the key to the development of China's capital market. It allows the listed companies and other major players to expand rapidly without a reputation that takes years to build. However, as shown above, it incurs substantial costs and constant redistribution of wealth.

2. Institutional Rent Seeking by SOEs

The growth and the liquidity of a stock market essentially depend on the demand for and the supply of the funds. It is often simply assumed that there is a strong demand for equity financing, but there is not. Modern corporate finance theory suggests that since the adverse selection problem is most severe in equity financing, outside investors will demand a higher rate of return on equity than on debt. Therefore, from the perspective of those inside the firm, retained earnings are a better source of funds than is debt, and debt is a better deal than equity financing. This is known as the pecking order theory (Myers, 1984; Myers and Majluf,

---

[20] 1998 Securities Law, Art 76 barred SOEs from share trading at all; in September 1999, the CSRC relaxed the restriction on the condition that the holding period should be no less than 6 months. 'Circular Regarding Legal Person Selling Off' (*Guanyu Faren Peishou Gupiao Youguan Wenti de Tongzhi*) available at http://www.csrc.gov.cn/n575458/n575742/n2529771/2619378.html.

1984). Empirical evidence finds strong support for this prediction (Hubbard, 1997).[21] In particular, despite having the most developed stock market, since 1994, American enterprises generally stopped raising funds through shares issuance. Instead, they largely repurchased outstanding shares. As a consequence, the net amounts of share issuance were actually negative (China Securities Journal, 15 December 1997).[22]

By contrast, Chinese listed companies display a strong preference for external financing, in particular, for equity financing. They would consider equity financing first, followed by debt and last retained earnings (Huang and Zhang, 2002; Wan et al. 2002). Aside from the intensive competition for IPOs, those already listed were also very keen for post-IPO issuance, even though this would dilute their shareholdings.[23] The excessive demand for equity financing is another important factor that explains the growth of China's stock market.

Then a question arises, why do Chinese companies have a different finance preference? What accounts for this peculiarity? I believe Chinese companies' strong preference for equity financing is mainly created by certain institutional arrangements that very much favour issuers and therefore provide them with considerable rents to capture.

2.1   Rents through equity issuance – a game of quan qian

In China's stock market, minority shareholders usually describe equity financing as *quan qian*, a phrase that means 'free lunch style' funds-raising. It sounds cynical, but the phrase does catch the core of the problem: in China's stock market, equity financing becomes an institutional expropriation of tradable shareholders by non-tradable shareholders. The game runs as follows.

In order to prevent state assets draining away, it provides that the conversion ratio of state capital stock to state net assets shall not be lower than 65 per cent, which means, 1 yuan of state assets shall be converted

---

[21]   It finds that during 1970s and 1980s, in 7 Western countries, the US, Canada, France, Germany, Italy, the UK and Japan, average internal financing constituted 55.71 per cent and external financing was 44.29 per cent, among which equity financing was only 10.86 per cent. See Hubbard (1997), quoted from Wan et al, (2002).

[22]   Data source: Federal Reserve Board, quoted from China Securities Journal, 15 December 1997.

[23]   From 31 January 1990 to 31 January 2011, 1017 listed companies made rights offerings and 799 made secondary offerings. Data source, TX Investment Consulting.

to at least 0.65 shares.[24] Suppose there is one SOE with total assets of 3000 yuan[25] and plans to raise funds of 7000 yuan via shares issuance. Taking the 65 per cent bottom line, 3000 yuan assets will convert into 1950 shares, 1.5 yuan per share. Now recall what we mentioned in Chapter 2, that in order to maintain state control over the company, only 30 per cent of shares are allowed to be issued to the public, that is to say, public investors pay 7000 yuan for 835 shares, about 8.3 yuan per share. After an IPO, the total assets of the company amount to 10 000 yuan with total 2785 shares. The non-tradable shareholder's initial investment was 3000 yuan now becomes 7000 yuan; by contrast, the tradable shareholders' invested 7000 yuan now decreases to 3000 yuan.

Next consider the case of a rights offering. The plan is that every ten shares are allotted four shares, at a price of 5 yuan. As in most cases, the non-tradable shareholder gives up its alloted shares and tradable shareholders fully subscribe to their allocated shares.[26] After the rights offering, the company now has 3119 shares and total assets of 11 670 yuan. Non-tradable shareholders now hold about 62.5 per cent of shares, worth 7293.8 yuan. Tradable shareholders now hold 37.5 per cent of shares, worth 4376.3 yuan.

This is followed by a secondary offering. The plan is to issue another 500 shares to the public investors, at a price of 20 yuan per share. Now the company has a total of 3619 shares and total assets of 21 670 yuan. Non-tradable shareholders' shareholding decreased to about 53.9 per cent, worth 11 680 yuan. Tradable shareholders' shareholding increased to 46.1 per cent, worth 9990 yuan.

Taken together, the non-tradable shareholders' initial investment of 3000 yuan now increases to 11 680 yuan. By contrast, public investors' invested total 18 670 yuan now becomes 9990 yuan. A sum of 8680 yuan has been transferred from tradable shareholders to non-tradable share-holders and I believe they are institutional rents designed for the issuers to capture. This is not a theoretical assumption but a real story that is occurring in China's stock market every day.

---

[24]   State-owned Assets Administration Bureau and State Commission for Economic Restructuring: Interim Measures for the Management of State Share-holding in Joint-stock Companies (*Gufen Youxian Gongsi Guoyu Guquan Guanli Zanxing Banfa*) 1994, Art 12.

[25]   A small figure is used for ease of calculation.

[26]   State shareholders on average subscribed to only about 30 per cent of the shares allocated to them; while tradable shareholders tended to fully subscribe to their allocated shares since rights offerings tended to be priced at 65 per cent of the current market price. See Wong (2006, pp. 404–405).

The weak corporate governance of Chinese listed companies also intensified the rent-seeking problem. The absolute dominance of non-tradable shareholders over the board and the shareholders' general meeting ensures that they can get whatever they want and leaves few options to tradable shareholders. Tradable shareholders can only vote with their feet or accept being diluted, both painful. For instance, on 21 January 2008 Ping An (601318) shocked the market by its 160 million yuan funds-raising plan, although it was less than one year since its IPO in the SHSE.[27] The funds plan was 4.19 times its IPO and 60 billion yuan more than its total net assets. More ridiculous, there was not even an investment plan. However, in spite of the fierce objection by retail shareholders, such a plan was still passed in general meeting with 92 per cent voting yes. Retail investors were forced to vote with their feet. By 25 February the stock price of Ping An had dropped from 98.21 yuan to 65.01 yuan (Southern Weekend, 21 March 2008). In addition, as pointed out in previous chapters, Chinese listed companies also suffer from an insider control problem. Thus, raising funds at the cost of shareholding dilution might not be in the controlling shareholder's interests, but it is clearly favoured by the management, whose private interests largely depend on the scale of free cash flow that they can control, particularly considering the short time horizon of Chinese management.

Table 4.2 provides IPO data of three listed companies and shows the rents captured by the state shareholder through IPOs.

It is worth noting that in the Chinese stock market, proceeds from post-IPO issuance are equivalent to that from IPO, sometimes even higher,[28] thus, the total rents scale should be nearly doubled.

2.2   Rents from entry regulation – the shell value

Until today, entry to and exit from the stock market has still been tightly controlled by the CSRC. Strict regulation makes listing qualification a scarce resource and thereby creates substantial rents for listed companies. Reflecting on stock prices, some companies still trade at a high price where the underlying value become negative and has lost the support of

---

[27]   Ping An launched its IPO in the SHSE on 1 March 2007. See Ping An of China, Listing Notice, available at http://ir.pingan.com/upload/201101270 81548810.pdf.

[28]   For instance, in 2008, proceeds were 103 438 billion yuan from IPO, 227 181 billion yuan from secondary offering, and 15 157 billion yuan from rights offering; see CSRC 2008 Annual Report.

Table 4.2   Rents captured by the state shareholder through IPOs

Name of shares	Wu Liang Ye (000858)	Jin Yu Group (000201)	Ben Gang Ban Cai (000761)
Total shares (million)	320	97	1136
Tradable A-shares (million)	80	35	120
Issuing Price (RMB yuan)	14.77	6.83	5.40
Conversion ratio of state capital stake/state net assets (%)	66.2	100	66.7
Shareholding of the first largest shareholder (%)	75	20.6	54.23
Proportion of capital contribution by the first largest shareholder (%)	23.5	6.6	42.9
Shareholding of public investors (%)	25	36.1	10.6
Proportion of capital contribution by public investors (%)	76.5	79.4	29.3
Increased value of state shares through IPO (%)	219.5	210.4	26.5
Lost value of public investors through IPO (%)	67.3	54.6	64.0

Notes:
Increased value of state shares = (pre-IPO net assets per share – post-IPO net assets per share)/pre-IPO net assets per share ×100%.
Lost value of public investors = (issuing price– post-IPO net assets per share)/issuing price × 100%.

Sources: Prospectus of each company

local governments.[29] This phenomenon can only be explained by regulatory rents: the stock price represents its shell value. Some estimated that the shell value was worth around 20 per cent of total market capitalization (21st Century Economic Report, 2 June 2002).[30]

In sum, rent seeking plays a significant role in the growth of China's stock market. According to Wong (2006), the growth of China's stock

---

[29]   Thus, it could exclude the factor of local governments' bail-out.
[30]   Liu's estimation based on joint research with Bai et al. (2004).

market was primarily driven by extensive expansion,[31] i.e. the increase in the supply of shares. During the period 1992–2003, extensive growth contributed to 73.03 per cent of the growth of China's A-share market.

3.   Financial Repression

If the above argument holds, the question arises: facing a clear risk of being expropriated, why do people still invest in the stock market? If there was no supply of funds, the market would wither. The answer is that Chinese people lack investment alternatives under a regime of financial repression. Financial repression refers to a policy regime that creates a wedge between the actual rate of return to financial assets and the nominal rate of return to the investors (Li, 2001). In its extreme forms, financial repression can render the return of holding financial assets negative. Financial repression has invariably stood at the centre of China's economic policy, which imposed rigid control over interest rates, bond markets, and convertibility of currency (RMB).

3.1   Interest rate control

The main alternative to the stock market is bank deposits. For most of the reform era, the interest rate on deposits has been kept positive, but very low. In some years, the actual rate was even negative. Since most banks are owned by the state, the low interest rate is thereby like an implicit tax on savers (Li, 2001; Bai et al., 1999). Li (2001) estimated the revenue from this implicit tax was, on average, 2.66 per cent of GDP during the period 1985–1995; and increased to 3.23 per cent during the period 1996–1998. Obviously, bank deposits are not a desirable investment. Figure 4.1 shows the effective interest rates during the period 1990–2007 in China.

3.2   Bond market control

In order to restrict competition so as to maintain the monopoly of the financial sector by SCBs, the Chinese government has imposed tight control over the bond market. As a consequence, China's bonds market, especially the corporate bond market, is lagging far behind other countries. By the end of 2007, the total outstanding value of the bond market was US$1.2 trillion, accounting for only 35.3 per cent of the year's GDP, far below that of overseas mature markets. Of this, 90.3 per cent was

---

[31]   Another source of stock market growth is intensive growth, which is due to the increase in the value of the old shares.

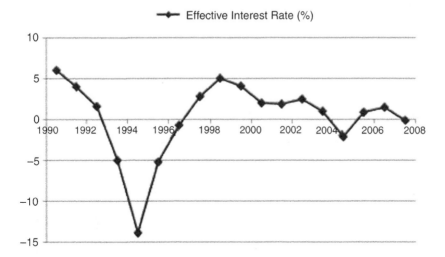

Source: PBOC.

Figure 4.1 Effective interest rates in China 1990–2007

treasury bonds and financial bonds, while corporate bonds accounted for only 4.2 per cent. The ratio of corporate bonds outstanding to GDP was only 1.5 per cent in 2007, far lower than that of other more mature markets.[32] In addition, China's domestic bond market is segregated into stock exchanges, the inter-bank bond market, and bank OTC retail markets and is thereby illiquid. Investor types are few and commercial banks are the dominant players holding 79 per cent of all bonds outstanding (PBOC, 2006). Figure 4.2 shows a comparison of selected countries' bond market sizes in relation to their GDP.

3.3 Inconvertibility of the currency

It is also hard for Chinese savers to invest in overseas markets. Up till today, RMB is still not freely convertible. Although the recent relaxation over foreign currency control allows more Chinese people to hold foreign currency, in order to invest in overseas markets they still need to open a foreign bank account which is not feasible for the majority. Additional obstacles include language, time difference, and so on. As a consequence, most people are constrained to the domestic market.

---

[32] Data source: CSRC and www.chinabond.com.cn.

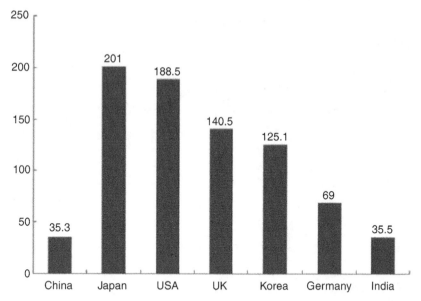

Note: China's data is as of the end of 2007, and the data for other countries is as of the end of 2006.

Source: CSRC, www.Chinabond.com.cn and World Bank.

Figure 4.2   Comparison of selected countries' bond market sizes in relation to their GDP

Financial repression drives a tremendous amount of savings into the stock market to pursue limited stocks (itself also part of financial repression). The direct consequence of this is that domestic investors have to pay about four times more than foreign investors do for the corresponding shares. This provides a sharp contrast with most markets with investment restrictions, in which foreigners pay a premium (Hardouvelis et al., 1994; Bailey, 1994; World Bank, 1995; Fernald and Rogers, 2002).[33] Take China Eastern Airlines for instance, on 25 November 2003 its A-share price was US$0.50; while its H share price was only US$0.16 (Walter and Howie, 2003).

---

[33]   On the typical premium, See Hardouvelis et al. (1994). On the Chinese foreign discount, see Bailey (1994); World Bank (1995); Fernald and Rogers (2002).

4.   A Speculation-driven Market

The last question we need to address is the high liquidity in the secondary market. How and why did active trading occur on China's stock exchanges? Lack of investment alternatives partly answered the question, but not fully. After all, investing in the stock market is highly risky and could easily end up with substantial losses. Unless the stock market could offer sufficient returns to compensate such risk, rational investors would not take part in it.[34] The stock market returns normally come from two sources: the appreciation of shares and dividend payments. The former, in turn, could result from the increase of value, or speculation. Given the overall poor performance of Chinese listed companies and low dividend yield, most companies have little investment value. Therefore, Chinese investors buy shares for capital gains, which are mainly driven by manipulation.

4.1   Low investment value of listed companies

The poor performance of China's listed companies has been documented by many studies and it was found that the performance of listed companies is even worse than before listing (Sun and Tong, 2003; Wang, Xu and Zhu, 2004). Considering the complex governance problems we identified before and the dubious listing process, this should not be a surprise at all. It is reported that the ratio of pre-tax operating profits to total assets declined from 7.34 per cent in 1993 to 2.7 per cent in 2003; the ratio of pre-tax total profits to total assets declined from 8.56 per cent in 1993 to 3.39 per cent in 2003; while the percentage of listed companies incurring negative operating (pre-tax total) profits increased from 1.7 (0.57) per cent in 1993 to 20.43 (12.59) per cent in 2003.[35]

During 1992–2003, on average, 50.7 per cent of Chinese listed companies issued cash dividends, among which the average cash dividends payout ratio was 35.75 per cent. Neither the payout percentage nor the payout ratios were too low (Wong, 2006, p. 413).[36] However, regardless of

[34]   Certainly, it is very likely that investors are simply guilty of overconfidence or misjudgment, but they are still 'rational' players in the sense that they come into the market because they *believe* it could offer them higher returns.

[35]   Data sources: China Stock Market and Accounting Research Databases, quoted from Wong (2006, p. 413).

[36]   There are a few reasons for this. First and foremost, the lion's share of dividend payments will go to controlling shareholders who hold majority shares at low costs. In fact, Lee and Xiao (2004) argue such dividend paying practice

their low profitability, the shares of Chinese listed companies are often traded at a P/E ratio of around 40–50 in secondary markets. It thereby led to an extremely low dividend yield[37] to shareholders. It is documented that dividend yields ranged from 0.5 per cent in 2000 to 3.4 per cent in 1995. The average dividend yield during 1992–2003 was 0.85 per cent, only half of the average deposits interest rate (1.78 per cent) for the same period (Wong, 2006). If we consider the fact that only 30 per cent of the dividends are distributed to public investors, the figure is even lower. Thus, the stocks of Chinese listed companies have very low long-term investment value. Table 4.3 shows the investment value of China's listed companies.

Table 4.3   Investment value of China's listed companies

Year	Number of listed companies	Percentage of companies distributing cash dividends	Dividend payout ratio (%)	Dividend yield (%)	One year saving rate (%)
1992	52	55.80	45.60	0.60	1.80
1993	176	29.00	9.50	0.30	2.54
1994	283	69.30	46.70	2.50	3.15
1995	307	80.80	130.60	3.40	3.15
1996	510	41.20	36.90	0.80	2.62
1997	715	54.30	38.50	1.00	1.91
1998	821	32.30	23.40	0.60	1.58
1999	918	35.70	26.80	0.60	1.18
2000	1054	60.40	34.20	0.50	0.99
2001	1132	61.00	32.20	0.60	0.99
2002	1188	52.10	29.90	0.80	0.74
2003	1263	48.70	33.40	0.80	0.72
Average		50.70	35.75	0.85	1.78

Source: China Stock Market & Accounting Research Database, quoted by Wong (2006, p. 415).

could be regarded as evidence of tunnelling. Second, the CSRC often linked the dividend payment with post-IPO issuance which forced those companies with equity financing plans to pay dividends (this became mandatory in 2006). Third, the news of dividends payout has often been used by insiders and market manipulators to push up share prices.

[37]   Dividend yield = annual dividend per share/price per share.

4.2   Speculation in secondary market

Given the low investment value of Chinese listed companies, trading activities are more likely to be driven by speculation rather than investment motives.

4.2.1   Highly speculative market   Take average turnover rate (defined as the total annual trading value divided by the average market capitalization), which is the most commonly used indicator for the degree of speculation in the stock market. It was found that during 1992–2003, the average turnover rate for the SZSE was 498 per cent and 543 per cent for the SHSE. The turnover rates were about ten times higher than those of other major markets in the world. In 1996, the turnover rate at SZSE even reached 1350 per cent.[38] The average shareholding duration was about only 3.44 months in SHSE and 3.65 months in SZSE, in contrast with 21.36 months in NYSE and 21 months in LSE.[39] The high turnover rate and short shareholding duration indicate China's stock market is highly speculative. Table 4.4 shows percentage turnover rates of major stock markets from 1994 to 2003.

Table 4.4   Turnover rates (%) of major stock markets 1994–2003

Year	SHSE	SZSE	NYSE	Tokyo	LSE	HKSE	Singapore
1994	1135	583	53	25	77	40	28
1995	529	255	59	27	78	37	18
1996	913	1350	52	27	58	44	14
1997	702	817	66	33	44	91	56
1998	454	407	70	34	47	62	64
1999	471	424	75	49	57	51	75
2000	493	509	88	59	69	61	59
2001	269	228	87	60	84	44	59
2002	214	198	95	68	97	40	54
2003	251	214	90	83	107	52	74
Average	543	499	74	47	72	52	50

Sources: China Securities and Futures Statistical Yearbook (2003); World Federation of Exchange (www.world-exchanges.org).

---

[38]   Data source: Chinese Securities and Futures Statistical Yearbook 2003.

[39]   The author's own calculation. Data Source: Chinese Securities and Futures Statistical Yearbook 2003, World Federation of Exchange. China's stock market statistics for the SHSE were from 1993 to 2003; for the SZSE from 1992 to 2003; for the NYSE and LSE, from 1992 to 1998.

4.2.2 Factors leading to high speculation With a few exceptions (Walter and Howie, 2003; Green, 2004), most studies viewed China's stock market as one dominated by small investors, and their lack of knowledge and inexperience are blamed for the widespread speculation. It is undeniable that the immaturity of small investors did play an important role in speculation, but their role has been largely overstated. I believe there are some other significant factors accounting for the prevalence of speculation.

4.2.2.1 WHO ARE THE MAJOR SPECULATORS?   First we need to identify who are the speculators in the Chinese stock market. Certainly, small individual investors are one group. However, although great in numbers, the shortage of funds and information has made them fellow travellers at most. The SZSE data has shown a very uneven distribution of A-share ownership: 91 per cent of shareholders controlled only 41 per cent of total A-shares; 58 per cent of A-shares were controlled by 9 per cent of shareholders.[40] Similarly, of the 1182 companies that provided data at the end of September 2002, 64 per cent had fewer than 50 000 shareholders and fewer than 5 per cent had more than 150 000 shareholders.[41] If we consider the fact that hundreds of accounts are often controlled by the same trader, the concentration of A-shares ownership is even higher. The role of small investors in speculation is apparently overstated. Table 4.5 shows Shenzhen Market A-share holdings and company control.

Table 4.5   Shenzhen Market A-share holdings and company control

Shareholder categories	Percentage of holders	Percentage of control	Average value (RMB)
1000 shares	52.8	10.2	4562
1000–5000	38.1	31.1	20 495
5000–10 000	4.3	11.3	73 932
10 000–50 000	3.6	22.3	214 777
50 000–100 000	0.7	8.7	770 220
>100 000	0.4	16.3	2 971 951

Source: SZSE, FY 2001, quoted from Walter and Howie (2003, p. 134).

[40]   SZSE, FY 2001, quoted from Walter and Howie (2003, p. 134).
[41]   Data source, Wind Information.

Nearly 60 per cent of A-shares are controlled by 9 per cent of share-holders, who are, in most cases, institutional investors.[42] In the Chinese stock market, institutional investors consist of securities companies, fund management companies, insurance companies, pension funds, social security funds, Qualified Foreign Institutional Investors (QFII), and various underground privately placed funds (*Simu Jijin*). The prevailing claim that institutional investors are of small scale mainly came from the calculation that excluded privately placed funds which are much larger than formal funds. Privately placed funds often took the form of financial management and financial trust companies and included the asset management services offered by the securities companies. They are institutional investors in everything but formal registration. Because privately placed funds usually operated underground, it is hard to estimate their real scale. A study by Xia Bin, a senior official at the PBOC, estimated by year end 2000, there were at least 7000 privately placed funds operating in Shanghai, Shenzhen, Beijing and hundreds more dotted around the country. They were worth about 700 billion yuan, about 8.7 times more than formal funds and some 40 per cent of the total tradable market capitalization at year end 2000 (Caijing, 5 July 2001). Among formal institutional investors, insurance, pension and security funds remain small and securities companies and fund management companies are major players.[43]

These institutional investors, with their capital and knowledge advantage, have played a dominant role in speculation. In the Chinese stock market, they are known as market manipulators (*Zhuang Jia*).[44] Market manipulation once became so prevalent that almost every stock had an institutional investor as a banker (*Wugu Buzhuang*). Major securities companies have often manipulated more than one stock at one time. For instance, after their collapse, it was revealed that Nangfang securities company had controlled 90 per cent of the tradable stocks of Harbin Pharmaceutical Group (600664) and Hafei Aviation Industry (600038); Dapeng securities company controlled 90 per cent of tradable shares of

---

[42]   There are, in particular in the early stages, some wealthy individual investors. But with the growth of the market, they gradually fade away.

[43]   By the end of 2007, the combined market share of the National Social Security Fund, insurance funds and pension funds was 3.31 per cent, while funds management companies had 25.7 per cent and securities companies had 1.4 per cent. Because most fund management companies are set up by securities companies, I believe they should be considered together. See the CSRC 2008 Development Report.

[44]   *Zhuang jia* means 'banker' in a gambling game.

Min-metals Development (600058) and Huaxia securities company controlled about 70 per cent of tradable stocks of Taiji Group (600129) and Tibet Mineral Development (000762). The failure of manipulation in the secondary market was the direct reason for the crisis of the securities industry during 2004.

Fund management companies did not look much better. In October 2000 Caijing published 'The Black Funds Scandal' which was based on a SHSE report on fund industry performance.[45] The exchange analyst had closely monitored fund trading during the periods 9 August 1999 to 3 December 1999 and 3 December 1999 to 28 April 2000. It was revealed that fund management companies traded shares between existing funds and newly listed funds, using the latter to solve the performance of the former and the wide use of churning (*Dui Dao*)[46] to create trading volume to attract other investors into the market. Once the share price had been driven up, the manipulators could cash out at a profit. There was a variety of collusion between funds under the same fund management company or between different fund management companies, between proprietary trading operations of the securities companies and their related fund management companies (Caijing, 8 October 2000).[47]

The prevalence of market manipulation left little option to small investors. For them, the only possibility of making profits is to ride on the manipulators. Thus, one could hardly blame them for paying little attention to fundamentals, while focusing on 'how to identify manipulators' (*Ruohe Shibie Zhuangjia*) or 'dancing with manipulators' (*Yu Zhuang Gongwu*). The highly speculative nature of the market should primarily be attributed to institutional investors.

4.2.2.2   THE SEGMENTATION OF THE MARKET   The segmentation of the Chinese stock market also plays an important role in speculation. Normally, market manipulation is very costly, requiring tremendous amounts of funds. However, in the Chinese stock market, there only one-third of shares are tradable, which means that manipulators only need one-third of the funds normally required to move stock prices. The

---

[45]   Ridiculously, the SHSE analyst Zhao Yugang, who wrote the report, received a serious warning for violation of confidential rules in the SHSE after this report made public by Caijing.

[46]   Churning referred to a series of transactions in which stocks were dumped by one fund into another.

[47]   Most fund management companies were established by securities companies and securities companies usually have holdings in two or three different funds management companies.

segmentation of the market has considerably lowered the costs of manipulation and thereby spurred speculation.

4.2.2.3 SOFT BUDGET CONSTRAINT   Even though manipulation is less costly in the Chinese stock market, it still requires considerable amounts of funds. Where do the funds come from? Part are institutional investors' own funds, and some come from wealthy individuals, or non-state firms, but the lion's share come from various SOEs, including listed companies. As disclosed in Xia Bin's report and later proved in the security industry crisis, SOEs were the main source of privately placed funds.[48] Operated with soft budget constraints, these SOEs had a strong incentive to engage in investment with high risk and high returns: any losses from such trading could be passed on to the public finances while any profits could be retained. Weak governance exacerbated the problem: managers were often offered rebates for lending funds. Yuan (2004) questioned the gap between the returns of asset management that were publicly admitted by the securities companies and those displayed in their SOE clients' balance sheets. It is reasonable to believe that the minimum 3 per cent gap went into the managers' own pockets.[49]

4.2.2.4 WEAK ENFORCEMENT OF INSIDER TRADING   Weak enforcement was another important factor that incentivized speculation. Contrary to normal thinking, manipulation is in fact very risky. If the manipulators cannot attract a copycat site, if the capital chains split, or if uncontrollable factors cause the market to fall, the manipulators have to bear the

---

[48]   Xia's report suggested that 69.3 per cent of clients are enterprises, companies. Although he did not further clarify the ownership of these enterprises, it is reasonable to believe that most of them are state-owned: there was direct proof of this, in 2004 when the state assets management commission tightened SOE's asset management business and the stock market immediately plunged. Because some enterprises are not listed, and some listed companies never make announcements regarding asset management funds, it is hard to get accurate data. In addition, according to the debts revealed by the bankrupt securities companies, institutional debts constituted the overwhelming majority and most institutional debtors were state-owned enterprises or listed companies.

[49]   A footnote to this is the China Life Reinsurance Company scandal. It revealed that China Life Reinsurance lost 0.4 billion yuan asset management funds, following the collapse of Hantang Securities Company in 2004. It further disclosed that although 0.4 billion yuan was half of its registered capital, neither the shareholders' general meeting nor the board of directors was informed about the asset management plan. It was completely decided by the general manager, Feng Hongjuan, alone. See Securities Market Weekly, 28 November 2005.

weight. The risk of manipulation could be seen no more clearly than in the securities industry crisis where most securities companies were tied to the stocks that they manipulated. Why then are the institutional investors so keen to engage in such risky trading? Besides the low investment value of listed companies, probably the single most important reason is that it provides insiders abundant opportunities to make a fortune, not only at the cost of small investors, but also at the cost of manipulators.

Rat trading has long been recognized as one of the most serious problems in the Chinese stock market (Zheng, 2009). Riding on the efforts of securities companies or fund management companies, managers, traders, other elites and their associates reaped substantial riskless profits. The other side of the bankruptcy of the securities industry was the emergence of thousands of millionaires.[50] However, it was not until very recently that the CSRC started taking measures against rat trading. The first case against fund managers for rat trading occurred in 2007. So far, a total of six fund managers have received administrative penalties, and among these, only one case was transferred to the police[51] (Phoenix Finance, Special Report).

In sum, institutional investors, rather than individual investors, should take primary responsibility for the excessive speculation in the Chinese stock market.

IV. A MARKET UNDER WEAK ENFORCEMENT

In the absence of effective enforcement, the Chinese stock market rapidly expanded, but it is a market driven by state guarantee, rent seeking, speculation and financial repression. With lack of support by intrinsic value, the stock market deviates seriously from the macro economy and is extremely volatile.

---

[50]   Take Hua Xia Securities company for instance. It lost 8 billion yuan in manipulating the stocks of Taiji Group (600129). The widespread story was, in order to help insiders cash out at 30 yuan, the company gave up cashing out at 22 yuan and further drove the price to 37.97 yuan at the time of the market going down, other investors selling off. See Caijing, 23 February 2005.

[51]   The former manager of the Great Wall fund management company, Han Gang, received a penalty of 1 year in prison in addition to fines of 300 000 yuan in 2011. See China Securities Journal, 23 May 2011.

1. Deviating from the Macro Economy

The Chinese stock market displays a serious deviation from the macro economy. From 1994 to 1999, as the GDP growth rate declined, the stock index kept going up. While, during the period 2001–2005, when the GDP growth rate increased, the stock market experienced four consecutive years' bear market. The obvious deviation from the macro economy indicates that the Chinese stock market is seriously distorted and therefore unlikely to fulfil its fundamental function – effectively allocating capital. Figure 4.3 shows the relationship between GDP and the SHSE composite index.

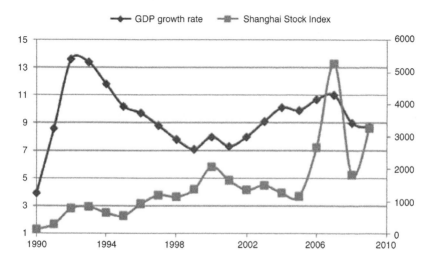

Source: SHSE, China's Statistics Bureau.

Figure 4.3 Relationship between GDP and SHSE composite index

2. Extreme Volatility

The Chinese stock market also seemed to be extremely volatile, despite a strict trading ceiling at a range of 10 per cent imposed by the exchanges. In its 20-year history, it has experienced a couple of boom-and-busts. In each boom-and-bust cycle, millions of wealth evaporated and thousands of small investors suffered from considerable losses. Thus, the Chinese capital is more a place of wealth-destruction than wealth-creation. Table 4.6 shows the volatility of the SHSE Composite Index during the period of 1990–2009.

Table 4.6   Volatility of SHSE Composite Index 1990–2009

Time	Duration (months)	SHSE Index	Volatility (%)
12/90–05/92	17	95.79–1234.71	1189
06/92–10/92	5	1175.69–507.25	–56.86
11/92–04/93	6	471.18–1358.78	188.38
05/93–07/94	15	1365.15–333.92	–75.54
08/94–09/94	2	394.87–791.15	100.35
10/94–01/96	15	770.9–561.36	–27.18
02/96–04/97	15	536.24–1393.74	160
05/97–05/99	25	1398.14–1279.32	–8.49
06/99–06/01	25	1283.3–2218.02	72.8
07/01–09/05	51	2220.41–1129.05	–49.15
10/05–10/07	25	1153.67–5952.4	415.95
11/07–10/08	12	5978.94–1728.79	–71.08
11/08–12/09	12	1713.76–3277.14	91.22

Source: SHSE.

CONCLUDING REMARKS

This chapter has attempted to explain the growth of China's stock market which quickly expanded in spite of weak enforcement. I disagree with Pistor and Xu (2005) who attribute the development of the Chinese stock market to the quota system. I believe it is mainly driven by state guarantee, rent seeking, speculation and financial repression.

As illustrated in the end, a market which expanded in this way deviates severely from the macro economy and is extremely volatile. The serious deviation and extreme volatility indicate that China's stock market is highly inefficient in allocating capital and it is more wealth destructive than wealth creative. Therefore, I believe the growth of the Chinese stock market does not constitute a challenge to my 'enforcement matters' thesis. In the absence of effective enforcement, the stock market might be able to grow in size as a result of some special reasons, but it is unlikely to be efficient nor sustainable. In order to cultivate a sustainable, efficient stock market, effective enforcement is a must.

In addition, since the key factor in the growth of China's stock market – the prevailing state ownership – does not exist in other economies, the experience of China cannot be generalized.

5. Conclusion

Chapter 5 concludes this book by reiterating its central arguments and major contribution. It also suggests the broad implications of China's experience for developing and transition economies in their pursuit of financial development. Finally, it briefly discusses the future of China's stock market.

I. CENTRAL ARGUMENTS

This book concentrates on the enforcement problem that is believed to be central to corporate governance and financial development, at least in transition and developing countries where there is often a big gap between 'law on the books' and 'law in practice'. In this book, corporate governance is regarded as a problem of how to enforce the financial contracts between external financiers and corporate controllers.

Relying on the NIE insights, it first establishes a general conceptual framework for contract enforcement and then applies it to a corporate context. In the stock market, the role of formal enforcement seems to be particularly important because the financial contracts are often too complex for small investors to understand and the gains from cheating often too large to be constrained by the consideration of future costs. In the absence of effective formal enforcement, various informal enforcement mechanisms, such as concentrated ownership, self-regulation, or relation of trust, might arise to respond to the weakness and could facilitate growth of the capital market to some extent. But they are only a partial substitute for formal enforcement, which would incur substantial costs in the long run. For sustainable development, a capital market must build on effective formal enforcement.

Nonetheless, the importance of formal enforcement should not be overstated. Information and litigation costs imposed serious limit on its role. The primary role of informal enforcement remains. For a healthy capital market to develop, it requires some form of combination of formal and informal enforcement.

The Chinese stock market emerged from a unique historical background. The sustained losses of SOEs forced the government to seek out new sources of finance. Meanwhile, the CCP had to ensure its control over SOEs, which is crucial to its political survival. As a result, China's stock market is characterized by four distinctive features: It is dominated by state-owned listed companies, two-thirds of shares are not free floating, the shares of the same company trade in different markets at different prices, and most market participants are owned or controlled by the party-state.

The unusual market features and ownership structure fundamentally changed the incentive of market players and therefore had a significant impact on the function of various enforcement mechanisms: self enforcement is largely undermined, non-state third-party enforcement is dysfunctional and formal enforcement is very weak.

Nevertheless, the Chinese stock market has quickly expanded in the past two decades regardless of the weak enforcement. I disagree with Pistor and Xu (2005) who argued that the quota system filled the governance vacuum at the initial stage and therefore fostered the growth of the Chinese stock market. I believe the development of the Chinese stock market should be attributed to state guarantee, institutionalized rent seeking, speculation and financial repression.

In the absence of effective enforcement, the Chinese stock market rapidly developed. However, it is a market big in size and low in efficiency. The stock market displayed serious deviation from the macro economy and is extremely volatile. It failed to fulfil the fundamental function of a capital market – effectively allocating capital. Instead, it caused substantial waste of resources.

II. MAJOR CONTRIBUTION

This book has developed a conceptual framework for enforcement study in the corporate context. Although the importance of enforcement has been widely recognized, the existing research mainly focuses on one or two particular enforcement mechanisms and lack of a unified conceptual framework. This book made an attempt to fill this gap. Our framework is mainly based on the findings of the NIE. Contract enforcement has been well developed by the NIE over the past decades, but this is the first time it has been applied to corporate governance study. Under this framework, findings in previous corporate governance studies, in particular, 'law and economics' and 'law and finance' literature, could be put together to be compared and evaluated. It thereby enabled me to answer the following important questions: to what extent does legal protection matter? What is the relationship between legal protection and alternative governance mechanisms? My conclusion is different from the 'law and economics' school, which claimed that contractual arrangements are sufficient to solve the governance problem and the role of law is marginal. Nor is it consistent with the 'law and finance' school, which suggested that legal protection is the precondition for capital market development. I believe legal protection is crucial to capital market development, but might not be necessary in the early stages. Informal mechanisms such as stock exchanges and investment bankers could foster capital markets to develop to a certain extent. But with the growth of the market, legal protection becomes necessary. In the absence of effective legal protection, informal enforcement mechanisms would incur substantial costs and endanger the sustained growth of the market in the long run.

Second, the book has offered a novel explanation to the rapid growth of the Chinese stock market. Previous studies have already revealed that legal protection of shareholders in China's stock market is very weak (Allen et al., 2005; Pistor and Xu, 2005). It has thereby raised a challenge to the 'law and finance' literature, which claimed legal protection is crucial to capital market development. In this book, I have also found that informal enforcement in the Chinese stock market is ineffective. Thus, the growth of the Chinese stock market cannot be explained by any existing literature. I challenged the argument by Pistor and Xu (2005) and suggested that the Chinese stock market is driven by state guarantee, financial repression, institutionalized rent seeking and speculation.

This book has also provided a comprehensive examination of enforcement in China's stock market, which was not previously available. It has presented a large amount of empirical evidence that covers major aspects of the stock market, ranging from business life and legal practice to social events. Several assumptions such as the 'bonding effect' (Coffee, 1999b), reputational intermediaries (Gilson and Kraakman, 1984; Kraakman, 1986) and the media (Dyck and Zingales, 2002a) have been tested in the Chinese stock market.

III.   IMPLICATIONS FOR DEVELOPING AND TRANSITION ECONOMIES

The findings of this book have important policy implications. First, they cast some doubts on the idea of the optimal model or 'best practice' for corporate governance. Over the past two decades, regardless of their differences, both 'law and economics' and 'law and finance' schools actually support the same idea that the Anglo-American governance model has outperformed others and therefore should be adopted by countries that attempt to develop their capital market. As a consequence, a large number of codes of corporate governance and legislations based on the Anglo-American model have been produced and spread around the world. As discussed in this book, sustained growth of capital markets relies upon effective enforcement, which in turn requires a combination of informal and formal enforcement. Nevertheless, it does not indicate that there can be only one particular combination. I believe there are a variety of combinations and that each could be equally efficient. The Anglo-American model is one that combines reputation, non-state third-party enforcement and formal enforcement. There could be other effective models, for instance one that combines a large shareholder, reputation and formal enforcement. Thus, for countries that attempt to develop their capital markets, it is not always necessary to imitate the Anglo-American model. Instead, they should choose a model that best suits local conditions.

Second, it is suggested that the sequence of institutional building is taken into account. As shown in this book, each different stage of the capital market has different institutional requirements. In the early stages, it could rely on informal mechanisms such as stock exchanges or investment bankers and formal legal enforcement becomes significant only when the market grows big. Thus, countries could choose the focus of institution building according to their development level.

Third, legal reform should be viewed with more caution. The 'law and finance' literature seemed to trigger a new wave of legal reform. However, the findings of this book call for more caution in legal reform. For one thing, as has been repeatedly emphasized, although formal protection is important, by reason of information and litigation costs, its role is inevitably limited. Downplaying the role of law is undoubtedly harmful, but overstating its importance is unlikely to be a good thing either. For another thing, as North et al. (2009) found, the weakness of a legal system is deeply rooted in the nature of the state. Like China, most developing and transition countries remain in the stage of 'natural state' where the elites are bound by the power of other elites not by law, and the legal system is inherently weak. This weakness cannot be overcome before the transition from 'natural state' to 'open access order' is completed. Thus, placing too much hope on legal reform might lead to disappointment.

Fourth, China's experience cannot be generalized. As discussed in this book, in the absence of effective enforcement, the growth of the Chinese stock market is driven by state guarantee, institutionalized rent seeking by SOEs, financial repression and speculation. The first two factors are unique to China and do not exist in other economies. Thus, the experience of China cannot be generalised. In addition, as shown in the book, a stock market thus developed is highly inefficient. What China provided is in fact more a lesson than an experience.

IV. THE FUTURE OF CHINA'S STOCK MARKET

On 30 December 2011 the SHSE composite index closed at 2199.42, below the level of ten years ago, although China's economics maintained outstanding growth during the same period. The capitalization of free-floating shares reduced by about 2.8867 trillion yuan in 2011, which means each investor lost about 42 000 yuan on average.[1] On the other hand, from 2001 to 2010, listed companies raised funds totalling 3.15 trillion yuan through IPO, secondary issuing and rights issuing in the SHSE and SZSE.[2] In the three-year 2009–2011, the IPO proceeds in China's A-share market ranked first in the world, 56 per cent higher than that in the US market and 115 per cent higher than the combined amount of all Western European markets.[3]

This stark contrast triggered a new wave of fierce debate over the role of China's stock market. Even the *People's Daily* expressed concern that the stock market was becoming a jungle hunting for people's wealth (People's Daily, 30 January 2012). The new president of the CSRC, Guo Shuqing,[4] announced three new policies: fostering dividend payouts by listed companies;[5] reforming the delisting system in ChiNext;[6] and cracking down on insider trading.[7] Although Guo is a well-known pro-market reformer and he has shown his determination to resolve some entrenched problems in the Chinese stock market, could this bring fundamental changes to the Chinese stock market? The answer is no

At the core of the problem in the Chinese stock market is the poor governance quality of listed companies. As argued in this book, state

---

[1] If one were to consider active investors only, then the figure would be much bigger.

[2] Data source: Wind Information.

[3] Data source: Genius Finance.

[4] Guo Shuqing was the president of the CCB before he took office in the CSRC.

[5] This is hardly new since the CSRC announced similar rules in 2008.

[6] ChiNext is a NASDAQ-style Growth Enterprises Market which was opened on 23 October 2009 in Shenzhen.

[7] For Guo Shuqing's speeches, see the CSRC website http://www.csrc.gov.cn/pub/newsite/.

ownership is the primary reason for the governance problem in most listed firms. However, state ownership is crucial to the survival of the CCP regime and therefore cannot be expected to change. Without ownership reform, the majority of listed companies are unlikely to operate as real market participants and all the market-based enforcement mechanisms cannot function well.

Except for ownership reform, reform of public governance in general, and of the legal system in particular, is also critical to the sustainable development of the stock market. Nevertheless, such reform requires imposing credible constraints on the CCP power, which does not seem to be feasible in the near future. In addition, the thousand-years'-long tradition of centralization and deep suspicion of pluralism and decentralization impedes non-state third-party enforcers like stock exchanges and securities associations from playing their part. Compared to political and legal reform, changes in culture or belief will take an even longer time.

The possibility that the Chinese stock market will completely collapse is also small, in particular after the listing of the economic giants such as the four SCBs and PetroChina. Most likely, the same routine will be repeated. The bear market will last for a few years until there are new funds flowing in. Then a new boom-bust cycle will begin again.

References

21st Century Economic Report, 2 June 2002, Liu, Q., 'The "Shell" of Chinese Listed Companies Worth RMB 800 Billion' (*Zhongguo Shangshi Gongsi Ke Zhi 800 Billion*) available at http://finance.anhuinews.com/system/2002/06/02/000027743.shtml

21st Century Economic Report, 24 November 2004, Mo, F., 'The MOF, PBOC along with CSRC Work Together to Solve the Securities Companies' Original Sin Once for All with 60 Billion' (*Caizhengbu, Yanghang, Zhenjianhui Lianshou, 600 yi Zhengti Jiejue Quanshang Yuanzui*) available at http://media.163.com/04/1126/09/163RS2230014182T.html

21st Century Economic Report, 24 December 2007, Zhu, Y., 'UBS AG Accumulated Wealth in PetroChina IPO' (*Ruiyin Zhongshiyou Liancai*) available at http://www.21cbh.com/HTML/2007–12–26/127253.html

21st Century Economic Report, 20 April 2010, Zhu, Y., 'Tracing the 20 years' Footsteps of Goldman & Sachs in China' (*Goldman&Sachs Zhongguo 20nian Meiying Zhuizong*) http://www.21cbh.com/HTML/2010–5–4/xOMDAwMDE3NTMxOQ.html

Abreu, D. (1986), 'Extreal Equilibria of Oligopolistic Supergames', *Journal of Economic Theory*, 39 (1), 191–225

Abreu, D., D. Pearce and E. Stacchetti (1990), 'Toward a Theory of Discounted Repeated Games with Imperfect Monitoring', *Econometrica*, 58 (5), 1041–1063

Acemoglu, D., S. Johnson and J. Robinson (2001), 'The Colonial Origins of Comparative Development: An Empirical Investigation', *American Economic Review*, 91, 1369–1401

Akerlof, G. (1970), 'The Market for Lemons: Quality Uncertainty and the Market Mechanism', *Quarterly Journal of Economics*, 84 (3), 488–500

Allen, F., J. Qian and M. Qian (2005), 'Law, Finance and Economic Growth in China', *Journal of Financial Economics*, 77 (1), 57–116

Anderson, D. (2000), 'Taking Stock in China: Company Disclosure and Information in China's Stock Market', *The Georgetown Law Journal*, 88, 1919–1952

Asia Times Online, 9 May 2003, Li, Y., 'China's Equity Markets: Buyer Beware', available at http://www.atimes.com/atimes/China/EE09Ad01.html

Asia Times Online, 8 July 2008, Lam, W., 'The Party Squeezes China's Judiciary', available at http://www.atimes.com/atimes/China/JG10Ad 01.html

Asian Wall Street Journal, 2 November 2004, Buckman, R., 'China Plans Job Shifts for Telecom Executives; Changes to Come Ahead of Mobile-License Awards and China Netcom's IPO', 23 December 2004, 'China's Biggest Lender is Ripe for December Recapitalization'

Atkinson, A. and J. Stiglitz (1980), *Lectures on Public Economics*, London: McGraw-Hill

Axelrod, R. (1984), *The Evolution of Cooperation*, New York: Basic Books

Bai, C., D. Li., Y. Qian and Y. Wang (1999), 'Anonymous Banking and Financial Repression: How Did China's Reform Limit Government Predation without Reducing Its Revenue?', CEPR Working Paper, London

Bai, C., Q. Liu and F. Song (2004), 'Bad News is Good News: Propping and Tunneling Evidence from China', University of Hong Kong Working Paper, available at http://www.hiebs.hku.hk/working_paper_updates/pdf/wp1094.pdf

Bailey, W. (1994), 'Risk and Return on China's New Stock Markets: Some Preliminary Evidence', *Pacific Basin Finance Journal*, 2 (2–3), 243–260

Bandiera, O. (2003), 'Land Reform, The Market for Protection and the Origins of the Sicilian Mafia: Theory and Evidence', *Journal of Law, Economics, and Organization*, 19, 218–244

Banner, S. (1998), *Anglo-American Securities Regulation: Cultural and Political Roots 1690–1860*, Cambridge: Cambridge University Press

Barca, F. (1995), 'On Corporate Governance in Italy: Issues, Facts and Agency', manuscript, Bank of Italy, Rome

Bardhan, P. (2005), 'Institutions Matter, but Which Ones?', *Economics of Transition*, 13 (3), 499–532

Barth, J. and G. Caprio (2007), 'China's Changing Financial System: Can It Catch Up With, or even Drive Growth?', available at http://papers.ssrn.com/sol3/papers.cfm?abstract_id=985580

Barzel, Y. (2002), *A Theory of the State, Economic Rights, Legal Rights and the Scope of the State*, Cambridge: Cambridge University Press

Bebchuk, L. and Z. Neeman (2007), 'Investor Protection and Interest Group Politics', Harvard Law School Online Discussion Paper No. 603

Becht, M., P. Bolton and A. Roell (2005), 'Corporate Governance and Control', available at http://ssrn.com/abstract-id=343461

Beck, T., R. Levine and N. Loayza (2000), 'Finance and the Sources of Growth', *Journal of Financial Economics*, 58 (1–2), 261–300

Beck, T. and R. Levine (2002), 'Industry Growth and Capital Allocation: Does Having A Market or Bank-Based System Matter?', *Journal of Financial Economics*, 64 (2), 147–180

Becker, G. (1968), 'Crime and Punishment: An Economic Approach', *Journal of Political Economy*, 76 (2), 169–217

Beijing Youth Daily, 25 July 2004, Wang, R., 'Non-performing Assets Rate is above 51 per cent, 129 Investment Banks Facing Life and Death' (*Buliang Zichanglü Chaoguo Wucheng, 129 Jia Quanshang Zhimian Shengsijie*)

Berglof, E. and S. Claessens (2004), 'Enforcement and Corporate Governance', World Bank Policy Research Working Paper No. 3409 available at http://papers.ssrn.com/sol3/papers.cfm?abstract_id=625286

Berglof, E. and A. Pajuste (2005), 'What Do Firms Disclose and Why? Enforcing Corporate Governance and Transparency in Central and Eastern Europe', *Oxford Review of Economic Policy*, 21 (2), 178–197

Berglof, E. and E. Perotti (1994), 'The Governance Structure of the Japanese Financial Keiretsu', *Journal of Financial Economics*, 36 (2), 259–284

Berglof, E. and E. Von Thadden (1999), 'The Changing Paradigm: Implications for Transition and Developing Countries', available at http://www.ecgr.org/research/accession/991014204.pdf

Bernstein, L. (1992), 'Opting Out of the Legal System: External Contractual Relations in the Diamond Industry', *Journal of Legal Studies*, 21 (1), 115–157

Bernstein, L. (1996) 'Merchant Law in a Merchant Court: Rethinking the Code's Search for Immanent Business Norms', *University of Pennsylvania Law Review*, 144 (5), 1765–1821

Bernstein, L. (2001) 'Private Commercial Law in the Cotton Industry: Creating Cooperation through Rules, Norms, and Institutions', *Michigan Law Review*, 99, 1724–1788

Bhattacharya, U. and H. Daouk (2002), 'The World Price of Insider Trading', *Journal of Finance*, 57 (1), 75–108

Black, B. (1990), 'Is Corporate Trivial? A Political and Economic Analysis', *Northwestern University Law Review*, 84, 542–597

Black, B. (2000), 'The Core Institutions that Support Strong Securities Markets', *The Business Lawyer*, 55, 1565–1607

Black, B. and R. Kraakman (1996), 'A Self-enforcing Model of Corporate Law', *Harvard Law Review*, 109 (8), 1911–1982

Black, B., R. Kraakman and A. Tarassova (2000), 'Russian Privatization and Corporate Governance: What Went Wrong?', *Stanford Law Review*, 52 (6), 1731–1808

Blair, M. (1996), *Ownership and Control: Rethinking Corporate Governance for the Twenty-First Century*, Washington D.C.: The Brookings Institution

Booth, J. and R. Smith (1986), 'Capital Raising, Underwriting and the Certification Process', *Journal of Financial Economics*, 15 (1–2), 261–281

Boycko, M., A. Shleifer and R. Vishny (1996), 'A Theory of Privatization, Paish lecture', *Economic Journal*, 106 (435), 309–319

Brennan, G. and J. Buchanan (1980), *The Power to Tax: Analytical Foundations of a Fiscal Constitution*, Cambridge: Cambridge University Press

Bruno, V. and S. Claessens (2008), 'Corporate Governance and Regulation: Can There be too Much of a Good Thing?', CEPR Discussion Paper No. 603

Cai, H. (2007), 'Bonding, Law Enforcement and Corporate Governance in China', *Stanford Journal of Law, Business & Finance,* 13, 82–121

Caijing Magazine, 8 October 2000, Ping, H. and Q. Li, 'The Black Funds Scandal' (*Jijin Heimu*)

Caijing Magazine, 7 February 2001, Hu, S., Q. Li and J. Li, 'The Professional Manipulator, Lüliang' (*Zhuangjia Lüliang*)

Caijing Magazine, 5 July 2001, Xia, B., 'A Report on China's Privately-placed Funds' (*Zhongguo Simu Jijin Baogao*)

Caijing Magazine, 7 August 2001, Ling, H. and L. Wang, 'Yin Guangxia Falls into the Trough' (*Yin Guangxia Xianjing*)

Caijing Magazine, 5 November 2001, 'Chinese Managers Survey' (*Woguo Jingli Diaocha*)

Caijing Magazine, 20 December 2001, Wen, H., 'The Predicament of CPA' (*CPA Kunju*)

Caijing Magazine, 20 December 2001, Li, J., 'The Fall of Zhong Tianqin' (*Zhong Tianqin Bengta*)

Caijing Magazine, 18 June 2002, Ling, W. and J. Li, 'The Death of Zhong Jing Kai' (*Zhong Jingkai zhi Si*)

Caijing Magazine, 20 June 2003, Ling, H., 'The Rise and Fall of Zhou Zhengyi' (*Zhou Zhengyi Xingshuai*)

Caijing Magazine, 5 November 2003, Anderson, J., 'How to Fix China's Banking System?' (English Newsletter)

Caijing Magazine, 20 March 2004, Lu, Y., 'Southern Metropolitan Case is In the First Trial' (*Nandu an Yishen Kaiting*)

Caijing Magazine, 5 May 2004, Pan, X. and F. Wang, 'The Kaiping Case Returns to the Spotlight' (*Zaijie Kaiping an*)

Caijing Magazine, 5 June 2004, Pan, X., 'Remarkable Uncertainties in Southern Metropolitan Case Appeared' (*Nanduanan Chuxian Xianzhu Bianshu*)

Caijing Magazine, 24 January 2005, Duan, H. and W. Kang, 'Financial Fraud Exposes Governance Weaknesses at the Bank of China' (English Newsletter)

Caijing Magazine, 23 February 2005, Li, J. and N. Yu, 'Hua Xia Securities Company is Between Life and Death' (*Hua Xia Zhengquan Shengsi Zhijian*)

Caijing Magazine, 13 November 2006, Su, D., 'Gu Chujun on Trial' (*Gu Chujun Shoushen*)

Caijing Magazine, 6 January 2007, Wang, X., 'Whose Luneng?' (*Shui de Luneng?*)

Caijing Magazine, 14 May 2007, Yu, N., 'In Like a Lion, Out Like a Lamb, Nan Fang Securities Company Case Closed' (*Nanfang Zhengquanan Hutoushewei*)

Caijing Magazine, 5 June 2009, Li, J. and X. Qiao, 'The Senior Manager of Guotai Junan Hong Kong, Fan Xiaowei is Under Investigation' (*Guotai Junan Hong Kong Gongsi Gaoguan Fan Xiaowei bei Diaocha*)

Caijing Magazine, 28 July 2010, Zhang, Y. and K. Xu, 'Correspondent Was Wanted by the Local Police for Disclosing Inside Stories of a Company' (*Jizhe Baodao Gongsi Neimu zao Shudi Jingfang Quanguo Tongji*)

Caijing Magazine, 3 August 2010, Hu, J., 'Wang Huayuan and the old story of Southern Metropolitan Daily' (*Wang Huayuan yu Nandu Wangshi*)

Caijing Magazine, 9 May 2011, Tan, Y. and Y. Zhang, 'An Unexpected Ending of the Gray Alliance in Stock Market' (*Ziben Shichang Huise Lianmeng yiwai Shouchang*)

Caprio, G., L. Laeven and R. Levine (2003), 'Governance and Bank Valuation', University of Minnesota, mimeo

Casella, A. (1996), 'On Market Integration and the Development of Institutions: the Case of International Commercial Arbitration', *European Economic Review*, 40 (1), 155–186

Casella, A. and J. Rauch (2002), 'Anonymous Market and Group Ties in International Trade', *Journal of International Economics*, 58 (1), 19–47

Charny, D. (1990), 'Non-Legal Sanctions in Commercial Relations', *Harvard Law Review*, 104 (2), 375–462

Cheffins, B. (1997), *Company Law: Theory, Structure and Operation*, Oxford: Clarendon Press

Cheffins, B. (2003) 'Law as Bedrock: The Foundations of an Economy Dominated by Widely Held Public Companies', *Oxford Journal of Legal Studies*, 23 (1), 1–23

Chen, C. and H. Shih (2003), 'Initial Public Offering and Corporate Governance in China's Transitional Economy', NBER working paper No. 9574

Chen, D., J. Fan and T. Wong (2004), 'Political Connected CEOs, Corporate Governance and Post-IPO Performance of China's Partially Privatized Firms', mimeo, Chinese University of Hong Kong

Chen, G. (1997), *Compilation of Chinese Securities Rules and Regulations* (*Zhongguo Zhengquan Fagui Zonghui*), Beijing: Renmin University Press

Chen, G., M. Firth., D. Gao and O. Rui (2005), 'Is China's Securities Regulatory Agency a Toothless Tiger? Evidence from Enforcement Actions', *Journal of Accounting and Public Policy*, 24 (6), 451–488

Chen, Z. (2003), 'Capital Markets and Legal Development, the China Case', *China Economic Review*, 14 (4), 451–472

Chen, Z. (2006), 'Stock Market in China's Modernization Process – Its Past, Present and Future Prospects', Yale School of Management working paper available at http://www.ckgsb.edu.cn/web2005/files/forum0607/rhjdzgzqs_chenzhiwu.pdf

Chen, Z. and X. Peng (2002), 'The Illiquidity Discount in China', International Centre for Financial Research, Yale University, available at http://people.stern.nyu.edu/lpederse/courses/LAP/papers/Overview/IlliquidAssets_China.pdf

Cheng, S. (2001), 11 May, 'Speech on The First Meeting of the National People's Congress Standing Committee's the "Implementation of Securities Law" Review Panel', available at http://www.fsou.com/html/text/bela/5704255/570425500.html

Chi, J. and C. Padgett (2005), 'Short-run Underpricing and its Characteristics In Chinese IPO Markets', *Research in International Business and Finance*, 19 (1), 71–93

China Daily, 15 February 2005, 'Three Chinese Indicted in New York for BOC Fraud'

China Law and Governance Review (2004) June, No. 2., 'Enforcement of Civil Judgments: Harder than Reaching the Sky' (*Zhixing nan, nanyu Shangqingtian*), available at http://www.chinareview.info

China News Week, 1 October 2004, Qiu, F., 'Seeking for the Legitimacy of Ownership Reform of SOEs' (*Xunzhao Chanquan Zhidu Gaige de Zhengdangxing*)

China News Week, 18 October 2004, 'Monitoring State Assets: The SASAC is Facing a Supervision Deficiency' (*Guoyouzichan Jianguan: Guoziwei Mianlin Jiandu Buli*)

China Securities Journal, 15 December 1997, Li, Y., 'A Study Regarding Several Problems in China's Capital Market' (*Woguo Ziben Shichang Ruogan Wenti Yanjiu*)

China Securities Journal, 20 August 2001, 'Crazy Financial Fabrication by Hubei Lihua Accounting Firm Shocked the Market' (*Hubei Lihua*

Kuaiji Shiwusuo Fengkuang Zaojia Lingren Zhenjing), available at http://money.163.com/editor/010820/010820_57836.html

China Securities Journal, 30 December 2003, Hao, M., 'Construction of Legalization will Speed Up in 2004 – An Interview With Dr Liu Junhai, Research Fellow of Chinese Academy of Social Science, Legal Research Institute' (*2004 Fazhihua Jiang Jiasu Qianjin – Fang Zhongguo Shehui Kexueyuan Faxuesuo Yanjiuyuan Liu Junhai Boshi*), available at http://202.84.17.28/csnews/20031230/452246.asp

China Securities Journal, 28 July 2005, 'A Survey on China's Independent Directors and Reflection on the Institutions' (*Zhongguo Dudong Diaocha ji Zhidu Fansi*), available at http://www.cs.com.cn/sylm/04/t20050728_723933.htm

China Securities Journal, 23 November 2005, Shen, C., 'Deloitte's Three Sins: Immoral, Unprofessional, Unrepentant' (*Deqin Sanzongzui, Budaode, Buzhuanye, Buhuigai*) available at http://www.chinaacc.com/new/184/185/2006/3/ma4356135131132360025512–0.htm

China Securities Journal, 25 October 2007, 'Zhou Mingchun's Speech' (*the Financial Director of Petro China*) in Petro China IPO online Road show in 2007, available at http://business.sohu.com/20071025/n252857779.shtml

China Securities Journal, 23 May 2011, Jiang, X., 'Han Gang Was Sentenced One Year in Prison for Illegal Trading, The First Rat Trading Case Raised the Alarm' (*Han Gang Weigui Jiaoyi Huoxing Yinian, Shouli Laoshucang Ruxingan Qiao Jingzhong*) available at http://finance.qq.com/a/20110523/002586.htm

China Youth Daily, 14 January 2002, Zhang, W. and J. Li, 'Gansu Dunhuang Government Issues Document, Imposes Obstructions to News Reporting' (*Gansu Dunhuang Zhengfu Fawenjian dui Xinwen Caifang Shezhi Zhangai*) available at http:///www.yifannet.com/xinwen/guonei/2002/01/14/3285873828792.html

China Youth Daily, 22 September 2003, Guo, S., 'How People's Daily Seeks Justice for Itself' (*Renming Ribao Ruhe wei Ziji Taoshuofa?*) available at http://news.163.com/editor/030922/030922_802003.html

Chow, D. (2003), *The Legal System of the People's Republic of China in a Nutshell*, St Paul: West Group

Claessens, S. (2006), 'Corporate Governance and Development', *World Bank Research Observer*, 21(1), 91–122

Claessens, S., S. Djankov., J. Fan and L. Lang (2002), 'Disentangling the Incentive and Entrenchment Effects of Large Shareholdings', *Journal of Finance*, 57 (6), 2741–2771

Clarke, D. (1996), 'Power and Politics in the Chinese Court System: The Enforcement of Civil Judgements', *Columbia Journal of Asian Law*, 10 (1), 1–92

Clarke, D. (2006), 'Independent Directors in Chinese Corporate Governance', *Delaware Journal of Comparative Law*, 31 (1), 125–228

Clarke, D. (2008), 'The Ecology of Corporate Governance in China', The George Washington University Law School Public Law and Legal Theory Working Paper No. 433 available at http://unpan1.un.org/intradoc/groups/public/documents/APCITY/UNPAN033859.pdf

Clarke, D., P. Murrell and S. Whiting (2006), 'The Role of Law in China's Economic Development,' available at http://papers.ssrn.com/sol3/papers.cfm?abstract_id=878672

CNPC News, 9 April 2008, 'Sinopec Performed Well in 2007' (*Zhongshihua 2007 nian Qude Lianghao Yeji*) available at http://news.cnpc.com.cn/system/2008/04/09/001168366.shtml

Coase, R. (1937), 'The Nature of the Firm', *Economica*, 4 (16), 386–405

Coffee, J. (1999a), 'Privatization and Corporate Governance: The Lessons from Securities Market Failure', *Journal of Corporation Law*, 25, 1–40

Coffee, J. (1999b), 'The Future as History: The Prospects for Global Convergence in Corporate Governance and Its Implications', *Northwestern University Law Review*, 93, 641–708

Coffee, J. (2001a), 'The Rise of Dispersed Ownership: The Roles of Law and the States in the Separation of Ownership and Control', *The Yale Law Journal*, 111, 1–82

Coffee, J. (2001b), 'The Acquiescent Gatekeeper: Reputational Intermediaries, Auditor Independence and the Governance of Accounting', Columbia Law School, The Center for Law and Economics Studies Working Paper No. 191 available at http://www.bmibourse.org/Report%5CFiles%5CSSRN-id270944.pdf

Coffee, J. (2002), 'Understanding Enron: It is About the Gatekeepers: Stupid', *The Business Lawyer*, 57 (4), 1403–1420

Coffee, J. (2006a), *Gatekeepers: The Professions and Corporate Governance*, Oxford: Oxford University Press

Coffee, J. (2006b), 'Reforming the Securities Class Action: An Essay on Deterrence and its Implementation', *Columbia Law Review*, 106 (7), 1534–1586

Coffee, J. (2007), 'Law and the Market, the Impact of Enforcement', *University of Pennsylvania Law Review*, 56 (2), 229–312

Cox, J., R. Thomas and D. Kiku (2003), 'SEC Enforcement Heuristics: An Empirical Inquiry', *Duke Law Journal*, 53 (2), 737–779

CSRC, 2008 Annual Report, available at http://www.csrc.gov.cn/pub/csrc_en/Informations/publication/200910/P020091028538385313599.pdf

CSRC, 2008 China Capital Markets Development Report, available at http://www.csrc.gov.cn/pub/csrc_en/Informations/publication/200911/P 020091103520222505841.pdf

Cull, R. and L. Xu (2000), 'Bureaucrats, State Banks and the Efficiency of Credit Allocation: The Experience of Chinese State-owned Enterprises', *Journal of Comparative Economics*, 28 (1), 1–31

Cull, R. and L. Xu (2003), 'Who Gets Credit? The Behavior of Bureaucrats and State Banks in Allocating Credit to Chinese State-owned Enterprises', *Journal of Development Economics*, 71 (2), 533–559

Daily Telegraph, 11 October 2002, 'City Scribblers Smarting Over Questions of Competence'

Dam, K. (2006a), 'Judiciary and Economic Development', available at http://ssrn.com/abstract_id=892030.

Dam, K. (2006b), 'China as a Test Case: Is the Rule of Law Essential for Economic Growth?', University of Chicago Law and Economics Online Working Paper No. 275, available at http://papers.ssrn.com/sol3/papers.cfm?abstract_id=880125

Datar, V. and D. Mao (1998), 'Initial Public Offerings in China: Why is Underpricing So Severe?', Seattle University Working Paper

Defond, M. and M. Hung (2003), 'Investor Protection and Corporate Governance: Evidence from Worldwide CEO Turnover', mimeo, University of Southern California, Leventhal School of Accounting

Defond, M., T. Wong and S. Li (1999), 'The Impact of Improved Auditor Independence on Audit Market Concentration in China', *Journal of Accounting and Economics*, 28 (3), 269–305

Delong, B., A. Shleifer, L. Summers and R. Waldmann (1989), 'The Size and Incidence of the Losses from Noise Trading', *Journal of Finance*, 44, 681–696

Delong, B., A. Shleifer, L. Summers and R. Waldmann (1990) 'Noise Trade Risk in Financial Markets', *Journal of Political Economy*, 98 (4), 703–738

Demirguc–Kunt, A. and V. Maksimovic (1998), 'Law, Finance and Firm Growth', *Journal of Finance*, 53 (6), 2107–2137

Denis, D. and J. McConnell (2003), 'International Corporate Governance', *Journal of Financial and Quantitative Analysis*, 38 (1), 1–36

De Soto, H. (1990), *The Other Path: The Invisible Revolution in the Third World*, New York: HarperCollins

Dezalay, Y. and B. Garth (1996), *Dealing in Virtue: International Commercial Arbitration and the Construction of a Transnational Order*, Chicago: University of Chicago Press

Diamond, D. (1984), 'Financial Intermediation and Delegated Monitoring', *Review of Economic Studies*, 51 (3), 393–414

Ding, X. (2000), 'Systematic Irregularity and Spontaneous Property Transformation in the Chinese Financial System', *China Quarterly*, 163, 655–676

Dittmer, L. (1995), 'Chinese Informal Politics', *The China Journal*, 34, 1–34

Dixit, A. (2004), *Lawlessness and Economics: Alternative Modes of Governance*, Princeton, N.J., Oxford: Princeton University Press

Djankov, S., O. Hart., C. McLiesh and A. Shleifer (2008), 'Debt Enforcement around the World', *Journal of Political Economy,* 116 (6), 1105–1149

Djankov, S., R. La Porta., F. Lopez-de-Silanes and A. Shleifer (2008), 'The Law and Economics of Self-dealing', *Journal of Financial Economics*, 88 (3), 430–465

Donahue, J. (1989), *The Privatization Decision*, New York: Basic Books

Dong, D. (2010), '29 Junk Stocks should be Delisted Immediately' (*29 Jia Laji Gongsi Yinggai Zhijie Tuishi*) available at http://blog. caijing.com.cn/expert_article-151355-5891.shtml.

Douglas, R. (1901), *Society in China*, London: Ward, Lock & Co.

Dower, J. (1999), *Embracing Defeat: Japan in the Wake of World War II*, New York: W.W. Norton

Dyck, A. and L. Zingales (2002a), 'The Corporate Governance Role of the Media', in R. Islam (ed.) *The Right to Tell: The Role of Mass Media in Economic Development*, Washington, D.C.: The World Bank

Dyck, A. and L. Zingales (2002b), 'The Bubble and The Media', in Comelius, P. and B. Kogut (eds), *Corporate Governance and Capital Flows in A Global Economy*, New York, Oxford: Oxford University Press

Dyck, A. and L. Zingales (2003), 'The Media and Asset Prices', unpublished paper, available at http://www.anderson.ucla.edu/faculty_pages/romain.wacziarg/mediapapers/DyckZingales.pdf

Dyck, A. and L. Zingales (2008), 'The Corporate Governance Role of the Media: Evidence from Russia', *Journal of Finance*, 63 (3), 1093–1135

Easterbrook, F. and D. Fischel (1991), *The Economic Structure of Corporate Law*, Cambridge, MA: Harvard University Press

Economic Daily, 30 January 2003, 'SETC Vice Chairman Jiang Qiangui: Being a Faithful and Responsible Controlling Shareholder in Listed Companies' (*Guojia Jingmaowei Fuzhuren Jiang Qiangui: Zuo Shangshi Gongsi Chengxin Fuze de Konggu Gudong*)

Economic Daily, 13 June 2003, 'Rationally Lay Out Structural Adjustment, Develop a Great State-owned Economy – A Visit with the Chairman of the State Council's SASAC, Li Rongrong' (*Heli Buju Tiaozheng Jiegou, Fazhan Zhuangda Guoyou jingji-Fang Guowuyuan Guoyou Zichan Jiandu Guanli Weiyuanhui Zhuren Li Rongrong*)

Economics Monthly, October 2004, Zhou, Y., 'The Cult of Bank's Shareholding Reform' (*Yinhang Gugai Mixin*), available at http://www.jingji.com.cn/show.aspx?id=681

Economic Observer, 18 November 2001, Zong, S., 'Underwriters Belong to "The CSRC Clique"' (*Zhengjianhui xi Zhangguan xia de Quanshang*), available at http://finance.sina.com.cn/t/20011118/131317.html

Economic Observer, 30 August 2004, Zhang, W., 'Zhang Weiying's Response to Lang Xianping: Those Contributions to Our Society Deserve Good Treatment' (*Zhang Weiying Huiying Lang Xianping: Shandai Wei Shehui Zuochu Gongxian de Ren*), available at http://economy.enorth.com.cn/system/2004/08/30/000853872.shtm

Economic Observer, 11 September 2004, Zhou, Q., 'Why My Response to Lang Xianping?' (*Wo Weishenme Yao Huiying Lang Xianping*), available at http://finance.sina.com.cn/jingjixueren/20040911/16341016995.shtml

Economic Observer, 23 October 2005, Li, L. and H. Guo, 'Filling the Supervisory Vacuum in Jianyin, Funds Injection into Investment Banks Now Needs Approval of the CBRC' (*Jianyin Jianguan Zhenkong Zhongjie, Zhuzi Quanshang Xiankan Yinjianhui*), online http://finance.sina.com.cn/stock/t/20051023/10472055928.shtml

Economic Observer, 28 July 2010, 'A Stern Statement By Economic Observer' (*Jingji Guanchabao de Yanzheng Shengming*)

Edwards, J. and L. Fischer (1994), *Banks, Finance and Investment in West Germany since 1970*, London: Centre for Economic Policy

Ellickson, R. (1991), *Order without Law; How Neighbors Settle Disputes*, Cambridge, MA: Harvard University Press

Ellison, G. (1994), 'Cooperation in the Prisoner's Dilemma with Anonymous Random Matching', *Review of Economic Studies*, 61 (3), 567–588

Fafchamps, M. (1996), 'The Enforcement of Commercial Contracts in Ghana', *World Development*, 24 (3), 427–448

Fafchamps, M. (2004), *Market Institutions in Sub-Saharan Africa: Theory and Evidence*, Cambridge, MA, London: MIT Press

Fairbank, J. and M. Goldman (2006), *China, A New History*, (enlarged edn.) Cambridge, MA; London: Belknap Press of Harvard University Press

Fama, E. and M. Jensen (1983a), 'Separation of Ownership and Control', *Journal of Law and Economics*, 26 (2), 301–325

Fama, E. and M. Jensen (1983b), 'Agency Problems and Residual Claims', *Journal of Law and Economics*, 26 (2), 327–349

Fan, D., C. Lau and S. Wu (2000), 'Corporate Governance Mechanisms of Chinese Firms: Incentives and Performances' – Proceedings of the

Conference on Chinese Management, The Chinese University of Hong Kong and The Hong Kong University of Science and Technology

Fan, H., T. Wong and T. Zhang (2005), 'The Emergence of Corporate Pyramids in China', available at http://www–wiwi.uni–muenster.de/iw/downloads/Im%20Seminar/ss06/Litss06/Topic%2026%20China/7_pyramids–china_fan_ver2.pdf

Fang, L. (2007), 'The Legal Status of Stock Exchange – A reflection on Following International Practice' (*Zhengquanjiaoyisuo de falü diwei-Fansi yü Guoji Jiegui*), *Political and Legal Forum*, 1, 65–68

Fei, X. (1947), *From the Soil: the Foundations of Chinese Society*, translated by Hamilton, G and W. Zheng, Berkeley: University of California Press

Fernald, J. and J. Rogers (2002), 'Puzzles in the Chinese Stock Market', *The Review of Economics and Statistics*, 84 (3), 416–432

Fewsmith, J. (1983), 'From Guild to Interest Group: The Transformation of Public and Private in Late Qing', *China Comparative Studies in Society and History*, 25 (4), 617–640

Financial Reporting Council, London Stock Exchange (1992) *Report of the Committee on The Financial Aspects of Corporate Governance*, Gee & Co. Ltd., available at http://www.ecgi.org/codes/code.php?code_id=132

Financial Times, 10 September 1997, Walker, T., 'Unbinding China: Chinese Leaders Are Slowly Facing up to the Huge Task of Reforming Bankrupt State-owned Enterprise'

Financial Times, 28 January 2002, McGregor, R., 'Creative Chinese Accounting Creates Work for Andersen'

Financial Times, 18 August 2004, McGregor, R., 'Directors Loses Seat for Hiring Auditors'

Financial Times, 2 September 2004, Huang, Y. and B. Yeung, 'ASEAN's Institutions Are Still In Poor Shape'

Financial Times, 29 December 2004, Deepak, L., 'How Foreign Reserves Could Make China yet Stronger'

Financial Times, 21 January 2005, Burton. J., M. Dickie., F. Guerrera and J. Leahy, 'A Collapse that Waves a "Big Red Flag" about Business with Beijing'

Financial Times, 10 May 2005, Dyer G., 'Shanghai Stock Market Slides on News of State Holdings Sale'

Financial Times, 8 July 2009, Lex, 'China Loan Growth'

Financial Times, 29 March 2010, 'China: To the Money Born'

Financial Times, 14 May 2010, Anderlini, J., 'Audits Lay Bare the Challenges That Lie Ahead'

Financial Times Chinese, 10 January 2006, Zhou, Q., 'The Difficulties with Big' (*Da you da de Nanchu*), available at http://www.ftchinese.com/story/001002409

Financial Times Chinese, 28 July 2007, Ye, T., 'The Death of Chen Guojun and the Difficulties with SOEs Restructuring' (*Chen Guojun zhisi yu Guoqi Chongzu Kunjing*), available at http://www.ftchinese.com/story/001027815

Financial Times Chinese, 5 November 2007, Anderlini, J., 'Nervous Beijing Pump Prcies as Shortages Bite' (*Zhongguo de Youjia Zenme Hexi?*) available at http://www.ftchinese.com/story/001015196

Financial Times Chinese, 14 April 2008, Wu, Z., 'Price Control is Detrimental to Chinese Energy Safety' (*Jiage Guanzhi Yousun Zhongguo Nengyuan Anquan*), available at http://www.ftchinese.com/story/001018623

Financial Times Chinese, 17 July 2009, Whipp, L. and P. Waldmeir, 'Chinese Market Overtakes Japan's' (*Zhongguo Gushi Shizhi Chaoyue Riben Ju Quanqiu Dier*), available at http://www.ftchinese.com/story/001027633/en

Forbes, 2 August 2007, Kwok, V., 'Merrill Scarfs up Ren for China Deals', available at http://www.forbes.com/2007/02/08/margaret-ren-merrill-face-cx_vk_0208autofacescan03.html

Franks, J. and C. Mayer (1994), 'The Ownership and Control of German Corporations', manuscript, London Business School

Franks, J., C. Mayer and S. Rossi (2005a), 'Spending Less Time with the Family: the Decline of Family Ownership in the U.K.', in Morck, R. (ed.), *A History of Corporate Governance around the World*, Chicago, London: University of Chicago Press

Franks, J., C. Mayer and S. Rossi (2005b), 'Ownership: Evolution and Regulation', Working Paper European Corporate Governance Institute

Friedman, M. (1962), *Capitalism and Freedom*, Chicago: University of Chicago Press

Fu, H. and R. Cullen (1996), *Media Law in the PRC*, Hong Kong Asia Law and Practice Publishing

Fukuyama, F. (1995), *Trust: The Social Virtues and the Creation of Prosperity*, New York: Free Press

Gao, X. (2000), *Some Regulatory Issues in the PRC Securities Market, in China 2000: Emerging Investment, Funding and Advisory Opportunities for a New China*, online books, at http://www.asialaw.com/bookstore/china2000/chatper01.htm

Gaylord, M. and C. Armitage (1993), 'All in the Family: Corporate Structure, Business Culture and Insider Dealing in Hong Kong', *Asia Pacific Law Review*, 2 (1), 26–42

Gilson, R. and R. Kraakman (1984), 'The Mechanisms of Market Efficiency', *Virginia Law Review*, 70 (4), 549–644

Glaeser, E., S. Johnson and A. Shleifer (2001), 'Coase versus the Coasians', *The Quarterly Journal of Economics*, 116 (3), 853–899

Glaeser, E. and A. Shleifer (2003), 'The Rise of the Regulatory State', *Journal of Economic Literature*, 41 (2), 401–425

Goetz, C. and R. Scott (1981), 'Principles of Relational Contracts', *Virginia Law Review*, (67) 6, 1089–1150

Gomes, A. (1996), 'Dynamics of Stock Prices, Manager Ownership and Private Benefits of Control', manuscript, Harvard University

Gong, T. (2004), 'Dependent Judiciary and Unaccountable Judges: Judicial Corruption in Contemporary China', *The China Review*, 4 (2), 33–54

Gray, C. (1997), 'Reforming Legal Systems in Developing and Transition Countries', *Finance and Development*, 34 (3), 14–16

Green, S. (2004), *The Development of China's Stock Markets, 1984–2002 Equity Politics and Market Institutions*, London, New York: Routledge Curzon, 1st edn.

Greif, A. (1989), 'Reputation and Coalitions in Medieval Trade: Evidence on the Maghribi Traders', *The Journal of Economic History*, 49 (4), 857–882

Greif, A. (1993), 'Contract Enforceability and Economic Institutions in Early Trade: The Maghribi Traders' Coalition', *American Economic Review*, 83 (3), 525–548

Greif, A. (1994), 'Cultural Beliefs and the Organization of Society: a Historical and Theoretical Reflection on Collectivist and Individualist Societies', *Journal of Political Economy*, 102 (5), 912–950

Greif, A. (1996), 'Contracting, Enforcement, and Efficiency: Economics beyond the Law', in Annual World Bank Conference on Development Economics

Greif, A. (1997), 'On the Interrelations and Economic Implications of Economic, Social, Political and Normative Factors: Reflections from Two Late Medieval Societies', in Drobak, J. and J. Nye (eds), *The Frontiers of the New Institutional Economics*, San Diego, CA: Academic Press

Greif, A. (2006), *Institutions and the Path to the Modern Economy: Lessons from Medieval Trade*, Cambridge: Cambridge University Press

Greif, A. and E. Kandel (1995), 'Contract Enforcement Institutions: Historical Perspective and Current Status in Russia', in Lazear, E. (ed.) *Economic Transition in Eastern Europe and Russia: Realities of Reform*, Stanford: Hoover Institution Press

Grossman, S. and O. Hart (1986), 'The Costs and Benefits of Ownership: A Theory of Vertical and Lateral Integration', *Journal of Political Economy*, 94 (4), 691–719

Gul, F. and R. Zhao (2001), 'Ownership, Board Structures and Firm Performance: Some Evidence from Chinese Listed Companies', Working Paper, Department of Accountancy, City University of Hong Kong

Guo, X. (2001), 'Dimensions of Guanxi in Chinese Elite Politics', *The China Journal*, 46, 69–90

Hall, R. and C. Jones (1999), 'Why Do Some Countries Produce So Much More Output per Worker than Others?', *The Quarterly Journal of Economics*, 114 (1), 83–116

Hardouvelis, G., R. La Porta and T. Wizman (1994), 'What Moves the Discount on Country Equity Funds?' in Frankel, J. (ed.), *The Internationalization of Equity Markets*, Chicago: University of Chicago Press

Hart, O. and J. Moore (1990), 'Property Rights and the Nature of the Firm', *Journal of Political Economy*, 98 (6), 1119–1158

Hartmann, P., F. Heider., E. Papaioannou and M. Duca (2007), 'The Role of Financial Markets and Innovation in Productivity and Growth in Europe', European Central Bank Occasional Paper No. 72, available at http://ssrn.com/abstract=1005850

Hay, J. and A. Shleifer (1998), 'Private Enforcement of Public Laws, A Theory of Legal Reform', *American Economic Review*, 88 (2), 398–403

Hay, J., A. Shleifer and R. Vishny (1996), 'Toward a Theory of Legal Reform', *European Economic Review*, 40 (3–5), 559–567

He, J. (1999), 'Some Thoughts on the Reform of the System of Assessors' *(Peishen Zhidu Gaige Duanxiang)*, *China Lawyer*, 4, 12–13

Ho, S., P. Bowles and X. Dong (2003), 'Letting Go of the Small: An Analysis of the Privatisation of Rural Enterprises in Jiangsu and Shandong', *The Journal of Development Studies*, 39 (4), 1–26

Hoshi, T., A. Kashyap and D. Scharfstein (1993), 'The Choice Between Public and Private Debt: An Analysis of Post-deregulation Corporate Finance in Japan', National Bureau of Economic Research Working Paper 4421, Cambridge, MA

Hu, W. and J. Jiang (2005), 'A Study on the Current Structure of Auditing Market and Its Improvement' *(Woguo Shenji Shichang Jiegou Xiankuang ji Gaijin Celue Yanjiu)*, *Chinese Certificated Public Accountant*, October, 70–74

Huang, H. (2007), 'An Empirical Study of the Incidence of Insider Trading in China', http://papers.ssrn.com/sol3/papers.cfm?abstract_id=993341

Huang, R. and G. Orr (2007), 'China's State-owned Enterprises: Board Governance and the Communist Party', *McKinsey Quarterly* 1, 108–111

Huang, S. and G. Zhang (2002), 'Analysis of Chinese Listed Companies' Preference for Equity Financing' (*Zhongguo Shangshi Gongsi Guquanrongzi Pianhao Fenxi*) *Economic Research Journal*, 11, 12–20

Huang, X. (2004), 'Looking Back 2004, Securities Companies: To Be or Not to Be?' (*2004 Zhengquan Gongsi Quanjing Huisu, Quanshang: Shengcun Haishi Siwang?*) *Capital Market*, 12, 43–48, available at http://finance.sina.com.cn/review/20041221/10481239846.shtml

Huang, Y. (2002), *Selling China: Foreign Direct Investment during the Reform Era*, Cambridge: Cambridge University Press, 1st edn.

Hubbard, R. (1997), *Money, The Financial System and the Economy*, London: Addison-Wesley, 2nd edn.

IMF (2006), 'People's Republic of China: 2005 Article IV Consultation – Staff Report; Staff Supplement; and Public Information Notice on the Executive Board Discussion', Country Report 06/394

Int'l Herald Tribune, 17 March 1999, Green, P., 'Prague Exchange's Failed Reform Efforts Leaves Some Predicting Its Demise'

Jackson, H. (2006), 'Regulatory Intensity in the Regulation of Capital Markets: A Preliminary Comparison of Canadian and U.S. Approaches, Research Study Commissioned by the Task Force to Modernize Securities Regulation in Canada', available at http://www.tfmsl.ca/docs/v6(2)%20Jackson.pdf

Jackson, H. (2007), 'Variation in the Intensity of Financial Regulation: Preliminary Evidence and Potential Implications', *Yale Journal on Regulation*, 24, 253–292

Jackson, H. and M. Roe (2009), 'Public and Private Enforcement of Securities Laws: Resourced-based Evidence', *Journal of Financial Economics*, 93 (2), 207–238

Jensen, M. and W. Meckling (1976), 'Theory of the Firm: Managerial Behavior, Agency Costs and Ownership Structure', *Journal of Financial Economics*, 3 (7), 305–360

Jing Hua Times, 30 March 2002, 'Not Afraid of Beatings, Reporters Need Strong Support' (*Dabupa de Jizhe Xuyao Jiangqiang Houdun*), available at http://www.people.com.cn/GB/paper1787/5851/588784.html

Johnson, S., P. Boone., A. Breach and E. Friedman (2000), 'Corporate Governance in the Asian Financial Crisis', *Journal of Financial Economics*, 58 (1–2), 141–186

Johnson, S., D. Kaufman and A. Shleifer (1997), 'The Unofficial Economy in Transition', *Brookings Papers on Economic Activity*, 28 (2), 159–239

Jones, C. (1994), 'Capitalism, Globalization and Rule of Law: An Alternative Trajectory of Legal Change in China', *Social & Legal Studies*, 3 (2), 195–221

Jones, W. (1978), 'An Approach to Chinese Law', *Review of Socialist Law*, 4 (1), 3–25

Jones, W. (2003), 'Trying to Understand the Current Chinese Legal System', in Hsu, C. (ed.) *Understanding China's Legal System: Essays in Honor of Jerome A. Cohen*, New York, London: New York University Press

Kan, Z. (2010), *Ups and Downs, The Kan Zhidong's Story (Rongru ershinian, Wode gushi Rensheng)*, Beijing: Citic Publishing House

Kandori, M. (1992), 'Social Norms and Community Enforcement', *The Review of Economic Studies*, 59 (1), 63–80

Klein, B. (1980), 'Transaction Cost Determinants of "Unfair" Contractual Arrangements', *American Economic Review*, 70 (2), 356–362

Kornai, J. (1980), *Economics of Shortage*, Amsterdam: North Holland Press

Kornai, J. (1986), 'The Soft Budget Constraint', *Kyklos*, 39 (1), 3–30

Kraakman, R. (1986), 'Gatekeepers: The Anatomy of a Third-party Strategy', *Journal of Law, Economics and Organization*, 2 (1), 3–104

Kreps, D. (1990), 'Corporate Culture and Economic Theory', in Alt, J. and K. Shepsle, (eds.), *Perspectives on Positive Political Economy*, Cambridge: Cambridge University Press

Kronman, A. (1985), 'Contract Law and the State of Nature', *Journal of Law, Economics, and Organizations*, 1 (1), 5–32

Krugman, P. (1998), 'What Happened to Asia?', Mimeo

La Porta, R., F. Lopez-de-Silanes and A. Shleifer (2008), 'The Economic Consequences of Legal Origins', *Journal of Economic Literature*, 46 (2), 285–332

La Porta, R., F. Lopez-de-Silanes., A. Shleifer and R. Vishny (1997), 'Legal Determinants of External Finance', *Journal of Finance*, 52 (3), 1131–1150

La Porta, R., F. Lopez-de-Silanes., A. Shleifer and R. Vishny (1998), 'Law and Finance', *Journal of Political Economy*, 106 (6), 1113–1155

La Porta, R., F. Lopez-de-Silanes., A. Shleifer and R. Vishny (1999), 'Corporate Ownership around the World', *Journal of Finance*, 54 (2), 471–517

La Porta, R., F. Lopez-de-Silanes., A. Shleifer and R. Vishny (2000a), 'Agency Problem and Dividend Policies around the World', *Journal of Finance*, 55 (1), 1–33

La Porta, R., F. Lopez-de-Silanes., A. Shleifer and R. Vishny (2000b), 'Investor Protection and Corporate Governance', *Journal of Financial Economics*, 58 (1–2), 3–27

La Porta, R., F. Lopez-de-Silanes., A. Shleifer and R. Vishny (2002), 'Investor Protection and Corporate Valuation', *Journal of Finance*, 57 (3), 1147–1170

La Porta, R., F. Lopez-de-Silanes., A. Shleifer and R. Vishny (2006), 'What Works in Securities Laws?', *Journal of Finance*, 61 (1), 1–32

Landa, J. (1981), 'A Theory of Ethnically Homogeneous Middleman Group: An Institutional Alternative to Contract Law', *Journal of Legal Studies*, 10 (2), 349–362

Landis, J. (1938), *The Administrative Process*, New Haven: Yale University Press

Lang, H. and J. Wang (2002), 'Optimal Earnings Manipulation' (*Xunzhao Zuishidang Zaojia Lirunliu*), *New Fortune*, October, 2002

Lardy, N. (1998), *China's Unfinished Economic Revolution*, Washington, D.C.: Brookings Institution

Lavington, F. (1921), *The English Capital Market*, London: Methuen & Co. Ltd

Lazzarini, S., G. Miller and T. Zenger (2004), 'Order with Some Law: Complementarity versus Substitution of Formal and Informal Arrangements', *Journal of Law, Economics, and Organization*, 20 (2), 261–298

Lee, C. and X. Xiao (2004), 'Tunnelling Dividends', Mimeo, available at http://www.baf.cuhk.edu.hk/research/cig/pdf_download/LeeXiao.pdf

Legal Daily, 6 January 2010, Jiang, D., 'Several Nanjing Officials under Investigation, Gao Chun Ceramics Insider Trading Case Continues' (*Duoming Gunayuan Beicha, Gaochun Taoci Neimujiaoyian Xu*)

Leng, J. (2004), 'The Interaction between Domestic and Overseas Capital Markets and Corporate Governance of Chinese listed Companies', *Studies in International Financial, Economic and Technology Law*, 7, 273–340

Li, D. (2001), 'Beating the Trap of Financial Repression in China', *Cato Journal*, 21 (1), 77–91

Li, D. (2008), 'Elites' Dirty Deals' (*Quangui de Anzang Jiaoyi*), available at http://economy.guoxue.com/article.php/15519

Li, N. (2004), 'Civil Litigation against China's Listed Firms: Much Ado about Nothing?', Asia Programme Working Paper No. 13

Li, Z. (2000), *Finally Succeed: A Report on the Development of China's Stock Market* (*Zhongyu Chenggong: Zhongguo Gushi Fazhan Baogao*), Beijing: Shijie Zhishi Publication

Liang, S. (1963), *The Essence of Chinese Culture* (*Zhongguo Wenhua Yaoyi*), Taipei: Zhengzhong Books

Licht, A. (2003), 'Cross-listing and Corporate Governance: Bonding or Avoiding?', *Chicago Journal of International Law*, 4, 141–164

Liebman, B. (2005), 'Watchdog or Demagogue? The Media in the Chinese Legal System', *Columbia Law Review*, 105 (1), 1–157

Liebman, B. and C. Milhaupt (2008), 'Reputational Sanctions in China's Securities Market', *Columbia Law Review,* 108 (4), 929–983

Lincoln, K. (1995), 'Fire When Ready', *Far Eastern Economic Review,* Feb, 23, 50

Liu, B. (1990), *A Higher Kind of Loyalty,* New York: Pantheon Books

Liu, F. and F. Zhou (2007), 'Does Big Four Mean High Quality Auditing? A Test Based on Accounting Conservatism Preliminary Evidence from A-share Market' (*Guoji Sida Yiweizhe Gaozhiliang Shenji ma? Jiyu Kuaiji Wenjianxing de Jiaodu Jianyan*), *Accounting Research,* 3, 79–87

Liu, G. and P. Sun (2003), 'Identifying Ultimate Controlling Shareholders in Chinese Public Corporations: An Empirical Survey', Asia Program Working Paper, No. 2, available at http://www.chathamhouse.org.uk/files/3096_stateshareholding.pdf

Liu, Q. (2006), 'Corporate Governance in China: Current Practices, Economic Effects and Institutional Determinants', *CESifo Economic Studies,* 52 (2), 415–453

Liu, T. (2003), 'Investment without Risk, an Empirical Investigation of IPO Under-pricing in China', Royal Institute of International Affairs, China Project Report No. 4

Liu, Y. and P. Xiong (2005), 'Equity Separate, Government Control and Chinese IPO Underpricing Puzzle' (*Guquanfenzhi, Zhengfu Guanzhi he Zhongguo IPO yijia*), FED Working Papers Series No.FC20050031

Lou, F. and H. Yuan (2002), 'The Independent Director System: Western Research and Problems in Chinese Practice' (*Duli Dongshi Zhidu: Xifang de Yanjiu he Zhongguo Shijian Zhong de Wenti*), *GaiGe,* 2, 51–55

Lubman, S. (1999), *Bird in a Cage: Legal Reform in China after Mao,* Stanford: Stanford University Press

Lynch. D. (1999), *After the Propaganda State: Media, Politics, and 'Thought Work' in Reformed China,* Stanford: Stanford University Press, 1st edn.

Macaulay, S. (1963), 'Non-contractual Relationships in Business: a Preliminary Study', *American Sociological Review,* 28 (1), 55–67

Macfarlane, A. (2000), *The Riddle of the Modern World: of Liberty, Wealth and Equality,* Basingstoke: Macmillan Press

Macneil, I. (1974), 'The Many Futures of Contracts', *Southern California Law Review,* 47 (3), 691–816

Mahoney, P. (2001), 'The Political Economy of the Securities Act of 1933', *The Journal of Legal Studies,* 30 (1), 1–31

Mako, W. and C. Zhang (2007), 'Why is China so Different from Other Transition Economies?' in Lieberman, W. and D. Kopt (eds.), *Privatization in Transition Economies: The Ongoing Story,* JAI Press

Mattli, W. (2001), 'Private Justice in a Global Economy: from Litigation to Arbitration', *International Organization*, 55 (4), 919–947

Mayer, C. (2008), 'Trust in Financial Markets', *European Financial Management*, 14 (4), 617–632

McMillan, J. and C. Woodruff (1999), 'Dispute Prevention without Courts in Vietnam', *Journal of Law, Economics, and Organization*, 15 (3), 637–658

McMillan, J. and C. Woodruff (2000), 'Private Order under Dysfunctional Public Order', *Michigan Law Review*, 98 (8), 2421–2458

Michie, R. (1987), *The London and New York Stock Exchanges, 1850–1914*, London: Allen & Unwin

Michie, R. (1999), *The London Stock Exchange: A History*, Oxford: Oxford University Press

Milgrom, P., D. North and B. Weingast (1990), 'The Role of Institutions in the Revival of Trade: The Law Merchant, Private Judges and the Champagne Fairs', *Economics and Politics*, 2 (1), 1–23

Milgrom, P. and J. Roberts (1992), *Economics, Organization and Management*, Upper Saddle River, N.J.: Prentice-Hall

Milhaupt, C. and K. Pistor (2008), *Law and Capitalism: What Corporate Crises Reveal about Legal System and Economic Development around the World*, Chicago, London: University of Chicago Press

Milhaupt, C. and M. West (2000), 'The Dark Side of Private Ordering: An Institutional and Empirical Analysis of Organized Crime', *The University of Chicago Law Review*, 67 (7), 41–98

Minzner, C. (2011), 'China's Turn against Law', *American Journal of Comparative Law*, 59 (4), 935–984

Miyazaki, I. (1980), 'The Administration of Justice during the Sung Dynasty', in Cohen, E. and C. Chen (eds.), *Essays on China's Legal Tradition*, Princeton: Princeton University Press

Mnookin, R. and L. Kornhauser (1979), 'Bargaining in the Shadow of the Law: The Case of Divorce', *Yale Law Journal*, 88 (5), 950–997

Morck, R., B. Yeung and W. Yu (2000), 'The Information Content of Stock Markets: Why Do Emerging Markets Have Synchronous Price Movements?' *Journal of Financial Economics*, 58 (1–2), 215–260

Murrel, P. (1996), 'How Far Has the Transition Progressed?' *Journal of Economic Perspectives*, 10 (2), 25–44

Myers, S. (1984), 'The Capital Structure Puzzle,' *Journal of Finance*, 39 (3), 575–592

Myers, S. and N. Majluf (1984), 'Corporate Financing and Investment Decisions: When Firms Have Information that Investors Do not Have', *Journal of Financial Economics*, 13 (2), 187–221

Nathan, A. (1973), 'A Factionalism Model for CCP politics', *The China Quarterly*, 53, 33–66

Nathan, A. (1985), *Chinese Democracy*, Berkeley: University of California Press

National Audit Office, 23 January 2003, 'The Investigation of Selected Auditor Firms Indicates that Quality of CPA's Service Is Worrying' (*Shenjishu dui Bufen Kuaijishi Shiwusuo de Jianchan Biaoming: CPA Shenji Yewu Zhiliang Lingrendanyou*), avaialble at http://www.audit. gov.cn/n1057/n1072/n1162/10626.html

New York Times, 1 June 2000, Bearak, B., 'In India, the Wheels of Justice Hardly Move'

North, D. (1981), *Structure and Change in Economic History*, New York, London: Norton

North, D. (1990), *Institutions, Institutional Change, and Economic Performance*, Cambridge: Cambridge University Press

North, D., J. Wallis and B. Weingast (2009), *Violence and Social Orders: A Conceptual Framework for Interpreting Recorded Human History*, Cambridge, New York: Cambridge University Press

OECD (2005), *Governance in China*, Paris

Olson, M. (1993), 'Democracy, Dictatorship, and Development', *American Political Science Review*, 87 (3), 567–576

Ostrom, E. (1990), *Governing the Commons: the Evolution of Institutions for Collective Action*, Cambridge: Cambridge University Press

Pagano, M. and A. Roell (1998), 'The Choice of Stock Ownership Structure: Agency Costs, Monitoring, and the Decision to Go Public', *Quarterly Journal of Economics*, 113 (1), 187–225

PBOC (2006), '2006 Report on China's Financial Market Development', available at http://finance1.jrj.com.cn/news/2007–05–30/000002283 199.html

Peerenboom, R. (2002), *China's Long March toward Rule of Law*, Cambridge: Cambridge University Press

Pei, M. (1998), 'The Political Economy of Banking Reforms in China 1993–1997', *Journal of Contemporary China*, 7 (18), 321–350

People's Court News, 23 May 2002, Cai, E., 'Calling Out for the Spring of Popular Opinion Supervision' (*Huhuan Yulun Jiandu de Chuntian*), available at http://www.hubce.edu.cn/jwc/jwc5/messages/6580.html

People's Daily, 16 December 1996, 'Correct Understanding of the Current Stock Market' (*Zhengque Renshi Dangqian Gupiao Shichang*), available at http://sc.stock.cnfol.com/081127/123,1764,5121358,00. shtml

People's Daily, 15 June 1999, 'Strengthen Confidence, Normal Development' (*Jiaqiang Xinxin, Guifan Fazhan*), available at http://www.stock star.com/focus/SS2007042530602835.shtml

People's Daily, 30 January 2012, Lin, L., 'Preventing the Capital Market from Becoming a Jungle Hunting for People's Wealth' (*Dujue Ziben*

Shichang cheng Liesha Laobaixing Caifu Conglin), available at http://finance.sina.com.cn/stock/stocktalk/20120130/072811269133.shtml

People's Procuracy, 27 August 2000, Lin, X., 'Where Are the Difficulties in Popular Opinion Supervision?' (*Yulun Jiandu Nanzai Hechu*)

Phoenix Finance, Special Report: 'The CSRC Crack Down on Rat Trading' (*Zhengjianhui Yanlidaji Laoshucang*), available at http://finance.ifeng.com/fund/special/ydlsc/

Phoenix Finance, 12 July 2010, 'Fan Xiaowei was Reported to Return to His Old Job in Guotai Junan, His Minor Problems were Disregarded' (*Fan Xiaowei beibao Chonggui Guotai Junan ren Yuanzhi, Xiaowenti bei Huluebuji*), available at http://finance.ifeng.com/stock/zqyw/20100712/2397757.shtml

Phoenix TV, 26 August 2004, Lang X., 'Cautions over the Collusive Expropriation of State Assets by Private and State Enterprises' (*Jingti Minqi Huotong Guoqi Hefa Tunbing Guoyou Zichan*)

Pistor, K., M. Raiser and S. Gelfer (2000), 'Law and Finance in Transition Economics', *Economics of Transition*, 8 (2), 325–368

Pistor, K. and C. Xu (2003), 'Incomplete Law', *Journal of International Law and Politics*, 35, 931–1014

Pistor, K. and C. Xu (2004), 'Addressing Deterrence and Regulatory Failure in Emerging Stock Market', American Law and Economics Association Annual Meeting Paper 72

Pistor, K. and C. Xu (2005), 'Governing Stock Markets in Transition Economies, Lessons from China', *American Law and Economics Review*, 7 (1), 184–210

Polinsky, A. and S. Shavell (2000), 'The Economic Theory of Public Enforcement of Law', *Journal of Economic Literature*, 38 (1), 45–76

Potter, P. (2002), *The Chinese Legal System, Globalization and Local Legal Culture*, London: Routledge

Procuratorate Daily, 19 December 2001, Zhao Z., 'The Alienation of Media Supervision and Media Self-Regulation' (*Yunlun Jiandu de Yihua yu Meiti Zilü*), available at http://www.jcrb.com/ournews/asp/readNews.asp?id=67678

Procuratorate Daily, 17 January 2002, Zhao, L., 'Calling Out for the Clear Blue Sky of Public Opinion Supervision' (*Huhuan Yulun Jiandu De Qingkong*), available at http://www.sc.cninfo.net/tanfo/dssh/laaw/block/html/2002011700614.html

Prowse, S. (1992), 'The Structure of Corporate Ownership in Japan', *Journal of Finance*, 47 (3), 1121–1140

Pye, L. (1981), *The Dynamics of Chinese Politics*, Cambridge, MA: Oelgeschlager, Gunn & Hain

Pye, L. (1985), *Asian Power and Politics: The Cultural Dimensions of Authority*, Cambridge, MA, London: Belknap Press of Harvard University Press

Pye, L. (1991), 'The State and The Individual: An Overview Interpretation', *The China Quarterly*, 127, 443–466

Pye, L. (1995), 'Factions and the Politics of Guanxi: Paradoxes in Chinese Administrative and Political Behavior', *The China Journal*, 34, 35–53

Qi, D., W. Wu and H. Zhang (2000), 'Shareholding Structure and Corporate Performance of Partially Privatized Firms: Evidence from Listed Chinese Companies', *Pacific Basin Finance Journal*, 8 (5), 587–610

Qiu, Y. (2008), 'A Study on Independent Directors in China's Listed Companies, Current Problems and Legal Solution' (*Woguo Shangshi Gongsi Dulidongshi de Xiancun Wenti yu Falü Duce Yanjiu*), available at http://www.chinacapitallaw.com/article/default.asp?id=1414

Rajan, R. and L. Zingales (2003), 'The Great Reversals, The Politics of Financial Development in the 20th Century', *Journal of Financial Economics*, 69 (1), 5–50

Rauch, J. (2001), 'Business and Social Networks in International Trade', *Journal of Economic Literature*, 39 (4), 1177–1203

Rawski, T. (1999), 'Reforming China's Economy: What Have We Learned?', *The China Journal*, 41, 139–156

Redding, G. (1990), *The Spirit of Chinese Capitalism*, Berlin: Walter de Gruyter & Co.

Redding, G. and M. Witt (2007), *The Future of Chinese Capitalism: Choices and Chances*, Oxford: Oxford University Press

Ren, H. (2004), 'How to Improve the Capital Structure of China's Listed Companies' (*Ruhe Youhua Woguo Shangshi Gongsi Ziben Jiegou*), *Shanghai Jinrong Xueyuan Xuebao*, 2, 60–63

Ren, X. (1997), *Tradition of the Law and Law of the Tradition: Law, State and Social Control in China*, Westport, Conn.: Greenwood Press

Reuters, 23 June 2003, Ansfield, J., 'China Stifles Curb-defying Magazines'

Reuters, 14 May 1995, Kaban, E., 'Shares Guns and Bodyguards in Russia's Courts'

Richman, B. (2004), 'Firms, Courts, and Reputation Mechanisms: Towards a Positive Theory of Private Ordering', *Columbia Law Review*, 104 (8), 2328–2368

Richman, B. (2006), 'How Community Institutions Create Economic Advantage: Jewish Diamond Merchants in New York', *Law and Social Inquiry*, 31 (2), 383–420

Rodrik, D., A. Subramanian and F. Trebbi (2004), 'Institutions Rule: The Primacy of Institutions over Geography and Integration in Economic Development', *Journal of Economic Growth*, 9 (2), 131–165

Roland, G. (2000), *Transition and Economics: Politics, Markets and Firms*, Cambridge, MA: MIT Press

Romano, R. (1993), *The Genius of American Corporate Law*, Washington, D.C.: American Enterprise Institute Press

Ross, S. (1973), 'The Economic Theory of Agency: The Principal's Problem', *American Economic Review*, 63 (2), 134–139

Royko, M. (1971), *Boss: Richard J. Daley of Chicago*, London: Barrie and Jenkins

Saich, T. (2000), 'Negotiating the State: The Development of Social Organizations in China', *The China Quarterly*, 161, 124–141

Sanlian Life Weekly, 26 November 2004, Xie, L., 'The Rent-seeking Chain in Shares Issuance was Exposed, Wang Xiaoshi Made Profits of Nearly 10 Million' (*Gupiao Faxing Xunzulian Baoguang, Wangxiaoshi Huoli Jin Qianwan*)

Schmitter, P. (1974), 'Still the Century of Corporatism?', *The Review of Politics*, 36 (1), 85–131

Schwartz, A. (1992), 'Relational Contracts in the Courts: An Analysis of Incomplete Agreements and Judicial Strategies', *Journal of Legal Studies*, 21 (2), 271–318

SEC, 2002 Annual Report, available at http://www.sec.gov/about/annrep02

SEC, 1 October 2003, 'International Reporting and Disclosure Issues in the Division of Corporation Finance', available at http://www.sec.gov

Securities Market Weekly, 30 June 2002, 'Semi-annual Reports' (2002 *Bannianbao*)

Securities Market Weekly, 25 September 2004, Chen Z., 'Preserving SOEs or Returning the Assets to People?' (*Yao Guoying Haishi Yao Huanchanyumin*)

Securities Market Weekly, 1 March 2008, Li, D., 'Who Approved the Listing of Pacific Securities Company?' (*Shui Pizhun le Taipingyang Zhengquan Shangshi*)

Securities Market Weekly, 13 June 2003, 'Rationally Lay Out Structural Adjustment, Develop a Great State-owned Economy; A Visit with the Chairman of the State Council's State Asset Supervision and Administration Commission, Li Rongrong' (*Heli Buju Tiaozheng Jiegou, Fazhan Zhuangda Guoyou Jingji-Fang Guowuyuan Guoyou Zichan Jiandu Guanli Weiyuanhui Zhuren Li Rongrong*)

SGX, 2005 Annual Report

Shanghai Morning Post, 18 June 2004, 'Yili Shareholding Dismissed Its Independent Directors, Is this Price of Independence?' (*Yili gufen*

Bamian Duli Dongshi, Zhejiushi Duli de Daijia), available at http://finance.sina.com.cn/t/20040618/0745820855.shtml

Shanghai Securities News, 28 April 2006, Wang, L., 'The Violation Costs of Fraud Listed Companies are only at 250 000 yuan' (*Zaojia Gongsi Weigui Chengben jin 25 Wanyuan*), available at http://www.stock star.com/focus/QJ2006042810194004.shtml

Shanghai Securities News, 5 December 2006, Wang, L., 'Some Exciting News: The Daqing Lianyi Case Finally Comes to End' (*Lingren Xingfen de Xiaoxi, Daqing Lianyian Zhongyu Huashang Juhao*), available at http://news.xinhuanet.com/stock/2006–12/05/content_5436052.htm

Shapiro, C. and D. Willig (1990), 'Economic Rationales for The Scope of Privatization', in Suleiman, E. and J. Waterbury (eds.), *The Political Economy of Public Sector Reform and Privatization*, London: Westview Press

Shapiro, M. (1975), 'Courts', in Greenstein, F. and N. Polsby (eds.), *Handbook of Political Science*, Addison-Wesley Educational Publishers Inc

Shirley, M. and C. Xu (2001), 'Empirical Evidence of Performance Contracts: Evidence from China', *Journal of Law, Economics, and Organization*, 17 (1), 168–200

Shleifer, A. and R. Vishny (1994), 'Politicians and Firms', *Quarterly Journal of Economics*, 109 (4), 995–1025

Shleifer, A. and R. Vishny (1997), 'A Survey of Corporate Governance', *Journal of Finance*, 52 (2), 737–783

SHSE (2009), 'A Report on the Institutional Design for Management Stock Incentive Plan in Listed Companies' (*Shangshi Gongsi Gaoguanjili Zhidusheji Baogaoshu*) SHSE Research Project, November 2009, available at http://static.sse.com.cn/cs/zhs/xxfw/research/plan/plan 20100311b.pdf

SIAS, 1 December 2004, 'China Aviation Oil's US$550 Million Derivatives Disaster', available at http://www.sias.org.sg

Sina.com, 3 August 2005, 'The Listed Lotus Gourmet Company Felt Helpless about the Crazy Funds Appropriation by Controlling Shareholder' (*Lianhua Weijing Dagudong Fengkuang Zhankuan, Shangshi Gongsi Monaihe*) available at http://finance.sina.com.cn/stock/t/2005 0803/09191858991.shtml

Sina.com, 9 August 2005, 'PwC Facing Fake Accounts Problem, Senior Partners are Still Lobbying Beijng' (*Puhuayongdao Jiazhang Yuboweiliao, Gaoceng Bejing Gongguan Weigui)*, available at http://finance.sina.com.cn/g/20050809/02261871634.shtm

Sina.com, 17 March 2010, 'The Former Vice President of the SPC Was Sentenced to Jail for Life' (*Qian Zuigaofayuan Fuyuanzhang bei pan*

Wuqituxing), available at http://news.sina.com.cn/c/2010–03–17/1238 19882663.shtm

Sinopec website: http://www.sinopec.com

Sohu Caijing, 17 June 2004, Lang X., 'Questioning the Method of Ownership Reform at TCL' (*Zhiyi TCL Chanquan Gaige Fangan*), available at http://business.sohu.com/2004/06/17/35/article/220573551. shtlml

Sohu Caijing, 2 August 2004, Lang, X., 'The Transformation of Haier: A complete Analysis of a Long and Complicated Process of MBO' (*Haier Bianxing ji: Manchang Quxian MBO Quanjiexi*), available at http://finance.sohu.com.cn/t/20040902/1417919523.shtml

Sohu Caijing, 19 October 2004, Liu, J., 'Leftism and Rightism both Harmful to Ownership Reform' (*Chanquan Geming Jiyao Fanzuo ye Yao Fangyou*), available at http://business.sohu.com/20042029/n22 2560185.shtml

Southern Weekend, 3 March 2003, Liu, W., 'Their Proposals: Something in Relation to Popular Opinion Supervision' (*Tamen de Tian: Yu Yulun Jiandu Youguan*), available at http://www.china-judge.com/fzhm/fzhm171.htm

Southern Weekend, 12 March 2008, Huang, H., 'Who Can Solve Ping An's Problem?' (*Shuijie Ping An Ju*), available at http://www.infzm.com/content/7493/2

Southern Weekend, 16 November 2009, Yang, X., 'Hu Shuli, Finally Walked Away' (*Hu Shuli, Zhongyu Chuzou*)

Stigler, G. (1964), 'Public Regulation of the Securities Market', *Journal of Business*, 37 (2), 117–142

Stigler, G. (1971), 'The Theory of Economic Regulation', *Bell Journal of Economics and Management Science*, 2 (1), 3–21

Strinivas, S. and D. Sitorus (2004), 'State-owned Banks in Indonesia', in Caprio, G., J. Fiechter., L. Roberte and M. Pomerleano (eds.), *The Future of State-owned Financial Institutions*, Washington, D.C.: Brookings Institution Press

Su, D. and B. Fleisher (1999), 'An Empirical Investigation of Underpricing in Chinese IPOs', *Pacific-Basin Finance Journal*, 7 (2), 173–202

Sun, Q. and W. Tong (2003), 'China Share Issue Privatization: the Extent of Its Success', *Journal of Financial Economics*, 70 (2), 183–222

Supreme People's Court, 1998 Annual Working Report, available at http://www.court.gov.cn/work/200302120012.htm

Supreme People's Court, 1999 Annual Working Report, available at http://www.court.gov.cn/work/200302120013.htm

Supreme People's Court, 2000 Annual Working Report, available at http://www.court.gov.cn/work/200302120014.htm

Supreme People's Court, 2005 Annual Working Report, available at http://www.court.gov.cn/work/200503180013.htm

SZSE (2007), October: 'A Report on the Analysis of Investor Structure and Behavior' (*Tou zizhe Jiegou yu Xingwei Fenxi Baogao*)

Tam, K. (2002), 'Ethical Issues in the Evolution of Corporate Governance in China', *Journal of Business Ethics*, 37 (3), 303–320

Tan, L. and J. Wang (2007), 'Modeling an Effective Corporate Governance System for China's Listed State-owned Enterprises: Issues and Challenges in a Transitional Economy', *Journal of Corporate Law Studies*, 17 (1), 143–183

Tang, D. (ed.) (1991), *Several Theoretical and Practical Problems in Civil Adjudication* (*Minshi Shenpan ruogan Lilun yu Shijian Wenti*), Jinlin Renmin Press

Tenev, S., C. Zhang and L. Brefort (2002), *Corporate Governance and Enterprises Reform in China, Building the Institutions of Modern Markets*, World Bank Publications

The Asian Banker data center, 2003, http://www.thesianbanker.com

The Economist, 22 January 1994, 'Two Half Revolutions', 330 (7847), 55–58

The Economist, 5 February 1994, 'European Airlines: Flights of Fancy', 330 (7849), 69–70

The Economist, 7 March 1998a, 'The Tigers Adrift', 346 (8058), 3–5

The Economist, 7 March 1998b, 'Six Deadly Sins', 346 (8058), 12–14

The Economist, 8 February 2003, 'Casino Capital, in the Weakest Link: A Survey of Asian Finance', 366 (8310), 10–12

The Economist, 20 March 2004, 'We Are the Champions', in *Behind the Mask: A Survey of Business in China*, 370 (8367), 13–15

The Economist, 8 February 2007, 'China's Stock Market Hot and Cold: Nervous Officials Talk Down the Market After Its Scorching Run', 382 (8515), 80

The Economist, 6 February 2010, 'Red Mist, China's Financial System', 394 (8668), 79–80

Tian, J. and C. Lau (2001), 'Board Composition, Leadership Structure and Performance in Chinese Shareholding Companies', *Asia Pacific Journal of Management*, 18 (2), 245–263

Tian, L. (2001), 'State Shareholding and the Value of Chinese Firms', Working Paper, London Business School

Tomasic, R. and J. Fu (2005), 'Legal Regulation and Corporate Governance of China's Top 100 Listed Companies', *The Company Lawyer*, 27 (9), 278–287

Trebilcock, M. and J. Leng (2006), 'The Role of Formal Contract Law and Enforcement in Economic Development', *Virginia Law Review*, 92 (7), 1517–1580

Tsou, T. (1976), 'Prolegomenon to the Study of Informal Groups in CCP Politics', *The China Quarterly*, 65, 98–117

Unger, R. (1976), *Law in Modern Society: Toward a Criticism of Social Theory*, New York: Free Press; London: Collier Macmillan

Upham, F. (1994), 'Speculations on Legal Informality: on "Winn's Relational Practices and the Marginalization of Law"': Comment', *Law & Society Review*, 28 (2), 233–241

Upham, F. (2002), 'Mythmaking in the Rule of Law Orthodoxy', Democracy & Rule of Law Project at the Carnegie Endowment for International Peace, Rule of Law Series, Working Paper No. 30

Van der Sprenkel, S. (1962), *Legal Institutions in Manchu China*, London: University of London, Athlone Press

Varese, F. (2001), *The Russian Mafia: Private Protection in a New Market Economy*, Oxford: Oxford University Press

Vernon, R. and Aharoni, Y. (eds.) (1981), *State-Owned Enterprises in Western Economies*, London: Croom Helm

Wall Street Journal, 10 September 2002, Wonacott, P., 'China's Stock Markets Open Doors'

Walter, C. and F. Howie (2003), *Privatizing China: The Stock Markets and Their Role in Corporate Reform*, Singapore: John Wiley and Sons (Asia)

Wan. C., C. Chu., X. Li., Y. Yuan and J. Zhou (2002), 'A Study on the Sources of External Financing in Listed Companies – An Empirical Research on Capital Structure and Cost of Capital of Listed Companies' (*Shangshi Gongsi de Waibuzijin Laiyuan Wenti Yanjiu – Shangshi Gongsi de Ziben Jiegou yu Rongzi Chengben Wenti de Shizheng Yanjiu*), available at http://static.sse.com.cn/cs/zhs/xxfw/research/plan/plan20020412e.pdf

Wang, X., L. Xu and T. Zhu (2004), 'State-owned Enterprises Going Public: The Case of China', *Economics of Transition*, 12 (3), 467–87

Wang, X. (2006), *The Crisis of Chinese Securities Companies* (*Zhongguo Zhengquan Gongsi Shengcun Weiji*), Ph.D thesis, Shanghai: Fudan University

Wang, Y. (2009), 'A Study on Illegal Accounting Information Disclosure in Listed Companies: Empirical Analysis Based on Administrative Sanctions By the CSRC From 2002–2007' (*Woguo Gufenyouxian Gongsi Kuaijixinxi Pilu Weifa Wenti Yanjiu – Jiyu Zhongguo Zhengjianhui 2002–2007 Xingzhen Chufa Juedingshu de Shizheng Fenxi*), *Journal of Anyang Institute of Technology*, 45–47

Weber, M. (1947), *The Theory of Social and Economic Organization*, New York: Free Press; London: Collier Macmillan

Wei, Y. (1999), 'Seeking Consensus between News and Law' (*Xunqiu Xinwen Yu Falü de Gongshi*), *China Reporter*, No. 6 available at:

http://www.zjonline.com.cn/node2/node26108/node30205/node30212/
node30213/userobject7ai1691.html

Weinstein, D. and Y. Yafeh (1994), 'On the Costs of A Bank-centered
Financial System: Evidence from The Changing Main Bank Relations
in Japan', manuscript, Harvard University

White, G., J. Howell and X. Shang (1996), *In Search of Civil Society:
Market Reform and Social Change in Contemporary China*, Oxford:
Clarendon Press

Whiting, R. (1999), *Tokyo Underworld*, New York: Random House

Williamson, O. (1983), 'Credible Commitments: Using Hostages to
Support Exchange', *American Economic Review*, 73 (4), 519–540

Williamson, O. (1985), *The Economic Institutions of Capitalism*, New
York: Free Press; London: Collier Macmillan

Williamson, O. (1991), 'Economic Institutions: Spontaneous and Intentional Governance', *Journal of Law, Economics, and Organization*, 7,
159–187

Williamson, O. (1996), *The Mechanisms of Governance*, New York,
Oxford: Oxford University Press

Wong, S., S. Opper and R. Hu (2004), 'Shareholding Structure, Depoliti-
cization and Enterprise Performance: Lessons from China's Listed
Companies', *Economics of Transition*, 12 (1), 29–66

Wong, S. (2006), 'China's Stock Market: A Marriage of Capitalism and
Socialism', *Cato Journal*, 26 (3), 389–424

Woodruff, C. (1998), 'Contract Enforceability and Trade Liberalization in
Mexico's Footwear Industry', *World Development*, 26 (6), 979–991

World Bank (1995), 'China: The Emerging Capital Market', Report No.
14501-CHA

World Bank (1997), *China's Management of Enterprises Assets*

World Bank (2005), *World Development Report 2005: A Better Investment Climate for Everyone*

World Bank (2006), *World Development Indicator 2006*

Wu, J. (2005), *Understanding and Interpreting Chinese Economic
Reform*, Australia: Thomson

Wu, J., J. Zhang., W. Lu., G. Long and C. Zhang (1998), *The Strategic
Restructuring of the State Sector (Guoyou Jingji de Zhanluexing
Gaizu)*, Beijing: China Development Press

Wu, J., J. Zhang., W. Lu., G. Long and C. Zhang (2005), 'China Reform
Will Fall into the Trap of Cronyism' (*Zhongguo Gaige Jiang Xianru
Quangui Zibenzhuyi Nikeng*) available at http://people.chinareform.
org.cn/W/wjl/Article/200501/t20050118_20204.htm

Wurgler, J. (2000), 'Financial Markets and the Allocation of Capital',
Journal of Financial Economics, 58 (1), 187–214

Xia, T. (1996), 'The Shanghai Exchange and Chinese Bond Law', *Columbia Journal of Asian Law*, 10, 281–304

Xiao, Z., J. Dahya and Z. Lin (2004), 'A Grounded Theory Exposition of the Role of the Supervisory Board in China', *British Journal of Management*, 15 (1), 39–55

Xie, P. and L. Lu (2003), 'A Research on Financial Corruption in China, From Qualitative to Quantitative' (*Zhongguo Jinrong Fubai Yanjiu: Cong Dingxing dao Dingliang*), *Bi Jiao*, September

Xinhua Net, 10 December 2003, 'The Former President of PCBC, Wang Xuebing Was Sentenced to Jail for 12 Years' (*Yuan Zhongguo Jianshe Yinhang Hangzhang Wang Xuebing Yishen Beipan Youqintuxing 12 nian*), available at http://news.xinhuanet.com/legal/2003–12/10/content_1224132.htm

Xinhua Net, 3 November 2006, 'The Former President of the PCBC, Zhang Enzhao Was Sentenced to Jail for 15 Years' (*Zhongguo Jianshe Yinhang yuan Dongshizhang Zhang Enzhao Yishen beipan 15 nian*), available at http://news.xinhuanet.com/legal/2006–11/03/content_5285792.htm

Xinmin Weekly, 28 July 2010, 'How Stock Market "Black Mouth" Took Shape?' (*Gushi heizui Shi Zenyang Liancheng de?*), available at http://finance.sina.com.cn/stock/stockarticle/20100728/10448378010.shtml

Xu, L. (2004), *Types of Large shareholders, Corporate Governance and Firm Performance, Evidence from China*, Ph.D thesis, The Hong Kong Polytechnic University, available at: http://hdl.handle.net/10397/1064

Xu, X. and Y. Wang (1999), 'Ownership Structure and Corporate Governance in Chinese Stock Companies', *China Economic Review*, 10, 75–98

Xu, X. (2010), 'We are Striding Back and Moving Towards Cronyism' (*Women Zhengzai Dabuhoutui, Buxiang Quanguizibenzhuyi*), available at http://blog.sina.com.cn/s/blog_4c7711270100ngck.html

Yang, X. (1996), 'Property Rights, Government and Marketization – A Case Study on Spontaneous Stock Market in Chendu', (*Chanquan, Zhengfu yu Jingjishichanghua – Chendu Zifa Gupiao Jiaoyishichang de Anli*) in Zhang, S. (ed.), *Case Studies on Institutional Transformation in China (Zhongguo Zhidubianqian de Anliyanjiu)*, Vol. 1, Shanghai: Shanghai People Publication

Yang Cheng Evening News, 13 August 2005, 'Liu Jinbao Was Sentenced to Death Penalty with a Suspension of Execution in First Trial' (*Liu Jinbao Yishen Sihuan*) available at http://www.ycwb.com/gb/content/2005–08/13/content_961354.htm

Yin, H. (2007), 'The Effective Check of Formation Mechanism of Reputation in CPA firms – Based on the Case of Kelon-Delloit'

(*Kuaijishi Shiwusuo Shengyu Xingchen Jizhi Youxiaoxing Jianyan*), *Communication of Finance and Accounting*, 3, 36–39

Yuan, J. (2004), *A Critique of Chinese Securities Market* (*Zhongguo Zhengquan Shichang Pipan*), Beijing: China Social Science Press

Zhang, P. and F. Ma (2006), 'A Reflection on the CSRC's Punishment Bulletin' (*Zhengjianhui Chufagonggao Fenxi Yinqi de Sikao*), *Journal of Xi'an University of Post and Telecommunications*, 11 (4), 72–74

Zhang, W. (1999), '10 Years in Jail for Providing Information to Radio Free Asia on Labor Protests inside China', *The Christian Science Monitor*, 24 Feb, 6

Zhang, Z. (2007), 'Legal Deterrence, the Foundation of Corporate Governance, Evidence from China', *Corporate Governance: An International Review*, 15 (5), 741–767

Zhao, Y. (1998), *Media, Market and Democracy in China: Between the Party Line and Bottom Line*, Urbana: University of Illinois Press

Zhao, Y. (2004), 'The State, The Market, and Media Control in China', in Thomas, P. and Z. Nain (eds.), *Who Owns the Media? Global Trends and Local Resistances*, London: Zed Books, 1st edn.

Zheng, Z. (2009), 'Back to the Era of Manipulators, Rat Trading is Prevailing' (*Chonghui Zhuanggu Shidai, Laoshucang Fanlan*), *Nanfengchuang*, 10, 75–78

Zingales, L. (2004), 'The Costs and Benefits of Financial Market Regulation', ECGI Working Paper 21/2004

Index